AMERICAN AIR POWER
THE FIRST 75 YEARS

AMERICAN AIR POWER
THE FIRST 75 YEARS

BY JOE CHRISTY

TAB BOOKS Inc.
BLUE RIDGE SUMMIT, PA 17214

FIRST EDITION

FIRST PRINTING

Copyright © 1982 by TAB BOOKS Inc.

Printed in the United States of America

Reproduction or publication of the content in any manner, without express permission of the publisher, is prohibited. No liability is assumed with respect to the use of the information herein.

Library of Congress Cataloging in Publication Data

Christy, Joe.
    American air power.
    Includes index.
    1. Aeronautics, Military—United States—History.
I. Title.
UG633.C523   358.4′00973   82-5825
ISBN 0-8306-2327-2   AACR2

Contents

Introduction vii

1 The First Air War 1
  The 1st Aero Squadron
  Chasing Villa in Mexico
  The U.S. in WWI
  The First Fighter Airplane
  U.S. Aircraft and Engine Production
  Airpower Prophet
  U.S. Naval Air in WWI
  Combat

2 The Wings Grow Stronger 28
  First Atlantic Flight
  Army and Navy Racers
  First World Flight

3 Naval Air and Billy Mitchell 40
  Navy Aircraft Engine Development
  The First Navy Dirigibles
  Mitchell Court-Martialed

4 The New Deal and U.S. Airpower 49
  "Neither Rain, Nor Snow, Nor Politics . . ."
  Engine Development Paces the Industry
  Navy Airships *Akron* and *Macon*
  Transition: The Biplane Era Passes
  A New Generation of Aircraft

5 WWII: The Desperate Months 73
  The Philippines Lost
  Coral Sea and Midway
  New Guinea and the Solomons

6 The War in Europe 93
  North Africa and Italy
  The Italian Campaign
  Assault on Fortress Europe
  Overlord: The Cross-Channel Invasion

7 Victory and the Unreal Wars 117
  The Aleutian Campaign
  Over the Hump with the AVG and the 14th AF
  The Assam Trucking Company
  The CBI Fighters
  The Final Thrust

8 Uneasy Peace, and Another War 138
  Berlin Big Lift
  Birth of the B-52
  The Korean War

9 Johnson's War—and After 158
  Airpower and the Flexible Response
  McNamara's Brand
  Faith, Hope, and Parity

Index 193

Introduction

Among all of Mankind's inventions, the airplane was one of the most inevitable. Man has always looked heavenward; from the mythical Icarus to the Wright brothers the dream persisted. Leonardo da Vinci was making sketches of manned aircraft when Columbus first sailed to the New World, and in 1799 a remarkable Englishman, Sir George Cayley, accurately described the logical shape of a self-propelled heavier-than-air vehicle.

Many experimenters appeared during the nineteenth century—Stringfellow, Wenham, Loup, Du Temple, Penaud, Montgomery—but it was the work of Otto Lilienthal in Germany that inspired the Wrights. Beginning in 1891, Lilienthal constructed a number of gliders and, sailing from the Stollner Hills near Rhinow, achieved glides up to 750 feet in length. He was killed in the crash of one of his gliders in 1896, still a long way from producing a controllable self-propelled flying machine, although the flights he had made far overshadowed all previous attempts put together.

Today, too many of us look upon the Wright brothers' original machine with small appreciation of what it actually represented at the beginning of the twentieth century. It seems so simple, so obvious, so crude. But it was a giant step forward in the science of applied physics. It was an incredible feat viewed against the background of what was then known about the science of manned flight.

Consider: The Wrights, both then in their thirties and largely self-educated, worked out a reasonably efficient airfoil to produce lift when next to nothing was known about that very complex subject. They designed and built their own propellers because, with marvelous perception, they alone recognized that an aircraft propeller is simply a wing acting upon the air in another direction. They designed and built their own engine because the gasoline engine manufacturers of that day declared it impossible to produce an engine possessing the power-to-weight ratio specified by the Wrights—25 lbs per horsepower. Most important of all, they discovered the aerodynamic principles which allowed them to control their machine in flight. Having accomplished all this, they still had to teach themselves to fly—which was, of course, the primary reason that their first flights were of short duration and but a few feet off the ground.

Not that they didn't try. Indeed, on that historic morning—17 December 1903—when Orville made the world's first successful powered flight (which covered 120 ft), the brothers made three additional flights, alternating at the controls, and on the fourth attempt Wilbur decided to fly all the way to the village of Kitty Hawk, nearly four miles away. He probably would have made it had he not overcontrolled and nosed into the sand. He was airborne for 59 seconds, covering a distance of 852 feet into a 21 mph wind. His landing left much to be desired, and the resulting damage to the *Flyer*, as they called their machine, ended their flying until the following spring.

As strange as it may seem now, instant fame did not come to the Wrights. The public, including newspaper editors, simply did not believe that man could fly. The Wrights' own hometown newspaper refused to print the story. Less than two months earlier, Simon Newcomb, a well-known scientist, had mathematically "proven" that human flight was impossible. Just nine days before the Wrights' success at Kitty Hawk, a well-publicized attempt, in a machine designed by Professor Samuel Langley (the secretary of the Smithsonian Institution, no less), had ingloriously failed. Clearly, manned flight should be regarded in the same light as perpetual motion. True, five people witnessed the original flights at Kitty Hawk (one took a picture just as Orville became airborne), but none seemed to have grasped the significance of the event until much later. Four were men from the Kill Devil Hill Life Saving Station about a mile away; the fifth was a visiting teenager.

The Wrights themselves were responsible for the skepticism that persisted for the next five years. They refused to make public any details of their Flyer and maintained their secrecy even after receiving patent protection because they hoped to sell their invention to the U.S. Army. However, the Army had suffered enough humiliation financing the Langley machine and wasn't interested. Not until the brothers had decided, in exasperation, to sell manufacturing rights to their machine in Britain and France, in 1908, did the U.S. Army at last agree to take a look at it.

Meanwhile, their secrets had become known through the patenting processes (France granted a patent before the U.S. Patent Office did) and through, perhaps, some spying by other inventors as the Wrights continued with experimental flights from a field some eight miles from their Dayton, Ohio, home. By the time the U.S. Army bought its first airplane, an improved version of the original Flyer, at the end of July 1909, a number of flying machines were airborne over France, and Frenchman Louis Bleriot had already flown across the English Channel, while in America motorcycle racer Glenn Curtiss had built two successful machines (the first financed by Alexander Graham Bell).

The Wrights would sue Curtiss and nearly a dozen others in the U.S., France, and Germany for patent infringement. In every case that went to trial, the Wrights won. Curtiss was their main target, and although they repeatedly beat Curtiss in court, Curtiss never stopped building airplanes. The patent pool, established by the government during WWI, effectively ended such lawsuits.

In the meantime, although the airplane had been invented in America, it was the French who contributed the most to its development prior to WWI. The British, who were quite prepared to believe that men could fly, had established the Royal Aeronautical Society in 1866 but were tardy in producing a useful airplane of their own. The Germans, distracted by Count von Zeppelin's giant gas-filled airships (the first of which took to the air three years before the first successful airplane), were also slow to grasp this new science. Not until 1910 were designers in England and Germany building flyable aircraft. The French, however, were clearly enchanted with the promise of charging noisily about the sky and indulging the anarchy in their souls. They embraced the airplane with enthusiasm, especially after Wilbur Wright made a number of public demonstration flights in France during 1908 while negotiating manufacturing rights in that country. While aircraft development languished in the U.S., French designers seemed to almost daily improve upon the Wrights' invention between 1908 and 1914—which is why so many present day aeronautical terms are of French origin: *fuselage, pitot, nacelle, chandelle, empennage, aileron, longeron.* (While on that subject, the British used the term "aeroplane" almost from the beginning, and still do. The word "airplane" first appeared in a 1916 U.S. aviation magazine.)

After purchasing the Wright Military Flyer in 1909, the U.S. Army bought an additional 23 airplanes during the following five years, ten of which were destroyed in accidents at a cost of 12 lives, which worked out to an average of one death for each 100 hours of flying time. Then, on 18 July 1914, Congress officially created the Aviation Section of the Signal Corps with an authorized strength of 60 officers and 260 enlisted men. (Today's United States Air Force claims 1907 as its birthdate, pointing to an order dated 1 August 1907 signed by Brigadier General James Allen, Chief Signal Officer, establishing an "Aeronautical Division" within the Signal Corps when the Army ordered a motorized gas bag from balloonist T. S. Baldwin. One officer and two enlisted men constituted the total personnel of this division.)

When the United States entered WWI on 6 April 1917, the Army had 55 airplanes in active service, 334 training planes on order, and 35 qualified pilots on active duty, plus a handful of civilian barnstormers quickly given uniforms and designated as instructors. The U.S. Navy entered WWI with 48 floatplanes, six flying boats, two balloons and 51 pilots. Of course, on Capitol Hill, the halls of Congress rang with promises to "darken the skies over Germany" with American warplanes. Then as now, the politicians had a single solution for every problem: Throw money at it. Less than 200 airplanes had been built in the United States since 1903, but the lawmakers appropriated money to build 20,000 within a year.

When WWI ended nineteen months later, the U.S. Air Service had 750 airplanes in the battle zone, most of which were bought from America's allies. The United States spent about a half-billion dollars for airplanes during WWI, but not a single American design saw combat. Automobile interests purchased the Wright and Curtiss operations, along with most of the other fledgling plane builders, and a goodly portion of the money spent for airplanes and airplane engines was clearly wasted. How much of it went to boondoggling and how much to simple incompetence is difficult to pin down.

It is generally accepted that aircraft development was advanced 20 years during the 1914-1918 war in Europe. Those advances were made by the French, British and Germans, while most of the money poured into America's infant aircraft industry produced no significant technological advances and did little to establish a permanent industry. Soon after the war ended on 11 November 1918, almost all of the companies formed to share in the wartime plane-building bonanza were quietly liquidated. Fortunately, there remained a handful of dedicated aviation pioneers—and a few farsighted investors—who were willing to suffer the lean years ahead, and who would give this nation a technologically sound (if financially weak) foundation upon which to build an industry that would, in years to come, affect the lives of every American, and constitute the deciding factor in the preservation of our freedom. Within two short decades the airplane would decide the fate of nations, but this fact, so obvious to a few, was completely lost on the governments of the United States and Great Britain during those twenty years of euphoria. The leaders of both these great nations appeared to believe that an earnest desire for peace was all that was necessary to achieve it, and the military planners of both countries, dominated by saddle-horse generals and battleship admirals, held firmly to the belief that the next war, if indeed it should ever come, would be fought exactly as the last.

One must keep in mind that the defense postures of the nations of the Free World are inexorably entwined with their domestic politics, and therefore, if we are to honestly examine U.S. airpower from its beginnings to the present, we cannot ignore the politics of defense. I trust you will not suspect that the political influences that are necessarily a part of this account were inspired by "Alice in Wonderland." Honest, this is the way it was, and is.

Chapter 1

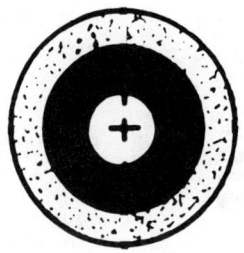

The First Air War

At the outbreak of World War I, in August 1914, there were no military aircraft in the world. True, France, Germany, Britain and the United States military forces all possessed airplanes by that time, but none were designed for any specific military mission. The airplane had been under development in Europe for less than six years, and most of that effort had been directed toward improving performance. The Wright Model A, or Military Flyer, of 1909 cruised at slightly over 40 mph. By 1914 a speed of 130 mph had been achieved in the British single-place SE-4, but since the Army generals could envision only one possible use for airplanes—the scouting of enemy troop movements—speed was not regarded as an asset.

Actually, in the United States, artillerymen had foreseen the possibility of employing airplanes to direct artillery fire three years earlier. A 1911 newspaper report is to be found in the files of the Field Artillery Museum at Fort Sill, Oklahoma:

"Junction City, Kansas—A successful aeroplane artillery test was conducted during the War Department's aeroplane maneuvers here. Battery E, Sixth Field Artillery, Lt. Palmer commanding, was stationed on the side of a hill. An imaginary enemy was placed on the other side. Lt. Milling, Aviator, with Lt. Sands as observer, flew over the hill obtaining the enemy's position. The messages giving the information secured were dropped to the artillerymen. No wireless tests were made."

The 1st Aero Squadron

At the time of the above mentioned experiment, the U.S. Signal Corps had a total of six airplanes in service or on order. Except for pilot training at San Antonio, Texas and College Park, Maryland, this appears to be the first field test of a U.S. Army airplane. In any case, whatever flying was done by the Army through 1912 was that of true pioneers feeling their way. Then, in January 1913, Lt. Harold E. Geiger inaugurated the Signal Corps Flying School at North Island, off San Diego, California, and in December of that year War Department General Order No. 75 authorized the

Fig. 1-1. The Army's Capt. C. DeF. Chandler (1) and Lt. Roy Kirtland in the Wright "B" airplane were first to fire a machine gun from an aircraft, 7 June 1912. (USAF)

First Aero Squadron, although this unit was not actually formed until 15 July 1915 from students trained at North Island.

On 26 July the squadron was sent to Fort Sill, Oklahoma, for duty with the Field Artillery School. The squadron consisted of 15 officers, 85 enlisted men and eight Curtiss JN-2 aircraft, Capt. Benjamin Foulois commanding.

According to official reports, the 1st Aero Squadron "carried out various exercises" at Fort Sill, including artillery spotting and some aerial photography. One pilot, Capt. G.H. Knox, and two aircraft were lost, which led to the squadron being re-equipped with Curtiss JN-3s (extended upper wings and improved engines). Then, in November 1915, the squadron was ordered to fly its eight aircraft to Fort Sam Houston, near San Antonio. This was done without serious mishap although it was undoubtedly the longest cross-country mass flight attempted up to that time.

An uneventful winter was spent at Fort Sam Houston erecting living quarters. Then, on 13 March 1916, the 1st Aero Squadron received orders to report to Gen. John J. "Black Jack" Pershing at Columbus, New Mexico, to serve with an American punitive expedition charged with the task of capturing the Mexican rebel leader Francisco "Pancho" Villa. Early in the morning of 9 March, Villa, with 400 men, had raided the border town of Columbus, killing nine civilians and seven United States troopers. More U.S. citizens certainly would have died had not Col. H.J. Slocum charged into town with the 13th Cavalry and chased the raiders back into Mexico.

Chasing Villa in Mexico

Gen. Pershing entered Mexico with 5000 men on the 15th of March, and the 1st Aero Squadron, with 10 officers and 80 enlisted men, began operations from Columbus on the 19th. The squadron's duties consisted mainly of reconnaissance, courier, and communications assignments. Pershing was an old horse soldier and clearly felt that the airplanes were more bother than help. Considering the state of aircraft development at that time, Pershing wasn't completely wrong.

Two of the eight airplanes were lost almost at once. Lt. T.S. Bowen escaped with only a broken nose when, in a high wind, his craft "dipped and plummeted in almost a straight 50-ft fall to the ground," according to a Fourth Army press release. And a news flash reported "Flight Lieutenants Edgar S. Gorrell and Robert H. Willis, Jr. overdue and apparently down somewhere in the Chihuahua desert." Fears for the downed fliers' safety deepened when it was pointed out that, in the great waste over which they were flying, men on foot could wander for days without reaching help. Each carried only three days' rations and two canteens of water. An additional danger was the possibility of capture by Villa's forces.

However, both survived with little ill effect. Willis walked 32 miles to the pueblo of Casas Grandes. Later, when a crew returned to his airplane, they found that the seats and instruments had been removed and the wings slashed. Only the engine was salvagable. Gorrell was found plodding along the road three miles from another village. He had gone down with a fuel leak two days earlier. A bit of solder and a can of gasoline were all that were needed to allow him to fly his airplane back to Columbus.

Another pilot, Lt. Dargue, and his observer, Capt. Willis, crashed on the side of a mountain while on a mission to reconnoiter the roads leading into Chihuahua City. Neither was seriously injured, but their walk back to the Mexican village of San Antonio covered about 60 miles of very rough terrain.

The actual campaign into Mexico was of short duration, and the squadron had but two serviceable airplanes left when it returned to Columbus after 33 days in the field. Still, a lot of lessons had been learned in that short time. Operating their primitive craft under harsh conditions over inhospitable desert and mountains (the Sierra Madres were often higher than the absolute ceiling of the JN-3), the men of the 1st Aero Squadron proved more durable than their machines.

Pancho Villa was never captured. He and his men remained under arms in the Sierra Madres until, in 1920, the Mexican Government coaxed him into retirement with the gift of a large estate. Three years later, he was assassinated.

Meanwhile, shortly before the 1st Aero Squadron was recalled from Mexico, President Wilson had sent an ultimatum to Germany demanding that U-boat (submarine) attacks on U.S. shipping be stopped. It would be another year before America would be forced into the war in Europe, and meanwhile the 1st Aero Squadron would remain at Columbus, New Mexico. After the U.S. entered the war, the squadron would go overseas in August 1917, and, following a six-month wait for airplanes, would enter combat in April 1918, flying French-built Salmson observation planes.

The U.S. in WWI

Now, the debate still continues among historians as to just how much the United States contributed to Allied victory in WWI, especially in the air. Starting with an army of 200,000 in April 1917, the United States had 2.8 million men under arms

Fig. 1-2. In November, 1910, civilian pilot Eugene Ely made the first aircraft takeoff from a ship when he flew a 50-hp Curtiss from a platform on the bow of the light cruiser *Birmingham* (USN)

Fig. 1-3. "Fly by wire" was method of launching the U.S. Navy's first airplane in 1912. The float-equipped Curtiss Triad took off from greased wires. Liason aircraft were similarly flown from Navy LSTs during WWII. (USN)

when the war ended, with 43 divisions overseas. True, they were sketchily trained and much of their armament came from France and Britain, but this was a typical American Army of "civilians in soldiers' suits," and they performed as Americans have always performed in battle. They griped and they joked and they fought superbly.

When Americans entered the battle zones in the spring of 1918, the war had been stalemated for more than three and a half years while 10,000,000 men died in the mud. But the Bolshevik revolution took Russia out of the war and freed the Germans on the Eastern Front for a series of spring offensives in France that may well have at last defeated the exhausted British and French but for the arrival of the Americans—commanded by Gen. "Black Jack" Pershing. In fact, long before the Americans arrived in force, the mere promise of their coming gave new resolve to the tottering Allies, and the popular cry "The Yanks are coming!" was alone probably worth a couple of new divisions on the Western Front.

The Americans did, of course, make all the difference in the key battles fought during the spring and summer of 1918. They stopped a major German offensive that had broken through Allied lines east of the Aisne River and which had advanced to within 40 miles of Paris. In July, eight U.S. divisions—two of them spearheading—led the Allies to victory in the Aisne-Marne Offensive which left the Allies with the initiative. Two months later, Pershing had 27 American divisions (11 of which he used) for the St. Mihiel offensive in a successful, totally American operation. That in turn allowed the joint American-French (630,000 Americans, 138,000 French) Meuse-Argonne Drive on 26 September 1918 which would end the war seven weeks later on 11 November.

Those are the essential facts, unclouded by detail, but the fact that all of it was accomplished in less than seven months and at what the Allies regarded as a small sacrifice (53,403 Americans killed, 202,261 wounded), and after they had suf-

Fig. 1-4. Glenn H. Curtiss began building successful flying machines in 1908; was repeatedly sued for patent infringement by the Wrights. Curtiss pioneered flying boat designs. (Joe R. Reed collection)

fered four years of unbelievable carnage fighting over that same ground, led some to downgrade America's role in the Allied victory when in truth it was American troops, American food, and the U.S. Navy guaranteeing the delivery of both, that ended the bloody stalemate in Flanders and allowed the Allies to dictate the terms of peace.

Those peace terms, spelled out in the Treaty of Versailles in 1919 and primarily drafted by France, were so harsh and unrealistic that they made the appearance of Hitler all but inevitable— about which, more later.

The 1914-1918 war in the air greatly accelerated aircraft development, but the airplane did not significantly influence the outcome of that conflict, and WWI in the air was not a dress rehearsal for future air warfare. Neither side had airplanes in sufficient numbers or of sufficient performance to make airpower a decisive factor. Important concepts in strategy and tactics emerged, but their implementation in each case was on a scale too small to establish their validity.

At the beginning of the war, airplanes on both sides were unarmed, and opposing machines often passed one another—sometimes exchanging pistol fire—on missions to scout one another's positions and troop movements. Of course, both sides recog-

Fig. 1-5. An early Curtiss triplane design, the Model L, crashed in test for the Army. (USAF)

Fig. 1-6. The 42nd airplane purchased by the U.S. Army was this Curtiss JN-2, forerunner of the famed JN-4 "Jenny." Engine of this 1915 aircraft was the Curtiss OX-5, evolved from a series of water-cooled V-8s designed by Curtiss dating back to 1908. (Boardman C. Reed collection)

nized the desirability of denying the enemy access to their skies while remaining free to invade enemy air, and that prompted the appearance of the first fighter planes. The Germans presaged the doctrine of strategic airpower with their dirigible raids on England as early as 1915; close air support of advancing ground troops was convincingly demonstrated by Col. Billy Mitchell's fliers during the Battle of St. Mihiel.

The First Fighter Airplane

The world's first fighter plane was the Morane-Saulnier Bullet, a single-place mid-wing monoplane operated by the French early in WWI. It became a fighter when an 1885 Hotchkiss infantry machine gun was mounted on its cowling, and a wedge-shaped steel deflector was attached to the back of each propeller blade to protect the prop from the estimated one bullet in seven that did not pass between the blades. French aviator Roland Garros is said to have shot down several German airplanes with this machine before going down behind enemy lines in April 1915.

The Germans inspected Garros' crude gun installation and soon had forward-firing, line-of-sight guns on their airplanes, although theirs utilized an interrupter gear activated by an engine-driven cam, allowing the gun to fire only between the prop blades. The British and French followed with similar systems.

The air war steadily intensified as aircraft on both sides improved. Throughout 1916, and for much of 1917, the Germans were generally better equipped. The Pfalz DIII, Albatros DIII, and Fokker DRI Triplane (the Red Baron's favorite mount) were excellent fighters for their time. Their most serious challenger was the French Spad VII, which entered combat in the fall of 1916. The British

Fig. 1-7. Curtiss R-4 of 1916 had red star on rudder, the first although unofficial attempt toward adoption of a national insignia for U.S. Army airplanes. (USAF)

SE-5a and Sopwith Camel were in service by mid-1917 and were, perhaps, the equal of any German fighters with the possible exception of the Fokker DVII, which entered combat at about the same time. So the Germans were never, for any significant length of time, confronted with Allied aircraft of superior performance.

Had WWI continued into 1919, the Allies would certainly have controlled the air; by that time, aircraft production in the United States would have, despite much wasted effort, become a major factor, as would the 10,000 American pilots in training when the war ended. Given time, America really would have "darkened the skies over Germany" with her warplanes.

While the United States could have produced a lot of airplanes through 1919, no notable American designs would have been among them. Most would have been deHavilland DH-4 observation planes. Perhaps some would have been the American-designed Orenco D and Thomas Morse MB-3 pursuits (fighters), had the 300-hp Hispano-Suiza engines been available for them. Both of these 150-mph craft appear to be copies of the French Spad (of which the U.S. ordered 6000 on three contracts, later cancelled).

U.S. Aircraft and Engine Production

The U.S. aircraft production effort during WWI is epitomized in the story of the Liberty engine.

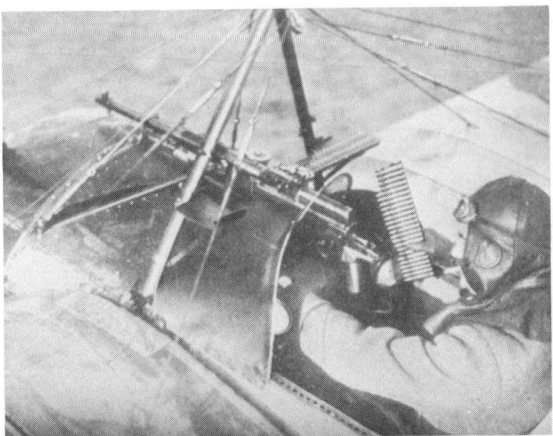

Fig. 1-8. World's first fighter airplane was the French Morane-Saulnier Bullet of 1914 which mounted an 1885 Hotchkiss machine gun for line-of-sight aiming by the pilot. Wedge-shaped steel deflectors on rear of propeller blades protected the blades from the estimated one-in-seven rounds that did not pass between. (National Archives)

Fig. 1-9. The British BE2 of 1914 served the Royal Flying Corps as an observation plane and light bomber early in WWI. Skids beneath nose were to prevent nose-over during landings.

Within days of America's entry into the war, a joint British-French commission arrived in the U.S. to aid manufacturers in selecting the most useful airframe and engine designs. This commission was directed to Detroit, where it was met by Jesse Vincent, the Packard Motor Car Company's vice president for engineering. As early as 1916, automobile interests had purchased the Wright patents and gained control of the Curtiss company. Therefore, aircraft and aircraft engine production would be in the hands of the car makers.

The commission recommended that U.S. factories build two-place fighter-bombers and engines of 200 to 400 horsepower. To save time, they suggested that those planes and engines be British and French designs already battle-proven. That was a realistic suggestion because, by 1917, the U.S. was years behind the combatant nations in aircraft development, and no U.S. manufacturer had any real experience in the volume production of airplanes—a product that had to be largely handbuilt.

But the automobile people were in control, and whatever the problems they would solve them, *profitably.*

Vincent went to Washington and conferred

Fig. 1-10. German Fokker E-1 Eindecker (monoplane) of 1915 was fitted with an 80-hp Oberursel rotary engine. Speed was 80 mph and the machine gun was synchronized by an interrupter gear to fire between the rotating propeller blades. (USAF)

Fig. 1-11. The L-30, a typical German military Zeppelin, appeared in 1916 and raided London and other cities in England as well as targets on the Eastern Front. L-30 was 649 ft in length, 78 ft in diameter, 90 ft high. She could carry five tons of bombs, had ten machine guns for defense, and cruised at 60 mph. (Wingfoot LTA Society)

with the automobile executives who had been appointed by President Wilson to the key aircraft procurement posts, Edward Deeds and Howard Coffin, top men of the hastily-created Aircraft Production Board. Deeds was an associate of Charles Kettering at Delco; Coffin was a Hudson Motor Company official.

This group determined that Packard should design and build the 400-hp engine needed. It would be known as the "U.S. Standard Aircraft Engine." This engine would power the deHavilland DH-4, the airplane selected by the board for mass production. The British Bristol Fighter was a newer, superior two-place fighter-bomber, but it would not accept the V-12 engine that Vincent planned. Vincent would later say that he and E.J. Hall designed the Standard Aircraft Engine, which became known as the *Liberty*, over a single weekend following his meeting with Deeds and Coffin, but the truth was that Vincent had been working on such a design for more than a year, and had actually built two test versions.

Fig. 1-12. The Germans lost a number of the world's first strategic bombers to Allied fighters, although most dirigible raids were made at night when few defensive airplanes were able to fly. (Joe R. Reed collection)

Fig. 1-13. A French Maurice Farman observation plane proceeding toward the Front in 1915. Engine was a 110-hp Le Rhone rotary. (USAF)

The Liberty was no better or no worse than most aircraft engines of its day. It was billed as a triumph of engineering, but it required hundreds of modifications during its first few years of service, and its official time-between-major-overhauls was 120 hours, although few Liberties ever ran that long without repair. (When the Army flew Liberty-powered planes around the world in 1924, engines were changed every 50 hours, but even that didn't prevent several engine failures on the four airplanes.)

The Liberty was a water-cooled engine, but its cylinders were not cast in a single block. What Vincent and Hall actually designed was a single cylinder which could be stuck into different crankcases to make engines of four, six, eight or twelve cylinders. It sounded good when stated that way, but there was nothing new about it, and the V-8 version could hardly have been taken seriously when the superior Hispano-Suiza, built under license by the Wright Corporation, had already proven itself. (Later the six-cylinder version of the Liberty—a six in-line, not a V-6—did enjoy minor success in the post-war civilian market.)

But the most interesting feature of the V-12 Liberty was its automobile-type Delco ignition system, a major component that was, of course, dear to Mr. Deed's heart. All other aircraft engines, then as today, used magnetos for a hotter spark and greater reliability.

Meanwhile, the car manufacturers and their financial backers divvied-up the market in an interesting way. Wright Aeronautical, controlled by a syndicate which owned the Simplex Automobile

Fig. 1-14. British F.E.2d fighter-bomber was often used to escort the vulnerable observation planes. Engine was a 250-hp Rolls-Royce. Forward gunner had a good field of fire. (USAF)

Fig. 1-15. Many American pilots trained in France in the Caudron C-3, which employed wing-warping for lateral control. (USAF)

Company (the principals being Richard Hoyt of Hayden, Stone; Thomas Chadbourne and Harvey Gibson of Manufacturers Trust, and Albert Wiggen of Chase National Bank) bought out the Glenn L. Martin Company (the third most important airplane builder behind Wright and Curtiss) and formed the Wright-Martin Company. With that kind of muscle, the Wright-Martin Company could put a hammerlock on the production of the 150—300-hp aircraft engine market.

Another "Wright" company was formed by wheeler-dealers Deeds, Coffin, Vincent, and Kettering. It was called Dayton-Wright (Orville Wright was listed as one of the original organizers, though he was not active in the company). Dayton-Wright was the prime contractor for the deHavilland DH-4.

At the Curtiss Aeroplane and Motor Company, John North Willys, who was something of a maverick among automobile biggies, seems to have had little or no influence with the "in" bunch comprising the Aircraft Production Board, but he didn't need it. Curtiss was well established as a purveyor of flying machines to the Signal Corps, already had substantial orders for its JN-4 trainer by the time the Aircraft Production Board was formed, and could hardly be denied additional orders for this craft which, known as the "Jenny," would be the standard Army training plane. On floats, it was the N-9 Navy trainer. Both versions were powered with the Curtiss OX-5 water-cooled V-8 engine of 90 hp. A total of 6750 Jennies were built by Curtiss and a couple of smaller war-born firms.

A total of 4846 DH-4s was produced: 3106 by Dayton-Wright, 1600 by Fisher Body (a GM subsidiary), and 140 by the Standard Aeroplane Company. About 1500 DH-4s were shipped overseas. However, Gen. Halsey Dunwoody, director of the Air Service's supply system, later said, "We never had a single plane that was fit for use." Those that reached the front had to be rebuilt by the A.E.F. aircraft production center at Romorantin, France.

Altogether, 13,574 Liberty engines were built before the war ended, by Packard, Ford, GM, and Marmon, but the first one did not fly over the fighting front in France until 7 August 1918.

For a reason never explained, Liberty engine production continued into 1920, by which time more than 22,000 had been built. The Army was

Fig. 1-16. Crash of a French Farman, 1917. (Charles W. Meyers)

stuck with these engines throughout the '20s, and Army observation planes designed ten years after WWI were forced to use them. The last Liberty was retired from service at Kelly Field, Texas, in 1935.

For all the money and effort invested, less than 200 American-built airplanes—Liberty-powered DH-4s—were in the battle zone and fit for service when WWI ended. The remaining 550 aircraft in American hands at the front were purchased from France and Britain. When the fighting stopped, there were 45 U.S. combat squadrons in action with a strength of 800 pilots and 500 aerial gunners and observers.

In seven months of combat, American losses were 289 planes and 48 observation balloons. U.S. pilots and gunners were credited with 781 enemy planes and 73 balloons shot down.

Eventually, in mid-1918, President Woodrow Wilson became aware of the Aircraft Production Board's blatant boondoggle and cleaned house. But the combines formed by Deeds and his cronies continued to possess their contracts, probably because there were no alternate sources at that late date. And since both public memory and political retribution are notably short-lived, both Deeds and Coffin would soon resurface in other positions of authority.

Airpower Prophet

The man who planned the highly successful U.S. Air Service tactics in WWI was Col. William "Billy" Mitchell. (We should pause to mention that the Aviation Section of the Signal Corps became the "Airplane Division" on 2 June 1917, although it was generally called the "Air Service." Separation from the Signal Corps came on 20 May 1918. On 4 June 1920 Congress approved the Army Reorganization Bill which officially recognized the "U.S. Air Service" as a "separate and coordinate branch of the Army." Then, on 2 July 1926 the Air Corps Act changed the Air Service to the "U.S. Army Air Corps," and it remained as such until 20 June 1941 when, with a new autonomy under Maj. Gen. Henry H. "Hap" Arnold, it became the "United States Army Air Forces" (USAAF). Today's independent United States Air Force (USAF) was created by the National Security Act of 1947, which became law on 18 September that year. We will try to use the appropriate term for each period discussed here.)

Mitchell had learned to fly at a civilian school and at his own expense while stationed in Washington, D.C. An excellent military record spanning 18 years service in the Signal Corps had resulted in assignment to the Signal Corps Headquarters staff and promotion to major. Mitchell had enlisted as a private in 1898 at the outbreak of the Spanish-American War, and had shown himself to be an innovative officer. Early in 1917, he convinced his superiors that he should be sent to Europe to study Allied air tactics. He was there when the U.S. declared war on Germany.

He flew as an observer with the French and went to England to talk with pilots and Royal Flying Corps brass. He was greatly impressed with Britain's Maj. Gen. Sir Hugh Trenchard, and Mitchell later wrote (Memoirs of WWI, *Liberty* magazine, 1928; Random House, 1960) that most of his philosophy on the proper use of airpower was based upon that of "Boom" Trenchard. Each clearly saw that a nation's air force should be an independent service, that a strategic air arm should be committed to the destruction of an enemy's critical industries, that tactical aircraft should be sent against the enemy's lines of supply and communication, and that close air support of an advancing ground force must include control of the air above that force.

Mitchell's immediate boss was Maj. Gen. Mason Patrick, Commander of the Army Air Services and an old classmate of Pershing's at West Point. Patrick never made any public statements about Mitchell, but there is evidence that he supported Mitchell whenever possible—not only in France, but years later, when Mitchell was publicly kicking a lot of sacred military cows, to the delight of the press and to the consternation of the War and Navy Departments. Gen. Patrick was almost certainly responsible for Mitchell's appointment to the post of Chief of Air Service, First Army, with a promotion in rank to colonel, because Pershing wasn't big on placing flying officers in command positions. Most flying officers were not "regular Army," and Pershing held the professional soldier's prejudices against reservists.

Mitchell was regular Army, and stretching friendship (with Patrick) only a little, that made him

Fig. 1-17. Albatros D-IIIs of Richthofen's Jagdstaffel 11, spring, 1917. A 160-hp Mercedes engine gave these fighters a speed of 120 mph. (USAF)

Fig. 1-18. Nieuport 17 fighters of the Lafayette Escadrille at Cachy, Somme, 1916. The Lafayette was made up of American volunteers flying for France prior to America's entry into WWI. (USAF)

acceptable to Pershing. However, Mitchell was not a West Pointer, and that definitely left him forever outside the council of the Army's General Staff. The highest permanent rank he could ever realistically expect was that of "bird" colonel. His later, temporary rank of brigadier general went with his job as the number two man in the Air Service—and it also went when he was relieved of that position.

The Army's policy of placing veteran regular Army officers in command of flying units generally worked very well. There's no substitute for experience, especially command experience. But it did produce a few unusual situations. At one flying school, when the new CO was informed that the students disliked their ancient Caudron training planes because they employed the old wing-warping principle for lateral control rather than hinged ailerons, he ordered the planes kept indoors and out of the sun when not in use to prevent such warping. An ex-cavalry major in charge of a squadron had a hitching post installed outside the Operations office and went about the aerodrome on horseback. (There were, in fact, so many ex-cavalry officers in the Air Service that spurs were part of the Air Service regulation uniform for several years.)

The most embarrassing example, perhaps, was the case of the major in charge of the 96th Bombardment Squadron who led a six-plane formation over Germany in marginal weather and eventually landed on a German aerodrome, believing it to be an Allied field. The Germans captured the whole outfit intact. The next day they dropped a note on the 96th's base which read: "We thank you for the fine airplanes and equipment you have sent us; but what shall we do with the major?" (When later reminded of the incident, Mitchell replied, "Needless to say, we did not reply about the major, as he was better off in Germany at that time than he would have been with us.")

Mitchell's chance to demonstrate some of his theories of aerial warfare finally came on 1 September 1918 when U.S. troops under Pershing began the great St. Mihiel Drive. From his headquarters at Ligny-en-Barrois, Mitchell commanded a force of 1476 aircraft, most of them placed at his disposal by the French, British and Italians. It constituted the greatest concentration of airpower the world had seen up to that time, and would appear to indicate that the French and Italian air commanders agreed with the Trenchard/Mitchell doctrine.

The St. Mihiel salient held by the Germans was shaped like a huge horseshoe, its foremost part on the Meuse River, its ends anchored on the German Border. Mitchell sent 400 planes to each end of the horseshoe to sever enemy lines at those points and split the enemy's air defences. Meanwhile, U.S. fighter-bombers (DH-4s, Breguets, Salmsons), along with elements of the U.S. 1st Pursuit Group, blasted in at treetop level across the horseshoe's center. While the American fliers were giving close support to the advancing infantry, the French and Italians far to the rear concentrated on the destruction of trains and trucks to immobilize all movement, effectively blocking both the possibilities of reinforcement and retreat. This was the employment of massed airpower as a tactical striking force as Mitchell envisioned it.

The operation was highly successful. The drive ended in quick victory for the American forces and the taking of thousands of prisoners who had been denied both help and an avenue of escape. Gen. Pershing was impressed; Mitchell was soon promoted to the temporary rank of Brig. Gen.

A few weeks later, Mitchell proposed to Pershing, via Patrick, that the U.S. Army form a paratroop division, but Pershing apparently did not take that suggestion seriously. Other Mitchell ideas (that the Air Service be a separate and equal department of the U.S. military, for example) *were* taken seriously—in fact, viewed with alarm. Just the hint that the upstart Air Service should someday independently take a share of the responsibility—and appropriations—for the nation's defense was enough to corrode a lot of brass. And well it might, for they were to hear a lot more from Billy Mitchell.

U.S. Naval Air in WWI

Some natural rivalry has always existed between the branches of the U.S. military, but seldom has it been more pronounced than in 1917-18 when the Army and Navy fought each other over aircraft procurement at home and the deployment of airplanes overseas. That may seem strange when one considers that *neither* service professed much faith in the effectiveness of aerial vehicles in their respective operations, but the generals and admirals, whatever their private or public positions concerning the value of military air machines, obviously felt that, since there *were* such things, *their* branch of the service should have the authority—preferably the *exclusive* authority—to operate them. In mid-1918, long before the U.S. Navy possessed a rigid dirigible (or could fathom any use for one), the Navy managed to obtain from the Secretary of War exclusive authority to operate rigid dirigibles. Upon America's entry into the war, the

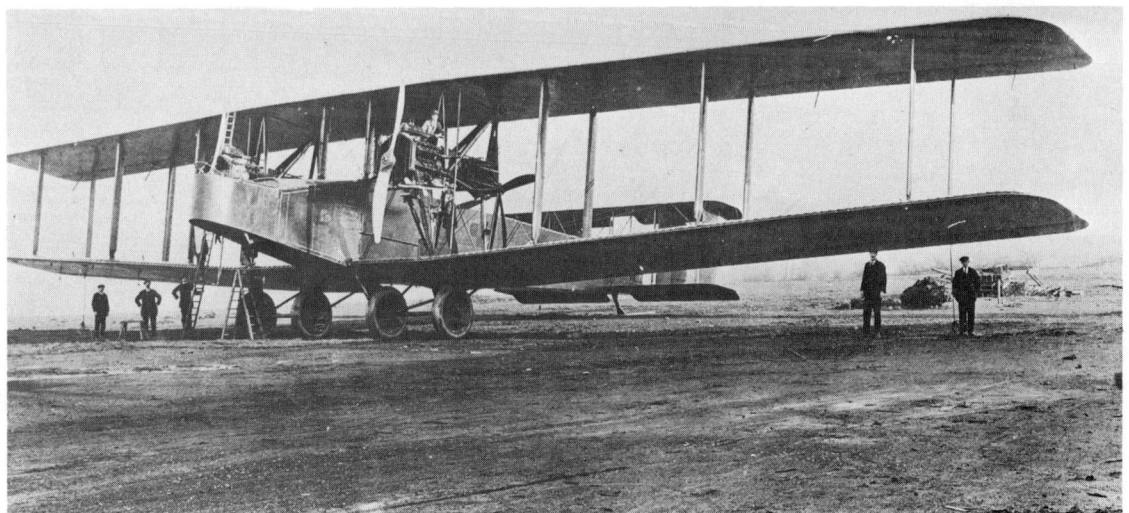

Fig. 1-19. The British Handley Page V/1500 of 1918 was designed to carry 1000 lbs of bombs to Berlin. Wingspan was 126 ft. (USAF)

Fig. 1-20. The Fokker DR-1 Driedecker (triplane) was Richthofen's favorite mount. Highly maneuverable, it was powered with the 110-hp Oberursel rotary engine and had a speed of 115 mph. (USAF)

Navy had rushed to sign contracts with all the major U.S. plane builders to tie up their entire production. The Army retaliated by taking charge of all sources of spruce (from which airframes were made). It was this bitter interservice squabble that hastened formation of the Aircraft Production Board.

Both services gave primary flight training to as many of its aviation enlistees as their limited facilities would permit, then shipped them overseas for advanced training (in some cases, all flight training). Therefore, many American pilots, in American uniforms, both Army and Navy, initially entered combat in French and British squadrons, because the U.S. had neither the airplanes nor the organized personnel and supporting equipment to establish its own air units until mid-March 1918. The Navy's first fighter ace, Lt. (jg) David S. Ingalls, scored all his air victories while flying with RAF Squadron 213.

The first aerial victory credited to a Navy airman went to Ens. Stephan Potter on 19 March 1918, when he shot down an enemy seaplane, one of several that attacked Potter's formation of flying boats as it attempted a reconnaissance mission along Germany's north coast.

The Navy air units were chiefly concerned with coastal patrol, but began offensive operations in August 1918, when Air Squadron One, Northern Bombing Group, made a single-plane night raid on enemy submarine docks at Ostend. The first raid in

Fig. 1-21. The body of Max Immelmann in wreckage of his Fokker Eindecker. The originator of the "Immelmann Turn" fell to the guns of Lt. George McCubbin, RFC, 18 June 1916. McCubbin was flying an F.E.2b. (USAF)

force by the Navy's Northern Bombing Group was made by eight aircraft of Marine Day Squadron Nine, which dropped 17 bombs, totalling 2,218 lbs, on the German-held railroad junction at Thielt Rivy, Belgium, 14 October.

When the armistice was signed ending the hostilities of WWI, the strength of Naval aviation had grown to a force of 6716 officers and 30,693 men in Navy units, and 282 officers, 2180 men in Marine Corps units, with 2107 airplanes and 230 lighter-than-air vehicles. Of these numbers, 18,000 officers and men and 570 aircraft were overseas, serving at 20 shore stations in France, England, Ireland, Gibraltar, Italy, and in the Azore Islands. The Navy's claims for its air units were modest: 27 enemy submarines sighted, 25 attacked, and 12 damaged. Naval aviators dropped 63 tons of bombs. The Navy's commander in chief, Adm. Mayo, refused to commend the war effort of Naval aviation, complaining that it had failed to work with his battleships.

Combat

Although the Americans made the difference

Fig. 1-22. More than two years of trench warfare took the lives of millions and left the war stalemated, the combatants exhausted, prior to the U.S. entry into the war in April, 1917.

in WWI, breaking the stalemate and spearheading Allied victory, we are allowed another perspective of the U.S. air contribution when we compare the number of aces (pilots officially credited with five or more enemy aircraft destroyed in aerial combat) produced by each country. Britain's RFC/RAF (the Royal Flying Corps became the Royal Air Force in

Fig. 1-23. The Curtiss H-12L flying boat used by the U.S. Navy during WWI as a patrol craft. Engines were 350-hp versions of the Army's Liberty. (USN)

Fig. 1-24. DeHavilland DH-4 at Fort Sill, Oklahoma, 1918. (Joe R. Reed collection)

mid-1918) could count 533 aces, their highest scorer being Maj. E. Mannock with 73 victories. There were 158 French aces, Capt. Rene Fonck being the greatest with 75. Of the 44 Italian aces, Maj. Francesco Baracca was tops with 34. Among the 360 German aces, Rttm. Manfred Frhr von Richthofen headed the list with 80 victories, and of the 83 American aces, Capt. Eddie Rickenbacker was the top scorer with 26 official victories.

These figures seem to suggest that U.S. Air Service pilots would have at least equalled the British record had the Americans been in combat a comparable length of time. It is a fair assumption. Gen. Trenchard himself remarked on the "aggressiveness of the Americans," and a look at the service records of a few U.S. aces underscores this factor. All were individualists, a trait not uncommon in a free society.

Take, for example, Elliot White Springs. His 12 air victories were topped by a half-dozen other U.S. pilots, but Springs typifies the attitudes, experiences, and the kind of young Americans who volunteered for the Air Service. Springs was a student at Princeton when the U.S. was forced into the war, a bright young man of small responsibility and large appetite for pleasure.

Thousands like Springs, in the best universities, were attracted to the Air Service because of newspaper accounts that had, throughout the previous year, lionized the aces and offered glowing accounts of chivalrous air duels in the skies of France. The air war was a romantic war, fought between fleet-winged machines in the crisp, unspoiled blue. The air war was a gentlemens' war.

Springs attended aviation ground school at Princeton, and in the fall of 1917 was sent to England with 209 others for flight training. Then, in May 1918, he was posted to RFC No. 85 Squadron, which was commanded by famed Canadian ace Maj. Billy Bishop (72 victories) and equipped with SE-5a fighters. The squadron was stationed near Petite-Synthe, France, and Bishop allowed his rookies a few short patrols but forbade them to fly near the front lines. That, however, was asking too much of the impatient Springs. He took off alone and flew into Germany looking for enemy aircraft.

Springs didn't find the enemy; the enemy—a flight of six Pfalzes—found him. Somehow he managed to escape and returned to his field in a badly damaged airplane. Attempting to land his crippled machine, he careened into Maj. Bishop's SE-5 and destroyed that one as well.

The next day, Bishop led six of his pilots, including Springs, on patrol in the Courtrai area where, with the advantage of altitude, they attacked a formation of 12 black Pfalz fighters. Springs, determined to vindicate himself, shot down one of the enemy as two others fell before the guns of his squadron mates. Then, returning to 85 Squadron's field, Springs, in high spirits, hot-dogged over a train for a dramatic landing—and wrecked his airplane.

Bishop determined that his eager rookie was unhurt, then sternly confronted him: "Well, Springs, pile up just two more SE-5s and you'll be a German ace. Whose side you on, anyway?"

The veteran Bishop knew, of course, that a fighter pilots's natural instincts should not be curbed, but directed. Springs would do well once a bit of responsibility was thrust upon him.

There followed a period of several weeks during which 85 Squadron escorted DH-9s of RFC 311 Squadron to bomb the U-boat pens on Germany's north coast (311 also contained Americans). Then, in June, 85 Squadron was transferred to St. Omer to help repulse what was to be the last great German offensive of the war.

While at St. Omer, Bishop was sent home to Canada to organize a Canadian air force (Canadians and other Commonwealth airmen had been fighting in the RFC), and Lt. Springs was promoted to flight commander.

Springs scored two more victories before he himself took a burst of fire in his engine during a battle with a Hannoveraner (an armored two-seater designed for trench strafing) and went down just behind British lines. His face smashed into his gun butts as his plane flipped end-over-end and he was pulled from the wreckage in shock. Four days later, he slipped out of the hospital in his pajamas and hitched a ride back to his squadron.

Meanwhile, as planes and equipment became available, Patrick and Mitchell were reclaiming American airmen from the British and French and forming U.S. combat squadrons. The first of these, the 12th and the 94th, had begun operations in April 1918, but Springs and a number of other Americans with the RFC did not make the transition until July, when they were at last able to fight under their own flag as the 148th Aero Squadron of the U.S. Air Service.

The 148th was equipped with Sopwith Camels, fighter planes the British were replacing with the superior SE-5, as Gen. Trenchard reorganized the Royal Flying Corps and the aircraft of the Royal Navy into the independent Royal Air Force (RAF).

Fig. 1-25. The Curtiss N-9H was the Navy's version of the JN-4 Jenny trainer. (Peter M. Bowers)

Fig. 1-26. French-built Nieuport 17 fighters at the U.S. Air Service training school, Issoudun, France, 1917. These aircraft were flown by all the leading Allied aces. (USAF)

The Camel had its good qualities. "It could turn so fast it could bite its own tail," according to Charlie Meyers, an instructor at the U.S. Air Service training base, Issoudun, France; it had a fast rate-of-roll and was a good machine in a dogfight—if one had mastered the manipulation of its rotary engine.

The rotary radial engines, used by both sides in WWI, seem a bit incredible today. Their crankshafts were bolted solidly to the airframe, while the cylinders and propeller rotated together around the crankshaft. A rotary always ran at full throttle, and power was controlled by a button on the pilot's control stick which cut out the ignition. A great deal of blipping with the cut-out button was required on every flight, along with adjustments to a two-lever fuel/air mixture control. Castor oil was used for lubrication, and the average time-between-overhaul on the rotaries was about 20 flying hours.

On 22 August, 148th Squadron was ordered to destroy a troublesome German observation balloon, a highly dangerous assignment because the *drachens* were tethered by steel cable to winch trucks that were surrounded by antiaircraft machine guns and fearsome devices known as "flaming onions" that formed a curtain of fire around the balloons. Meanwhile, these hydrogen-filled "rubber elephants" could be hauled down very quickly—they were seldom raised above 1500 ft—and the observer, suspended in a wicker basket, often took to his parachute when attacked, fearing a hydrogen explosion. (Balloon observers were the only airmen on either side equipped with parachutes until shortly before the war's end when some German pilots received them.)

Springs was unwilling to order any of his men to make the attack, so he took the mission himself, and assigned to his flight the job of keeping enemy fighters off of him while he was vulnerable at low altitude.

Springs planned the attack carefully, and dove on the *drachen* from out of the sun. He banked steeply away as it flamed and, continuing at low altitude through the hail of lead from the balloon's defenders, sped for home.

A few days later, while flying alone, Springs dove into a formation of five Fokkers, downing two of them before his guns jammed and he was forced to dive from the fray and make a run for his home field. He was on the ground just long enough to refuel and have his guns cleared, and then took off to aid an RAF observation plane under attack by three Fokkers over Bapaume.

Attacking out of the sun, Springs shot down one of the enemy fighters over Bapaume and, in a running fight that carried well into Germany, eventually downed the other two.

We single out Springs for this report not because of an unusual combat record, but rather because his actions were *not* unusual. The traits and abilities he displayed were fairly representative of all the young Americans who participated in that war. There were many others like him, in the trenches, at sea, and in the air. They were products of their time—naive, bold, idealistic. They were patriots, and they truly believed that they were fighting to "make the world safe for democracy."

The 148th Aero Squadron could count 66 enemy aircraft destroyed during its four months of combat. Rickenbacker's much-publicized 94th, in action three months longer, had a total of 69 air victories.

America's second-ranking ace of WWI was less typical. In fact, he was one of those rare people who defy understanding. He obviously believed in the same things that most of the rest of us claim as our standards, but he was so uncompromising in these beliefs—even when death was the only alternative to compromise—that we can only look at him with uncomprehending awe. Lt. Frank Luke, Jr scored 21 victories in a 17-day period—and nine of those days he did not fly. It is doubtful that any airman before or since has equalled that record. Luke's primary targets were as dangerous as any he could have chosen: German observation balloons. And if that is not enough to mark him as one-of-a-kind, consider this: Luke is the only man in the annals of flight to be awarded the Congressional Medal of Honor for a deed done while under military arrest.

Lt. Frank Luke's story would make an absorbing book in itself, but not enough is really known about him to ensure that such a work would be accurate. Much of it would have to be speculation. We *do* know that he tended to be a loner, but on the

Fig. 1-27. The Curtiss Jenny was the standard primary training plane of the U.S. Air Service during WWI. Powered with the 90-hp OX-5 engine, it had a top speed of about 75 mph. Approximately 6750 were built by Curtiss and several war-born firms, and surplus Jennies were the barnstormers' airplanes of the twenties. (Francis H. Dean collection)

Fig. 1-28. The Liberty engine was tested in eight-cylinder configuration atop Pike's Peak. Almost all Liberties were built as V-12s. (Air Force Museum)

other hand, former schoolmates characterized him as a pleasant fellow who made friends easily despite the fact that he wasn't much of a talker. A for-real John Wayne? Perhaps. As a native of Arizona, he spent much of his time as a teenager in the saddle. With a .30/30 carbine tucked in its scabbard close to his reins, he'd ride out of town trailing a pack animal and disappear for days. Some need within himself lured him into the heat-soaked desert and the silent mountains beyond. Perhaps it was a simple appreciation for raw nature—the desert is beautiful to those who truly know it—perhaps a subtler siren beckoned.

Luke learned of America's declaration of war one day in April 1917, when he rode into a small mining town after days in the trackless wasteland. He returned home and told his parents that he had to enlist because it was his duty. He was 20 years old.

Luke chose the Air Service, and after primary flight training at North Island, was sent overseas for advanced training at Issoudun, France. He then served as a ferry pilot for a time and was at last posted to combat duty with the 27th Aero Squadron late in July 1918. The 27th was commanded by Maj. Harold Hartney and equipped with the French-built Spad ("Spad" from the company that produced them, *Societe Pour Aviation et Derives*).

Fig. 1-29. Maj. Raoul Lufberry scored 17 victories as a member of the Lafayette Escadrille. He was killed soon after transferring to the U.S. Air Service. (USAF)

Luke's first combat patrol came on 15 August, but no enemy aircraft were encountered. Several days later, after more "milk runs," Luke deserted his formation and dove down to destroy a German observation balloon. His airplane was so badly damaged in the encounter that it had to be junked. Hartney chewed him out for leaving the formation without permission, but when Billy Mitchell saw the report of the incident, he phoned Hartney and said that if Lt. Luke really wanted to "bust balloons," allow him to do so. Other pilots dreaded the assignment, and since the enemy "sausages" directed a lot of artillery fire against the U.S. positions, their destruction was always gratefully acknowledged by ground commanders.

Luke accepted the mission, although Maj. Hartney warned that only one man could be spared to accompany Luke as top cover. Lt. Joseph Fritz Wehner immediately volunteered for that duty. He and Luke had become close friends during their brief acquaintance, perhaps because Wehner, too, had been cast from a different mold. Wehner had twice been arrested and questioned by Army intelligence people, apparently because of his German background, because he had worked for the YMCA in German prison camps before the U.S. entered the war, and possibly because he spoke fluent German.

While a new Spad—fitted with special .45-caliber machine guns, one of which would be armed with incendiary ammunition—was being made ready for Luke, the squadron moved up to Rembercourt, about 12 miles behind the front lines, to prepare for the great St. Mihiel offensive. Along with the move, the 27th Aero Squadron received a new commanding officer, Capt. Grant, as Hartney was promoted to Group Commander.

The St. Mihiel offensive began on 12 September, but Luke remained on the ground because his new machine wasn't ready. Then, on the 14th, he took Wehner with him and shot down two balloons. Wehner attacked a formation of eight Fokkers to keep them off of Luke, and the two of them made it safely back to base with no serious damage to their aircraft.

The next day, Luke got two more balloons. Wehner shot down two enemy fighters that were intent on attacking Luke, then peeled off and flamed a balloon that Frank had not seen. On the ground

Fig. 1-30. The Salmson observation plane was a superior French design operated by some U.S. units. The pilot had two forward-firing guns, and the observer two flex-mounted Lewis guns. (USAF)

Fig. 1-31. A German Hanoveraner CL-II observation craft forced down intact 2 October 1918 by U.S. pilots Reed Chambers and Eddie Rickenbacker after observer was killed and pilot wounded. (Joe Durham)

again, the two of them laughed uproariously over that one.

By this time, the enemy had come to know this pair of Spads very well. On the morning of the 16th,

Fig. 1-32. Crew of U.S. observation balloon prepare to launch. (Ft. Sill Field Artillery Museum)

when they appeared over the lines, every German balloon in the sector was quickly hauled down.

Frank and Joe returned to Rembercourt and waited for sunset. They decided to take off just before dark, stay low, and catch the *drachens* by surprise just before they were hauled down for the night. "We'll get three of them," Luke casually informed the squadron adjutant. "The first at 7:10, the second at 7:20, and the third at 7:30." They did. However, they were a few minutes late flaming the last one because they took time out to strafe an enemy truck convoy.

They remained on the ground the next day while the many bullet holes in their airplanes were patched, then returned to action on the 18th. Near Labeuville, they found a pair of balloons and Luke attacked while Wehner circled above.

It was an enemy trap. The sky was full of Fokkers before Luke completed his first pass. The enemy fighters had apparently managed to track

Fig. 1-33. U.S. sausage balloon explodes on ground, 1918. (Ft. Sill Field Artillery Museum)

Wehner and Luke directly up-sun where they could not be seen. Stubbornly, Luke held his dive, and as the first balloon began to burn from a short burst from his guns, he levelled off very low and came upon the second balloon from underneath. It exploded behind him as he made a steep climbing turn in a bid for altitude. A glance behind revealed two enemy fighters dropping on his tail. Wehner was right behind them, guns aflame, but the remaining Fokkers were closing in behind Wehner.

Luke nosed down again to gain speed, reversed direction with an Immelmann turn, rolled inverted, and split-essed to bring his guns to bear on the closest of Wehner's attackers. A short burst directly into the enemy's cockpit sent that one down. Rolling to his right, Luke got the next one as well before he was forced to level off only a few feet above the ground. It was frustrating trying to fight with so little space between him and the ground in which to maneuver. As his airspeed built up once again, he looked around to evaluate the situation. The remaining enemy fighters were breaking off the engagement. Wehner was nowhere in sight.

Low on fuel and with countless bullet holes in his machine, Luke turned for home. On the way, he stumbled onto a German observation plane and shot it down with a short burst into the pilot's cockpit. It was his fifth victory within ten minutes, but he did not know then that he would drink no toast with Joe Wehner that evening. The Fokkers had shot down Wehner over Labeuville.

Luke's official report of that mission is very brief and closes with: "Confirmations requested, two balloons, three planes . . . Lt. Wehner is entitled to share in the victories . . ." (Wehner had eight confirmed victories when he died.)

That evening, Maj. Hartney (an ace in his own right, and aware of the close bond between Luke and Wehner) came down from headquarters and ordered Luke to take a week's leave in Paris. Luke went, but was back at the end of three days, asking to be returned to duty. Hartney stalled for several days, believing that Luke needed rest, but by 26 September Luke was back in the air. Lt. Ivan Roberts volunteered to fly with him.

As they crossed the lines into enemy territory, they were joined by another Spad from a neighboring squadron. Then, in the vicinity of Consonvoye and Sivry, Luke spotted a large formation of Albatros fighters and led his three-plane element to the attack. Luke downed one of the enemy almost at once, but was forced to dive away from the fight when his guns jammed. Lt. Roberts did not return.

Luke seemd to brood over the loss of Roberts, apparently blaming himself. He took a motorcycle and left the field without permission, and when that drew a reprimand from Capt. Grant, Luke simply went to his plane and took off, also without permission.

He found a German balloon over Bantheville, but was unable to reach it before it was pulled down.

Fig. 1-34. Capt. Eddie Rickenbacker (l) was America's leading ace in WWI with 26 victories. Capt. Douglas Campbell (center) scored six victories. Maj. Kenneth Marr at right. (USAF)

Fig. 1-35. Lt. Frank Luke, Jr., and his Spad fighter. (USAF)

He turned away as if disinterested, but then, a few minutes later, roared in on the deck and exploded the *drachen* in its nest.

He did not return to the 27th's field, but spent the night with the *Cigognes* ("Storks"), a famed French fighter squadron, flying back to his own base the next day. Capt. Grant immediately grounded him. Luke responded by taking off again, telling his mechanic that he would have his plane serviced at a temporary forward aerodrome commanded by Capt. Vasconcelles. Grant's reaction to that was a phone call to Vasconcelles ordering Luke's arrest.

Vasconcelles apologetically relayed this order to Luke. But then, when Maj. Hartney landed there a few minutes later, Vasconcelles remained silent when Luke casually asked for—and received—Hartney's permission to attack three *drachens* hanging in the sky near Dun along the east bank of the Meuse River. Hartney was unaware of the arrest order.

Luke took off just at sunset. He stayed low and caught the first balloon crew by surprise, but left a flaming beacon in the air that quickly brought a flight of eight Fokkers that had apparently been waiting for the lone Spad and its sundown attacks.

Luke destroyed the second balloon before he was forced to turn on the Fokkers and attempt to deal with them. He shot down two of them (many believed that Luke was the best aerial marksman on the Western Front), then broke away to get the third balloon which was hastily being hauled down near Milly. As the third *drachen* exploded, Luke swung over the village of Murvaux and strafed a column of German infantry, then landed in a field beyond with a dead engine.

He jumped from his crippled plane, Colt .45 automatic in hand, and tried to escape toward the river, but enemy soldiers cut him off. From the gathering darkness, they called upon him to surrender. He replied with his Colt.

It was futile, of course, but Luke never gave an inch. He fell from chest wounds with an empty pistol in his hand.

On the Allied side of the lines, Luke was listed as "missing in action" until two months after war's end. Observers at the front had seen the three balloons go down, but that was all that was known about Luke's last flight until U.S. Graves Registration Officers reached the village of Murvaux in January 1919. Their first report read:

    From: Graves Registration Officer, Neufchateau Area No. 1.

Fig. 1-36. Lt. Joseph F. Wehner flew top cover for Luke. (USAF)

Fig. 1-37. Recently discovered rare photo is believed to be of Luke just as he flamed a German drachen. (Archiv Krueger)

To: Chief of Air Service, APO 717.
Subject: Grave, unknown American aviator.

1. Units of this service have located the grave of an unknown aviator killed on Sunday, 29 September 1918 in the village of Murvaux.

2. From inspection of the grave and interviews held with inhabitants of this town, the following information was learned in regard to this aviator and his heroism. He is reported as having light hair, young, of medium height, and of heavy stature.

3. Reported by the inhabitants that previous to being killed this man had brought down three German balloons, two German airplanes, and dropped hand bombs killing German soldiers and wounding others.

4. He was wounded himself in the shoulder and evidently had to make a forced landing. Upon landing he opened fire with his automatic pistol and fought until he was killed.

5. It is also reported that the Germans took his shoes, leggings, and money, leaving his grave unmarked.

Chester E. Staten,
Captain of Infantry,
G.R.S. Officer

Upon receipt of this report, Gen. Mitchell ordered further investigation that turned up Luke's wrist watch, which was under the sleeve of his flying suit and which the Germans had missed. An affidavit signed by the mayor and 14 inhabitants of Murvaux provided the eyewitness account upon which the Graves Registration officer's report was based. Later, this affidavit was verified by Lt. B. Mangels of Munster, Germany, who commanded German balloons numbers 35 and 64 of the 5th German Army, the last two destroyed by Luke that fateful Sunday. [*Note:* Your author is aware of previously published accounts of Luke's last flight which do not agree with this presentation. However, it appears that those versions were written without benefit of the official records, particularly, the report of Capt. Staten, and the much more detailed affidavit sworn to by the villagers of Murvaux. One such story mentions the affidavit, but then misquotes it. There is no need to tamper with the facts. The villagers' impression that Luke dropped "hand bombs" on the enemy infantry is the kind of natural mistake one expects when the witnesses are unfamiliar with airplanes. Luke's twin .45-caliber machine guns could create a lot of havoc in the narrow, dusty street of Murvaux. The villagers also believed that Luke landed in order to get a drink of water from the river, but in all other details their account agrees with that of Lt. Mangels, the German balloon commander.]

Luke's body was removed to the American cemetery at Romagne and buried with full military honors. He was posthumously awarded the Distinguished Service Cross, France's Croix-de-Guere, and the United States' highest military award, the Congressional Medal of Honor.

Chapter 2

The Wings Grow Stronger

U.S. military aircraft were improved during the two decades between WWI and WWII, but little credit for those advances can be given to America's leaders, either civilian or military. Military planning, at the highest levels, reverted to pre-WWI concepts. The Atlantic and Pacific Oceans were viewed as America's great natural barriers to foreign aggression, and the U.S. Navy was regarded as the primary defender of American shores—indeed, the entire Western Hemisphere. The Monroe Doctrine, which served notice to the world that the United States would tolerate no "outside" intervention into the affairs of any North, Central, or South American nation, was an unambiguous cornerstone of U.S. foreign policy.

Since every American knew that the United States was not going to start a war anywhere, there was really no need to maintain a large, well-equipped Army. American arms were for defense only. Such a posture seemed perfectly reasonable at the time. (If man were half as civilized as he should be, it would be reasonable today.) Unfortunately, the bitter seeds that would blossom into WWII were planted at the conclusion of WWI, and America's determination to avoid future involvement in Europe's squabbles would fade when it appeared that the Nazis could well become the rulers of all Europe, including Great Britain.

It was the terms of the peace treaty signed with Germany at the close of WWI—in a railway coach at Versailles, France, 28 June 1919—that led to the Nazi takeover of Germany. Had it not been the Nazis, a similar movement almost certainly would have evolved, because the Treaty of Versailles doomed Germany to economic servitude and the status of a second-class nation.

Germany was stripped of all her overseas territories, along with 25,000 square miles of Germany itself, and the Allies demanded that Germany pay billions in "reparations." There was no way that a bankrupt Germany could pay, in either money or goods, but the French, especially, were adamant and repeatedly sent troops into a prostrate Germany in attempts to force the Germans to pay.

Fig. 2-1. Military budgets of the early '20s forced the Air Service to fly the WWI DH-4s. A DH-4 training flight at Fort Sill ended against a barbed wire fence. (Mike Sweatt collection)

Many other sanctions were imposed, including the provision that Germany be allowed no military aircraft of any kind. In short, the Treaty of Versailles—which the United States refused to sign—made it impossible for Germany to regain political and economic stability. By 1923, German money was worthless and there were food riots in the streets of Berlin.

Nevertheless, the Allies did not relent, and in 1930 the final amount that Germany must pay in damages was set at 121 billion Reichmarks. Two years later, German unemployment passed the six million mark, and the following January Adolf Hitler was elected chancellor of Germany, brought to power by eleven years of political and economic turmoil. True, the Nazis received only 33 percent of the vote in the election and Hitler was, in effect, a compromise candidate. But all Germany, after years of deprivation and humiliation, was ready to follow a leader who could quicken its national pulse with visions of a new pride, prosperity, and Germany's return to its rightful place in the world.

During this period the American people, their representatives in Congress, and their Presidents believed that the United States could avoid future wars with other major powers, especially if no entangling commitments were made overseas. The U.S. Army shrunk to 137,000 officers and men during the '20s as military appropriations dwindled. The Air Service stood at the end of the line for its share. The Air Service/Air Corps' average yearly expenditure from authorized appropriations was 25 million dollars for the years 1921 through 1938 inclusive, while average personnel strength for those years was less than 14,000 officers and men.

For the first ten years after WWI Gen. Pershing dominated War Department policy. Although he had, during the closing weeks of the late war, been given a glimpse of the airplane's potential as a military weapon, he did not project that lesson into planning for the future defense of the nation. He removed Gen. Patrick from his post as Chief of Air Service and replaced him with Gen. Charles Menoher, an infantry commander with no background in aviation. Gen. Billy Mitchell was appointed Menoher's deputy, and that epitomized the War Department's attitude toward the Air Service: Mitchell was able. Menoher was Army. That priority of command would continue until the eve of WWII.

The Navy, meanwhile, actually had several top officers who recognized the airplane's potential value to the fleet, among them Admirals Fiske, Fullam and Sims. Primarily due to their influence, the Navy kept its aviation program alive after the war ended and, in 1919, decided to test the efficacy of large flying boats as long-range patrol craft by attempting to fly the Atlantic. That decision may have been given a little boost by the fact that Glenn Curtiss had built a flying boat early in 1914 expressly for that purpose, although war came before the flight could be attempted. Then, the Navy contracted with Curtiss to build four large flying boats that could be flown to Europe for submarine patrol. However, only the first of those, the NC-1, was completed by war's end.

First Atlantic Flight

Rear Adm. Douglas Taylor, apparently abetted by Cmdr. John Tower (one of the Navy's first pilot-seems to have been the one who initially pushed for the Atlantic flight and who obtained permission from the Secretary of the Navy Josephus Daniels to complete the NC-2 through NC-4 sister craft for that ambitious project. The NC-2 was cannibalized to provide components for aircraft Numbers One and Four which were damaged in a hangar fire. Then, on 8 May 1919, planes NC-1, NC-3 and NC-4 left Rockaway Beach, Long Island bound for Plymouth, England, by way of Newfoundland, the Azores, Portugal, and France.

The NCs (for "Navy-Curtiss;" inevitably

Fig. 2-2. The Orenco D fighter was a 1918 U.S. design which had a speed of 139 mph fitted with a 300-hp Hispano engine. Curtiss built 50 for the Air Service in 1920. (USAF)

Fig. 2-3. The Douglas C-1 was the standard Army transport of the '20s. It was Liberty-powered. (USAF)

called the "Nancies") were large for their time. Wingspan was 126 ft, hull length was 45 ft, and each was powered with four 400-hp Liberty engines mounted in nacelles between the wings, a tractor and a pusher mounted back-to-back in the center nacelle with a tractor on each side. All-up weight was 28,000 lbs and cruising speed was 77 mph.

Delayed by engine trouble and weather, the three planes at last left Newfoundland on 16 May headed for the Azores, 1200 miles away.

Approximately half of the flight was made in darkness and much of the rest through recurring patches of fog. The NC-1 landed on the ocean in dense fog about 300 miles short of its destination, and the NC-3 did the same 100 miles away. The crew of the NC-1 was picked up by a passing ship, although their airplane sank in heavy seas. Cmdr. Towers taxied the damaged NC-3 on the surface, arriving in the harbor at Horta, in the Azores, 60 hours later, his airplane a wave-battered wreck.

Meanwhile, Lt./Cmdr. Albert C. Read and his five-man crew aboard the NC-4 had flown nonstop from Newfoundland to Horta in 15 hours and 18 minutes. They left Horta on the 20th, after a two-day rest, and flew on to Lisbon by way of Ponta Delgada, and ended their epic flight at Plymouth, England on 31 May. The U.S. Navy was first to fly the Atlantic—but just barely.

Two weeks later, on 14 June 1919, RAF Captain John Alcock and Lt. Arthur Whitten-Brown took off from Newfoundland in a British bomber, the twin-engined Vickers Vimy and, after 16 hours and 28 minutes (1890 miles) at an average speed of 118.5 mph, landed at Clifden, Ireland to claim a cash prize of $50,000 offered by a British newspaper publisher for the first transatlantic nonstop flight. Then, two weeks after *that*, on 2 July 1919, the British rigid airship R.34 left Scotland bound for New York.

The R.34, commanded by RAF Maj. G.H. Scott and carrying a crew of 30, landed in New York on 6 July after covering a distance of 3600 miles in 108 hours. On 9 July, Scott turned his airship around and flew back to the British Isles, thus completing the first aerial round trip across the Atlantic.

Eight years later, Charles A. Lindbergh would fly alone nonstop from New York to Paris in a single-engine monoplane, and that would be the aerial crossing of the Atlantic that would capture the fancy of the world and convince people everywhere that the airplane had become a reliable and useful machine to serve mankind.

In the meantime, several other Atlantic flights were attempted. Most ended in disaster, although the German rigid airship, Zeppelin ZR-3, was flown to America in mid-October 1924, by a German aircrew commanded by Dr. Hugo Eckener, and presented to the U.S. Navy as part payment on war damages claimed by the United States. (The U.S. did ask for some reparations, although the amount was comparatively small and no serious effort to collect was made. The U.S. and Germany signed a separate peace treaty in 1921.)

The NC-4's successful Atlantic crossing had a predictable effect on Gen. Billy Mitchell. In the fall of 1919, he sent 60 of the Army's DH-4s across the United States in a "reliability" test. Thirty flew westward from New York as 30 others left San Francisco. Several were lost, and nothing much was proved, although it could be said that the Air Service had blazed a trail which the air mail (begun on a limited basis by Air Service planes in 1918) would later follow.

The following June (1920), four DHs, commanded by Capt. St. Clair Street, flew from New York to Nome, Alaska. They returned in October, having covered 4345 miles (much of it over uncharted wilderness) in 112 flying hours.

Army and Navy Racers

Since Air Service budgets—about five percent of the Army's total budgets—did not allow the acquisition of new airplanes in significant number, Mitchell convinced his boss, Gen. Patrick (who replaced Menoher in 1921), that what money they had should be spent on headline-grabbing flights that would impress the public in general and the Congress in particular, especially as such activities could be justified as useful research and development. Accordingly, the Air Service (quickly followed by the Navy, of course), fostered the design and construction of a series of racing planes to compete in several popular international air races during the early twenties. The Army and Navy Curtiss racers dominated these events; although the publicity returned no discernable benefits, and the U.S. Congress remained as stingy with appropriations as ever, the races did prove the new Curtiss D-12 engine of 435 hp—a vast improvement over the wartime Liberty—and the D-12 would

Fig. 2-4. The four Curtiss-built NC flying boats were designed at the Naval Aircraft Factory. Powered with four Liberties (one pusher and three tractors), three of these craft attempted the first Atlantic flight in 1919. (USN)

Fig. 2-5. The Navy's NC-4, commanded by Lt/Cmdr. A.C. Read, proudly taxies into the harbor at Lisbon, Portugal, 27 May 1919, after completing the first transatlantic flight from Trepassey, Newfoundland. (USN)

power Army fighter planes throughout the '20s and lead to the development of far more powerful engines of the same type.

The Curtiss D-12, a V-12 water-cooled engine, was developed by Finlay Porter from a design initiated by long-time Curtiss engineman Charles Kirkham. It featured cast cylinder blocks (which, up to that time, had not been successful in aircraft engines of that power). The British were so impressed with the D-12 that the Air Ministry purchased one and gave it to Rolls Royce, along with an appropriate government subsidy, to copy or improve. The result was the 1295 cubic-inch Kestrel of 480 hp which went into production in May, 1928. By 1937 the Kestrel XVI was rated at 750 hp as installed in the RAF's Hawker Fury fighters, and it was this engine, with its displacement raised to 1650, that became the famed Merlin of WWII.

Ironically, Curtiss, after developing the D-12 into the 600-hp Conqueror (which powered the last of America's biplane fighters) decided, in 1931, to discontinue development of liquid-cooled aircraft engines, and in America that role went by default to the (then) tiny Allison Division of General Motors.

Allison was given a Navy contract at that time to build five such engines for possible use on its big rigid dirigibles. That engine, the Allison V-1710, was never installed in a dirigible (by the time it was ready for delivery, the Navy's *Akron* and *Macon* had both crashed), but it was concurrently developed during the mid-30s with the British Merlin to become a principal WWII fighter airplane powerplant. But all this takes us ahead of our story.

First World Flight

Since the Navy gained as much from the well-publicized air races of the early '20s as did the Army, Billy Mitchell came up with another idea. Although his bombers had, at least to his own satisfaction, demonstrated in 1921, and again in 1923, that the most impregnable battleship was vulnerable to air attack (about which, more later), the Air Service needed to demonstrate its potential versatility in an even more dramatic fashion. Mitchell took his idea to Gen. Patrick and Patrick officially announced it late in 1923: The U.S. Army Air Service would fly around the world!

That was indeed a bold undertaking, viewed against the background of air progress up to that time. There would be few landing fields, no navigational aids, no radio, and no weather reports. The art of instrument flying was still far in the future, and the fliers themselves would have to perform all maintenance on their machines—a truly herculean task since it would include half a dozen complete engine changes in each of the four planes. They dared not trust the Liberty engine beyond 50 hours of flight, and it was the only engine of sufficient power available. (The new Curtiss D-12 was still in test and had been operated only for short periods in the military racers.)

A small California airframe builder, Donald Douglas, was awarded a contract to build five World Cruisers, four of which would attempt the journey with the fifth held in reserve. Douglas was 28 years old in 1920 when he opened for business in the rear of a barber shop with $600 in capital. But he had a degree from M.I.T.—earned in two years—and a year's experience working for Glenn Martin, during which time he designed the prototype of the Martin

Fig. 2-6. The Navy's Curtiss CR-2 racer, fitted with a Curtiss D-12 engine, attained an average speed of 193.2 mph around a closed course in the 1922 Pulitzer race. (USN)

Fig. 2-7. The Army Curtiss R3C-1 was first in the 1925 Pulitzer race with an average speed of 249 mph; engine was the new Curtiss Conqueror of 600-hp, a glycol-cooled V-12. (USAF)

Fig. 2-8. The Curtiss D-12 (V-1150) engine of 400 to 460 hp.

bombers in Army service during the '20s. Douglas had sold some torpedo planes to the Navy and, when he began design and construction of the World Cruisers, had a payroll of 112 and occupied an abandoned movie studio just off Wilshire Boulevard in eastern Santa Monica.

The World Cruisers, which were identical, had a wingspan of 50 ft, maximum weight of 8200 lbs, service ceiling of 8000 ft, and a normal cruise near 90 mph. These were hefty, two-place, open-cockpit biplanes with fittings for either floats or wheels because both would be needed in different parts of the world. Their crews were selected by Gen. Patrick from among hundreds of volunteers.

The crews and their planes were: Maj. F.L. Martin and Sgt. Alva Harvey in World Cruiser #1, the *Seattle*; Lts. Lowell Smith and Leslie Arnold in #2, the *Chicago*; Lt. Leigh Wade and Sgt. Henry Ogden in #3, the *Boston*, and Lts. Erik Nelson and John Harding in #4, the *New Orleans*.

Equipped with floats, the four planes left Seattle shortly after sunrise on 6 April 1924 and followed the Inside Passage to Alaska through spring blizzards—one of which claimed the *Seattle* when Maj. Martin, blinded by snow, literally flew into the ground. Neither he nor Harvey were seriously injured; they walked out to civilization on their own, while the remaining three cruisers continued across the North Pacific with Lt. Lowell Smith in command.

The adventures of the three remaining crews would (and did) fill a book in itself. Weather forced them down in Russian waters off the Komandorski Islands, but as the ceiling lifted Smith led the flight into Paramushiru, navigating (as he did the entire trip) by dead reckoning. The Air Service had accomplished the first aerial crossing of the Pacific.

The cruisers flew southward over Japan's 4000 home islands to Tokyo where, for the second time, the crews installed new engines, and then fought heavy rains down the South China Coast to Saigon in what was then French Indochina. The *Chicago's*

Fig. 2-9. The *New Orleans*, flown by Lts. Erik Nelson and Jack Harding, was one of the two Douglas World Cruisers to complete the first around-the-world flight, 6 April to 28 September 1924. (Douglas Aircraft Company)

Fig. 2-10. Uncovered forward fuselage reveals fuel tanks beneath seats of the Liberty-powered World Cruisers. (McDonnell Douglas Astronautics Co.)

engine blew up over the Gulf of Tonkin, but Smith hired a native to tow the plane with a fleet of sampans to a village dock where a new Liberty delivered by a Navy destroyer, was quickly installed. The *Chicago* joined the other two planes in Saigon from where the flight turned northwestward for Bangkok, Rangoon, and Calcutta.

Switching from floats to wheels, the three cruisers left Calcutta on the first of July and made good time across India despite a newspaperman stowaway in the *Boston's* tool compartment, sandstorms, and the oppressive heat until, a few miles short of Karachi, the *New Orleans'* engine began to disintegrate. With oil bathing the entire nose of his airplane, Lt. Nelson managed to reach Karachi.

Another engine change for the three aircraft required two days, then the fliers were off for Bag-

Fig. 2-11. The *Boston* goes down in the North Atlantic after rescue of her crew, Lts. Leigh Wade and Henry Ogden. (USAF)

Fig. 2-12. L to R: Lt. Lowell H. Smith, Secretary of War John Weeks, M./Gen. Mason Patrick, B./Gen. William Mitchell, Lts. Erik Nelson and Leigh Wade. (USAF)

dad on 7 July. Later, they were beset by sandstorms over the Arabian Desert and threaded their way through passes in the Taurus Mountains. (The Cruisers' 8000-ft service ceiling did not permit them to climb over the mountains.) They reached Constantinople on 11 July, and five days later were in London.

By then, the six airmen were international heros. This caused a problem because crowds awaited their arrival at every stop and officials in each city along their route planned ceremonies and dinners in their honor. The fliers understood that they were representing the United States and therefore had to smile through a lot of speeches and try to remain awake through a lot of formal dinners they would have much preferred to have skipped. It all took time, and they badly needed that time to rest and to work on their airplanes.

In England, the planes received new engines and had wheels replaced by floats once again, while the U.S. Navy positioned ships in the North Atlantic along the Cruisers' course and rushed fuel to planned stops in Iceland and Greenland. No airplane had ever been to either place.

The North Atlantic, however, would exact its price. The *Boston* was forced down at sea with a dead engine. Although the Navy ship *Billingsby* rescued Wade and Ogden, their airplane sank in heavy seas.

The *Chicago* and *New Orleans* continued the flight and, after a Navy-assisted engine change in each plane on the Greenland Coast, and a link-up with Wade and Ogden in Nova Scotia on 3 September (where Gen. Patrick had sent the reserve Cruiser, christened *Boston II*), the world fliers reached Boston on 6 September, and were back at their starting point at Seattle on 28 September 1924, having been mobbed and laden with gifts at every stop across the United States.

The total distance flown was 26,345 miles, and the *Chicago* and *New Orleans* had been in the air 363 hours and seven minutes at an average speed of 72.5 mph. The fact that the journey required 177 days elapsed time primarily reflected the inadequacies of the Cruisers' engines. Each plane used nine engines averaging slightly over 40 hours on each, yet the fliers still suffered four engine failures. When it is realized that the fliers themselves performed seven of those changes, usually under primitive conditions (the Liberty engine weighed more than 700 lbs) and attended to all other servicing of their aircraft, their feat appears all the more remarkable.

There wasn't much Navy fliers could do to top the Army's world flight, which undeniably added to the United States' prestige abroad, and except for Gen. Patrick and the crews of the World Cruisers, all of whom sent warm notes of thanks to the Navy, few others stopped to consider that the flight would not have been completed without the Navy's help, particularly over the North Atlantic.

Meanwhile, Gen. Billy Mitchell, looking to the future, had just completed an extensive tour of the Far East. On 24 October 1924, he submitted a 325-page secret report to the War Department in which he warned of a coming war with Japan:

"... the Japanese have specialized on their air force since 1918 ... it now appears that the Japanese are probably the second air power in the world with between 600 and 800 airplanes ... Japan estimates that, if war comes, America will begin the war with the methods and systems of the last war ... She knows that war is coming someday with the United States ... Air operations for the destruction of Pearl Harbor will be undertaken ... the attack to be made on Ford's Island at 7:30 a.m. ... nothing can stop it except air power ... the Philippines will be attacked in a similar manner ... The initial success, as things stand now, will probably be with the Japanese"

Mitchell's sadly prophetic 1924 secret report was ignored by the War Department (nowadays called the "Department of Defense"), and Mitchell became ever more public in his crusade for a strong and independent Air Force.

Chapter 3

Naval Air and Billy Mitchell

Rear Admiral William Adger Moffett demonstrated that a man may prevail against the errors of his friends if only his enemies will help a little. Adm. Moffett greatly advanced U.S. Naval aviation during the '20s. He did so despite anti-airplane prejudices held by the old sea dogs who were his superiors, because he was aided—unintentionally, of course—by a man he detested. That man was the Army's Brigadier General William Mitchell, who consistently made the issue of U.S. Airpower front-page news and thereby kept the blood pressures of the "battleship admirals" at dangerously high levels.

William Moffett had risen to the rank of captain in the battleship Navy when in March 1921 he was appointed "Director of Naval Aviation," an office tucked into the Navy's Planning Division, and which was not expected to do much directing. The office was useful primarily as the authority responsible for whatever went *wrong* in Naval air operations, while direct control of the air units was spread among the several commands to which the units were attached.

This piecemeal administration meant that no single voice possessing real authority could speak for Naval air, and that's just the way most of the ranking officers wanted it. The Chief of Naval Operations, Admiral William S. Benson, had spoken for the saltiest of them when he declared, "The Navy doesn't need airplanes. Aviation is just a lot of noise."

There were, however, a few top Naval officers who had a different view and the courage to say so. These included Admirals Bradley Fiske, William S. Sims, and W.F. Fullam. None was radical in his thinking, and none suggested that airplanes could supplant warships in the nation's defense. They were simply agreed that the Navy needed airplanes, and recommended to the Secretary of the Navy in 1919 a development program that would establish a Naval air service "capable of accompanying and operating with the fleet in all waters of the globe."

This recommendation—actually, the last of a series forwarded by the Navy's General Board—was endorsed in its essentials by Navy Secretary

Josephus Daniels. Daniels added an earlier request for funds to build a rigid dirigible, along with Admiral Sims' strong plea for an aircraft carrier, and then sought Congressional approval. That followed on 11 July 1919, with passage of the Naval Appropriations Act for fiscal 1920.

Congressional approval, while necessary, was not a guarantee. Money for Naval air was buried within the total Navy appropriation, and Naval Aviation would stand at the end of the line for its share when the Navy's Budget Bureau divvied-up the cash. Thus, the aircraft carrier that Adm. Sims had hoped for turned out to be a coal barge (the collier *Jupiter*, which was to be converted by addition of a flight deck), and the request for 108 fighter aircraft to equip America's first aircraft carrier was first cut to 75, and finally to ten.

Even that was too much to suit Adm. Benson. In the fall of 1920, he countermanded the order to convert the *Jupiter*. But Capt. Thomas T. Craven, who was then Director of Naval Aviation, managed to get a direct order from Secretary Daniels and work on the *Jupiter* was resumed.* That cost Craven his job. Shortly after the crews returned to work on the *Jupiter*, he was replaced by Capt. Moffett.

Moffett took over Craven's desk at a propitious time. Throughout the previous year, newspapers around the country had given a lot of space to Gen. Billy Mitchell's crusade for an independent air force, and his claim, made before several Senate committees, that the airplane had rendered the Navy's surface ships obsolete. Since 1920 was an election year, the issues Mitchell raised probably received more national attention than would have otherwise been the case. His seemingly far-out pronouncements on political/military matters were custom-made to fit charges of waste, outdated policies, and maladministration at high government levels.

---

*The office of Chief of Naval Operations was established 2 March 1915, and the scope of CNO's authority was challenged for years thereafter by the Navy bureau chiefs. Not until President Truman issued Executive Order 9635 on 29 September 1945 were CNO's authority and duties clearly defined.

Fig. 3-1. M./Gen. Patrick (l), and Billy Mitchell. Patrick, as Chief of Air Service, was Mitchell's boss and quiet supporter from 1921 until Mitchell was forced to leave the service four years later. (USAF).

Then, a few days before President Harding took office in March 1921, the War Department announced that several German warships, taken as prizes under terms of the Treaty of Versailles, would be destroyed in Naval ordnance tests. Gen. Mitchell reacted predictably, and the nation's press enthusiastically took up his challenge to the Navy that the Air Service be allowed to prove that airplanes could sink battleships.

This at last prodded the Navy into covering its own aviation bets. Clearly, if Mitchell's preachments should gain significant support in Congress, then it was at least possible that an independent air force, of (God forbid!) co-equal status, could emerge, and the effect of *that* on Naval appropriations was too frightening to consider. Therefore, prudence dictated that the Navy quickly establish a substantial legal equity in its own air service.

Fig. 3-2. Martin GMB (above) and Martin MB-2 were the bombers sent by Mitchell to prove that airplanes could sink battleships in 1921. (USAF)

Congress obliged on 1 July 1921 with an act that created a Naval Bureau of Aeronautics (BuAer), "possessing such responsibilities and authority pertaining to Naval Air as the Secretary shall prescribe." When this office began to function on the first of September Moffett, as its director, was elevated to the rank of rear admiral.

Meanwhile, on 21 July, an 11-plane formation of Mitchell's bombers had indeed sent the German battleship *Ostfriesland* to the bottom with two direct hits and four near-misses employing 2000-lb bombs. At the time, that seemed to prove everything or nothing, depending upon one's prejudices. Ultimate proof would wait upon another day—a Sunday morning in Hawaii, to be described as a day that would "live in infamy."

It should be noted that the Congresses of this period reflected little polarization of opinion over "Mitchellism." It occasioned no great debates on Capitol Hill, probably because most lawmakers saw no urgent need for major changes in the defense alignment in the absence of a definite threat; in any case, military spending was certain to remain at a minimal level for the foreseeable future. The nation was recovering from the effects of WWI, and Harding had won the Presidency with the slogan, "Back to Normalcy."

But whatever one's views on Mitchellism, it must be credited with aiding (however unintentionally) at a critical time the cause of that small band of visionaries within the Navy that recognized the developing need for a strong Naval air arm. With establishment of the Bureau of Aeronautics, headed by an officer of flag rank, Naval Aviation had its *Magna Carta*—albeit a poorly funded one—and a secure anchorage to attract gifted, airminded personnel.

Navy Aircraft Engine Development

Among such personnel was Lt. Cmdr. Bruce

G. Leighton, Naval Aviator No. 40, a pleasant, outgoing type chosen by Moffett to head up the bureau's Aircraft Engine Section. Leighton and his engine program typified the kind of officer and the kind of action that gave BuAer its special character under Moffett. The soft-spoken Moffett believed in encouraging initiative. He told his subordinates what he wanted, but seldom how to accomplish it. That sometimes resulted in methods he himself may not have chosen, but which he always stood ready to support. He knew that loyalty begets loyalty, and future commanders must learn to command. It was an approach that paid great returns in Leighton's case—not only for the Navy, but for the Army and civil aviation as well, because Lt./Cmdr. Leighton jawboned private industry into the development of the most successful aircraft piston engines ever built, the Wright Whirlwinds and the Pratt & Whitney Wasps.

Leighton was pointed in the right direction at the outset, because the officer previously responsible for the Navy's aircraft engines, Lt./Cmdr. S.M. Kraus in the Bureau of Steam Engineering, had determined that the air-cooled static radial engine ("static" as opposed to the rotary-type radial engines of WWI), if it could be made reliable, was best suited to the Navy's needs. It promised more horsepower for less weight, and would be easier and cheaper to maintain than the water-cooled engines then available. Therefore, Kraus had obtained some Navy money to foster development of the Lawrance Model J, a radial design of 200 hp with which Kraus hoped to power the small fighters that would be needed if and when Adm. Sims got his aircraft carrier.

The Lawrance J was the product of tiny Lawrance Aero Engines Company, operated by Charles Lanier Lawrance, who had switched from automobile to airplane engine design after working for Allesandro Anzani in Paris prior to WWI. Returning to the U.S. in 1914, Lawrance set up shop in a New York City loft where he produced, during the next four years, some two and three-cylinder air-cooled engines. In 1919, he designed an experimental nine-cylinder static radial engine for the U.S. Army Air Service. Early in 1920, after Adm. Sims (who had commanded U.S. Naval Forces in the Atlantic during WWI) gave his support to the air advocates

Fig. 3-3. Developed at Navy insistence, the Wright J-5 Whirlwind was America's first truly reliable and efficient air-cooled radial aircraft engine.

within the Navy and called for construction of U.S. aircraft carriers, Lawrance designed and built the Model J engine with Navy funds supplied by Lt./Cmdr. Kraus.

This prototype engine was running in test when Lt./Cmdr. Leighton was introduced to the program in March 1921. (This was actually four months before creation of BuAer, but Moffett had begun collecting his key people in anticipation of his new job.) Leighton studied the Model J and concluded that Kraus had bet on the right horse (power). Then, at the end of June 1921, Moffett backed Leighton's decision and approved purchase of 50 Lawrance J-1s, a deal apparently made possible because the Navy had some unspent monies in the fiscal 1921 budget that were about to be returned to the Treasury.

The first production J-1 passed a 50-hour test, producing its rated 200 hp, in February 1922, a month before metamorphosis of the *Jupiter* into the *USS Langley* was completed. In the meantime, Cmdr. Jerome C. Hunsaker, Moffett's chief of aircraft design at the Naval Aircraft Factory in Philadelphia, was constructing the first TS-1 fighters (43 were eventually built, 11 by Curtiss) to equip the *Langley*, so Lawrance was given a contract for an additional 200 J-1s—along with a lecture from Leighton on the need for increasing the engine's reliability factor.

By this time, however, it had become clear to Leighton that Lawrance was either unwilling or unable to find enough expansion capital to properly develop and efficiently produce engines in such quantities. In time of national emergency such a supplier would be of small value. Therefore, Leighton, knowing that both Curtiss and Packard were adamant in their stand against development of air-cooled aircraft engines, decided to pressure Wright Aeronautical Corporation into taking over the Lawrance design.

Wright Aeronautical's boss was Frederick Brant Rentschler, a sharp young man of sound family and an Ivy League education. Rentschler had served as an airplane engine inspector for the Air Service during the war and, in 1919, had formed Wright Aeronautical Corporation from the liquidated remains of the Wright-Martin Corp. Rentschler's principal products were Hispano-Suiza aircraft engines, excellent (for that time) water-cooled V-8s built under a license agreement with a French manufacturer. Both the Army Air Service and the Navy bought Wright "Hissos" in some numbers (Navy planes fitted with Hissos included the Curtiss N-9 trainer, Thomas Morse MB-3 fighter, and Vought VE-7 all-purpose aircraft); but by 1923 the Army, although stuck with thousands of war-surplus Liberties that it would have to use in its bombers and observation planes, was looking to the new Curtiss D-12 of 400 hp for its new fighters. Since there was no civil market for new airplane engines worth mentioning, that gave Leighton some muscle at Wright Aeronautical.

Leighton was just the man to use it. He told Rentschler that the Navy would buy no more Hissos or Hisso parts. Then he suggested that Wright buy out Lawrance and develop the engine the Navy wanted.

Rentschler had little trouble recognizing Dame Opportunity, especially when she stood by with a club in her hand. With his board of directors concurring, he acquired Lawrance Aero Engines for half a million dollars (and a Wright vice-presidency for Charles Lawrance). Then, Rentschler directed that his ablest engineers, George J. Mead and Andrew V.D. Willgoos, take over the J-1 engine project and crank in a large dose of reliability.

Mead and Willgoos had already learned a lot about air-cooled engine reliability—or rather, the lack of it—with their markedly-deficient Wright R-1 of 1920, a nine-cylinder radial built for the Air Service. But engine men, a stubborn and secretive lot who hear things in engine exhausts that are denied to the rest of us, have always worked empirically, aided only by the metallurgist, the petroleum chemist, and a good deal of intuition. This process allowed Mead and Willgoos to announce, in September 1923, the evolution of Lawrance's J-1 into the Wright J-3. Following additional slight improvements the next year, it became the Wright J-4, the first Whirlwind. That was the penultimate step in development of an engine destined to touch off a transportation revolution and provide the basic de-

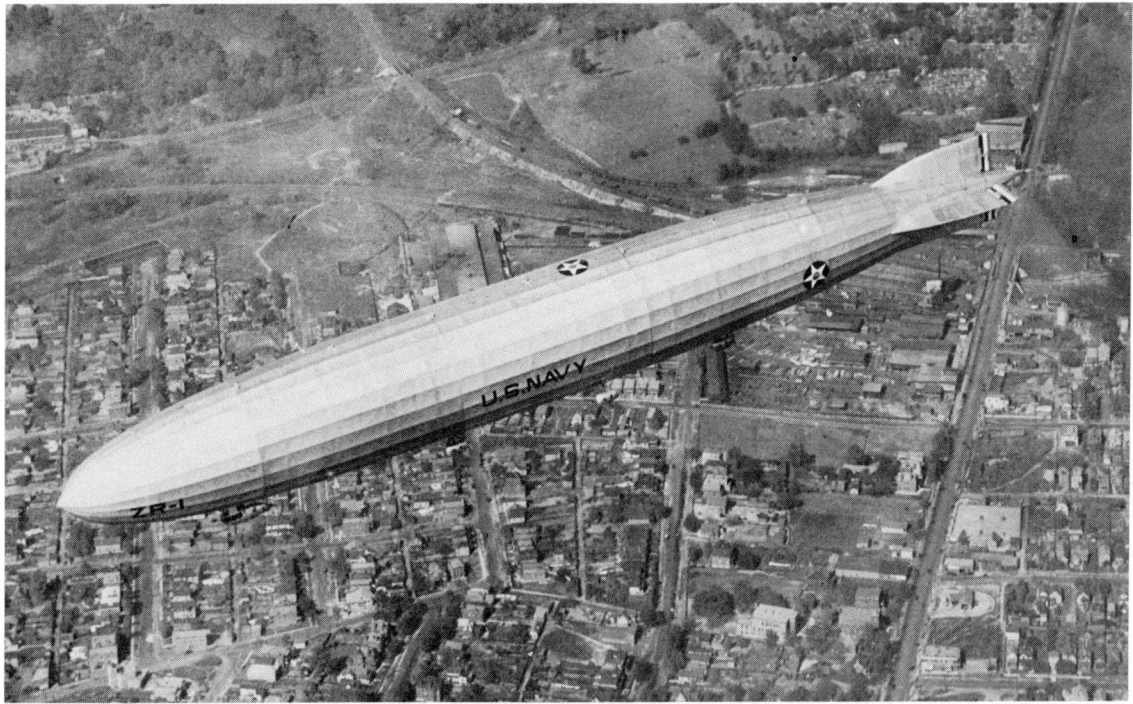

Fig. 3-4. The ZR-1 *Shenandoah* was completed in September 1923; it was lost two years later in a storm over Ohio. (Joe R. Reed collection)

sign for all Naval aircraft engines and a majority of Air Corps engines for two critical decades. (The Air Service would become the Army Air Corps in 1926.)

Meanwhile, nervously glancing over its shoulder at Billy Mitchell, the Navy decided to install turntable airplane catapults on some of its capital ships. Originally powered by compressed air, and later by gunpowder, the first of these devices was fitted to the stern of the *USS Maryland* in May 1922. After Lt. Andrew C. McFall's Vought VE-7 floatplane was successfully flung into the air by this mechanism, such launchings slowly became routine.

Recovery of these scout planes was tricky, however, because the aircraft had to land on the sea, taxi close to the ship, and be returned to the deck by crane. This could prove interesting in a rough sea.

During the next four years, 22 ships in the fleet were equipped with catapults (12 battleships and 10 light cruisers), and most of their captains grudgingly came to appreciate the far-ranging reports of their "slingshot" aviators. The fleet had extended its vision. It could, with its take-along scout planes, establish picket lines up to 200 miles in radius about the fleet. That constituted a security blanket of no small dimensions.

Patrol of the seas to greater distances by big, multiengined flying boats evolved more slowly. That was partly due to the lack of reliable engines of sufficient power, and partly due to Admiral Moffett's great faith in large, rigid dirigibles for such duty. It was Moffett's most serious hangup. His dirigible programs ended in disaster, and he himself died in one.

The First Navy Dirigibles

The Navy had established its right to operate U.S. military dirigibles at the end of WWI, and two such machines were included in the 1920 Navy budget. But that didn't necessarily mean that the top brass believed all that much in the usefulness of the big airships. There is a good bit of evidence that the Navy's primary concern was to prevent Gen. Mitchell from claiming such craft for the Air Service. Obviously, a lot of money could be spent for the air giants, and it would be much better to have those funds added to, rather than subtracted from, Naval appropriations. Besides, knowing Mitchell, one must expect that he would, if in possession of such craft, employ them in an attempt to usurp at least some of the Navy's rightful areas of responsibility.

The ZR-1 *Shenandoah* was completed in September 1923, and made its first flight from Lakehurst (NJ) Naval Air Station with Capt. F.R. McCrary in command. It was a copy of a WWI German rigid dirigible. ("Rigid" airships have a structural framework, fabric-covered, within which a number of individual "ballonets" contain a lifting gas. The "non-rigids" such as modern blimps have a single fabric envelope without internal framework.)

The ZR-2, purchased from Britain and called the "R-38" by the British, had been completed two years earlier, but during a trial flight broke in half and fell into the Humber River at Hull, England, carrying 28 Britons and 16 Americans to their deaths.

The Navy's ZR-3 *Los Angeles* was ordered from the Zeppelin works at Friedrichshafen, Germany in June 1922, after the Allied Reparations Commission levied a $33 billion "war damage" claim against Germany. As partial payment on this assessment, Germany built the ZR-3 for the U.S., along with similar craft for France and Italy. The *Los Angeles* was delivered in mid-October 1924, and served with the fleet for eight years until, during a fit of economizing, it was scrapped. It was the only dirigible to be successfully operated by the Navy.

Perhaps contributing to the *Los Angeles'* relatively long service was the fact that it was designed and built by those most experienced with such craft (Count von Zeppelin built his first dirigible before the Wright brothers flew), and because of the caution attending operation of the *Los Angeles* after the *Shenandoah* was lost. Caught in a line squall over Byesville, Ohio during the early morning hours of 3 September 1925, the *Shenandoah* was torn apart and its wreckage scattered. There were 29 survivors, but 14 were killed, including Lt./Cmdr. Zachary Lansdowne, the airship's commander.

This disaster stalled the Navy's airship programs for a time. It would be another three years before Adm. Moffett could get money for more—and bigger—dirigibles. But the *Shenandoah* tragedy served the Navy in an unexpected way: it provided the vehicle that carried Billy Mitchell to oblivion.

Mitchell Court-Martialed

After the sinking of the *Ostfriesland* in 1921, Mitchell was quietly supported in his abrasive crusade for a strong independent air force by his new boss, Maj./Gen. Mason Patrick, who replaced the more conservative Gen. Menoher as Chief of Air Service late that year.

Patrick also agreed with Mitchell on how best to get the most from tiny Air Service appropriations. Lacking funds to buy new airplanes in meaningful numbers, Gen. Patrick spent as much as possible on research and development. At some future date, the need to defend America in the air must become evident; when that time came superior planes must be ready. Therefore, Patrick okayed Air Service participation in national and international air racing, and daring long-distance flights as a means of developing high-horsepower aircraft engines and advanced airframe designs.

Such activity gathered favorable news coverage for the Air Service. This was important, because from the time that Mitchell began to kick up a fuss over the proper role and status of U.S. airpower, there was a federal investigation of some kind—20 in all, between 1919 and 1925—looking into the "aviation question." The most thorough of these was that of the Lampert-Perkins Committee in the House of Representatives (68th Congress) which, in 1924, made recommendations largely favorable to the Mitchell-Patrick position. But the Lampert-Perkins Committee report was soon submerged in another controversy when the Army's

Fig. 3-5. The ZR-3 *Los Angeles* was German-built and entered Navy service in 1924; retired in the early '30s. Improper handling resulted in this nosestand while anchored to mast in 1927. (USN)

General Staff decided that Mitchell should not be reappointed as Assistant Chief of the Air Service. Indeed, as his tour of duty ended he was "allowed" to revert to his permanent rank of colonel and transferred to Fort Sam Houston, Texas.

Mitchell probably expected as much. The Army General Staffs of that era were made up of old horse soldiers, dominated by Gen. John J. "Blackjack" Pershing, and to a man all were schooled in strategy and tactics that had not changed since the Civil War. Mitchell had become as bothersome to them as he was to the Navy.

Many newspapers cried "Shame!" and the public generally agreed that Mitchell was being punished for daring to disagree with his superiors. Columnist Mark Sullivan may have summed it up best when he observed: "The American people admire a man who has the courage to sass his bosses." There is small evidence that the people were actually much concerned with the issues raised by Mitchell. His public support was simply rooted in that basic human trait which compels us to cheer for the underdog.

Whether or not Mitchell understood that, he did know that the public constituted his only court of appeal. He recognized that his career was finished; the most he could do was to inform the people of the facts and let history be his judge. He therefore continued to make strong statements to the press, alleging gross mismanagement of America's military establishments, and he ignored orders to obtain prior approval from his superiors for these public utterances.

The inevitable showdown came two days after the *Shenandoah* went down (and while a Navy flying boat was missing over the Pacific), when Mitchell handed reporters a lengthy prepared statement in which he charged that these losses were due to the "incompetency, criminal negligence, and almost treasonable administration of the national defense by the War and Navy Departments."

Mitchell went on to accuse the Army and Navy of forcing officers to falsely testify before various Congressional committees, condemned the War Department for retaining the Air Service's obsolete "flying coffins," and concluded by saying: "I can no longer stand by and see these disgusting performances by the Navy and War Departments, at the expense of the lives of our people, and the delusion of the American public."

That, of course, resulted in headlines of arresting proportions, and before the stunned War and Navy Departments could regroup for a common defense, Mitchell followed up with a demand that the President appoint a panel of representative Americans to investigate these departments.

President Calvin Coolidge, a humorless, unimaginative man thrust into the White House by President Harding's sudden death in mid-1923, first directed that Mitchell be court-martialed under the 96th Article of War. Then Coolidge appointed a nine-member President's Aircraft Board "to make a study of the best means of developing and applying aircraft in national defense."

No one ever accused this board of being representative of the American people. It was headed by Coolidge's school chum Dwight Morrow, a partner in the J.P. Morgan banking firm, and contained Senator Hiram Bingham, already on record as opposed to Mitchellism; Maj. Gen. (ret) James Harbord, who had sought Mitchell's resignation earlier; and Howard Coffin who was, it will be recalled, chairman of the bungling Aircraft Production Board of WWI.

This hip-pocket assembly, popularly called the "Morrow Board," sat for about three weeks, and Coolidge timed release of its report to immediately precede the verdict in the Mitchell trial. This report summed up its rejection of Mitchell's proposals with the statement: "The next war may well start in the air, but in all probability it will wind up, as the last one did, in the mud." Then it dangled an aerial carrot, recommending acquisition of new and modern airplanes for Navy and Air Service.

As for the verdict in the Mitchell trial, there was never any doubt about that once the court ruled, shortly after the proceedings began on 28 October 1925, that *truth was not a defense*. Whether or not Mitchell's statements were true had no bearing on the case, the six generals sitting in judgment decided. Mitchell was *not* charged with lying, but with "conduct prejudicial to good order and military discipline." It was a catch-all canon applicable to everything from kicking a horse to making an improper advance to another officer's wife. And although Mitchell pleaded not guilty to each of eight counts, he knew that the whole procedure was mere formality. The proceedings were in the best Judge Roy Bean tradition: Give 'em a fair trial and then hang 'em.

Mitchell was eloquent, and managed to turn the whole affair into an indictment of his accusers—at least, for the record. Then he directed his legal counsel to withdraw from the case and make no closing argument.

The court's guilty verdict was announced on 17 December 1925. The only dissenting vote was cast by Gen. Douglas MacArthur. The court decreed that Col. Mitchell be suspended from rank, pay, and allowances for five years. Mitchell responded by resigning from the Army.

But nothing is so hard to destroy as the truth, and the principles that Mitchell championed were firmly held by others in both the Army and the Navy. The time would come when their counsel would be sorely needed.

Billy Mitchell, however, would not live to see that day. He would die five years before the Japanese attacked Pearl Harbor—exactly as he predicted they would, early on a Sunday morning.

Chapter 4

The New Deal and U.S. Airpower

The fact that President Franklin D. Roosevelt never admitted a mistake is insufficient evidence that he never made one. Of course, any President elected to four terms in that office, and whose supreme self-confidence leaves him unencumbered by doubt and provides him with the courage to make tough decisions without equivocation, is going to make mistakes. Nobody's perfect. And whether or not Roosevelt's "New Deal," which pointed the nation down the road to socialism, was a great mistake depends upon the politics of those who judge him, and is beyond the scope of this modest book. We are concerned here only with the effects of the New Deal on U.S. military aviation and the physical defense of our freedoms.

Still, in order to attain this limited objective we must take note of the atmosphere that gave birth to the New Deal and certain events that preceded it.

First, however, let us plainly state a couple of simple facts that our nation's leaders must heed in the planning of U.S. security: The American people will unite in support of war *only* when they believe that our very survival is at stake and that God is clearly on our side. It's just that simple. And a great many Americans view the maintenance of superior military forces as an invitation to trouble, rather than a deterrent to foreign aggressors.

These attitudes are not new; they date back to the Revolutionary War, and they were at least as pronounced during the '20s and '30s as they are today.

Nevertheless, the function of a leader is to lead, and a leader with a mandate from the people as great as that enjoyed by Franklin Roosevelt has little defense for his failures. The threat to the United States was clearly delineated long before he made any move to counter it, and America's tardiness in preparing to defend herself not only cost countless American lives, but encouraged military conquests that bore heavily on U.S. vital interests and, eventually, tempted attack on America herself. History offers no examples of a peace dictated from weakness.

America's reaction to the aggressions of Japan,

Fig. 4-1. McCook Field, located on the outskirts of Dayton, Ohio, was the most significant place in American aviation during the early '20s. Almost all new aerial hardware was either developed or tested there prior to 1927. (Merle Olmsted collection)

Germany, and Italy during the mid-'30s was funding for an Army of 165,000 and the Neutrality Acts passed between 1935 and 1937. As late as 1938, the Army Air Corps' appropriation was $58.8 million (compared to $35.1 million in 1921), and total Air Corps personnel numbered 21,089. At that time, our best fighter airplanes were some 70 Curtiss P-36s in service (plus 139 more on order), and our best heavy bombers were 14 service test YB-17s (plus 39 B-17Bs on order). Just one year later, Hitler would march into Poland to start the Second World War.

There is evidence that Roosevelt shared the anti-Air Corps sentiments held by the Navy Department's battleship admirals right up to the time of Pearl Harbor. Roosevelt, born to wealth and position, a Harvard graduate and amateur yachtsman (always expected of such young men), served as assistant secretary of the Navy 1913-1921, and was obviously much perturbed at Billy Mitchell's claim that the airplane had made the battle ship obsolete. "It is highly unlikely that an airplane, or a fleet of them, could ever sink a fleet of Navy vessels under battle conditions," he told the press in 1921.

Later, following Mitchell's demonstrations,

Roosevelt was asked by a reporter if he'd changed his mind, to which he replied, "I once saw a man kill a lion with a .30/30 rifle . . . but that does not mean that a .30/30 is a lion gun."

Thirteen years later, the Air Corps would provide him an even greater embarrassment.

"Neither Rain, Nor Snow, Nor Politics . . ."

Early in February 1934, Roosevelt cancelled all air mail contracts with the airlines and directed that the Army fly the mail. The Air Corps took over the mail routes on 19 February, and although the 27,000-mile airway system was reduced to a basic 9,000 miles and no passengers were to be carried, it was an impossible assignment. With only ten days preparation, obsolete aircraft, and non-instrument pilots, the Air Corps tried to fly unfamiliar routes—often without so much as a compass—during the worst weather of the year. At the end of a week, five pilots were dead and six critically injured. The newspapers made the most of it.

Now, we should digress to explain that the airline system in the United States was originally made possible by the 1925 Kelly Bill which provided for payment to private contractors to fly the mail. In 1931, the McNary-Watres Act changed the rate of payment for as much as $3.10 per pound to a much larger amount based upon the cubic feet of capacity in the contractor's aircraft available for mail. This legislation, amounting to an outright subsidy, was intended to encourage the airmail contractors to place in service large, multi-engine aircraft (most had been flying the mail in open cockpit biplanes), which in turn would lead to scheduled passenger flights since it would cost the operators very little more to fill all that empty space with people.

The Post Office Department felt that this subsidy would not long be needed as the public began paying for that space, and the Post Office (in the person of President Hoover's Postmaster General, Walter Folger Brown) was right. By the time FDR

Fig. 4-2. The Curtiss Hawk series of biplane fighters, 247 in all, were procured 1925 through 1931 inclusive. Above is a P-1F at Kelly Field. (USAF)

Fig. 4-3. Lt. Otto Wienecke, one of 12 Army fliers to be killed flying the mail during the 1934 airmail moratorium, died in this Curtiss 0-39 observation plane when he crashed near Cleveland in a snowstorm. (UPI)

took office early in 1933, postal payments to the airlines was rapidly decreasing as the public began to accept scheduled airline service in the Ford and Fokker Tri-Motor airliners.

The only trouble was that these early airliners simply were not efficient. With passenger capacities of 12 to 15, some mail pay was still necessary—was, in fact, the difference between profit and loss. However, this policy was about to bear other fruit, because it fostered development of the Douglas DC-2/DC-3 series, the first of which appeared a few days before Roosevelt ordered the Air Corps to fly the mail, and these airplanes were capable of returning profits to their operators with passenger revenues alone.

Meanwhile, the New Dealers had discovered, soon after they took possession of the White House, that ex-Postmaster General Walter Folger Brown had built America's airline system with the employment of some rather undemocratic methods. Brown had not bothered with such things as competitive bidding for the routes or a fair shake for the small, poorly financed operator. He had forced mergers and favored the well-financed bidders, and his high-handed methods had left a trail of enemies in his wake. About all that could be said in Brown's favor was that he had, using his mail pay whip, given the United States the best domestic airline system in the world.

The Democrats gleefully smelled collusion and thievery and appointed a Senate committee to investigate the "Air Mail Scandals" of the previous Republican administration. This committee was headed by a senator from Alabama, Hugo L. Black (whose law degree, he later admitted, came from a correspondence school), and it is difficult to understand why, today, reading transcripts of the testimony given before the Black Committee, that the New Dealers should have pursued the matter, because the only provable fact was that Brown had been a dictator—a charge that Brown himself cheerfully agreed to, pointing out that his power had been bestowed upon him by the Congress of the United States.

Nevertheless, citing the Black Committee report, President Roosevelt cancelled all air mail contracts, charging that the airways system had been mapped out in a series of "spoils conferences" by W.G. Brown and a handful of his favored airline cronies. The Army Air Corps would fly the mail, the President said, until such time as the New Dealers should present their own plan for the awarding of airline routes.

But the Air Corps, though it made a valiant effort, lacked both the equipment and the trained

Fig. 4-4. This crash, 2 February 1934, claimed the life of Lt. Ed Lowry about 50 miles southwest of Toledo. Mail bags were scattered far from the scene. (USAF)

Fig. 4-5. The P&W R-1340 Wasp was introduced in May 1926, rated at 400 hp; by 1938 it had evolved into a 600-hp engine. A smaller version, the R-985 Wasp Jr, similarly grew from 300 to 450 hp.

pilots to perform the task, and by the second week in March the mounting death toll among the Army fliers appalled the nation. The President had to find a way out. On 10 March he announced that the air mail would be returned to the airlines as soon as possible.

A total of 12 Army fliers died before the mail could be returned to its former contractors.[*Author's Note:* Now, lest I be accused of party bias in recording this episode, I am willing to concede that had the situation been reversed—that is, had the Republicans rather than the Democrats taken over the White House in 1933 after 12 long years of the other party's rule—they, too, would have been looking for signs of maladministration to discredit their political enemies. The point is that the Democrats acted too hastily in starting a vendetta against the airlines and the Republicans because no thievery could be proved. There was probably plenty of it to be proved had they looked in the right places, but once the "Air Mail Scandals" became a media event, the New Dealers had to follow through as best they could.]

In an attempt to save face, Roosevelt decreed that no airline company represented at the 1929 meetings ("spoils conferences") with W.F. Brown, when the air routes were parceled out, should be allowed to carry the mail in the future. That, too, became a farce, because that edict was easily handled by the airlines which, at that point, had the President over the proverbial barrel: American Airways suddenly became American Air Lines; Eastern Air Transport repainted its signs to read "Eastern Air Lines." TWA, a bit bolder, merely added "Inc." to its name, and United Air Lines remained unchanged because its original contract had been awarded to a United subsidiary.

The New Dealers gained no political mileage from the tragic witch hunt, and nothing was changed for the small, poorly financed operators in whose name all the fuss had been made in the first place. Roosevelt's Postmaster General, James Farley, continued to award air mail contracts only to those companies which had the capital to buy the best equipment and the organization to operate the most responsibly, while the small operators continued to be squeezed out and gobbled up by the growing major airlines.

The whole episode was an embarrassment to Roosevelt, and he was not the kind of man to forget an embarrassment. During the ensuing four or five years he appears to have ignored the Army Air Corps as much as possible, while the Navy received authority to build no less than 34 new battleships and battle cruisers (a program that was modified after WWII began and the importance of the aircraft carrier became evident).

Engine Development Paces the Industry

You will recall from Chapter 3 that Fred Rentschler and his two top enginemen at Wright Aeronautical Corporation had brought the Wright Whirlwind J-4 to the threshold of success by 1924. Although Rentschler never admitted it, it appears most likely that he recognized the opportunity of a lifetime at that point. Rather than enrich Wright Aeronautical with his foresight, he decided to start his own company. It was a decision worth millions.

Rentschler correctly judged that the 200-hp Whirlwind, when fully developed, would have a great impact on aviation and make a great deal of money for Wright. However, he also knew about the work of Sam Heron and Edward T. Jones at the Air Corps' McCook Field experimental center, which had resulted in development of the first truly reliable air-cooled cylinders in several sizes, and which featured Heron's sodium-filled exhaust valves. Further realizing that here was the key to much bigger aircraft engines that would match the Whirlwind's reliability, Rentschler resigned from

Fig. 4-6. The Allison V-1710 powered the P-40s, P-39s, P-63s, P-38s, A-36s and F-82s. Pictured is the V-1710-39, which was fitted to the P-40D and P-40E as well as the early Kittyhawks. (Allison Division, GM)

Fig. 4-7. Two Sparrohawks return to the trapeze beneath the *Macon*. The *Macon's* engines were inside her hull. Normal crew was 10 officers and 50 enlisted men, plus four Sparrowhawk pilots. (USN)

Wright in September, 1924, taking his best enginemen (Mead, Willgoos, and Brown) with him.

Then, with a truly first-class dream to sell, he was able to secure the backing of the owners of the idle Pratt and Whitney Tool Company factory for production of his new 400-hp Wasp engine, Model R-1340. This engine (and others of the same basic construction that followed) were so successful that by 1933, the 1375 shares of Pratt & Whitney stock that Rentschler had purchased for $275 in 1925 had grown to more than $21,000,000—that's correct, *twenty-one million.*

It also appears that Rentschler's principal advisor—that is, the man who encouraged him to build the Wasp engine—was none other than Adm. William Moffett, chief of the Navy's Bureau of Aeronautics. Moffett wasn't concerned with the money to be made from the production of such an engine. The Navy badly needed an aircraft powerplant of that size, and Moffett had decided that the Navy would use air-cooled radials exclusively for the foreseeable future, principally because they were much easier to service than the big liquid-cooled powerplants.

But Rentschler did not need to be told that the Air Corps and the airlines would also come knocking at his door if he had a reliable high-horsepower air-cooled radial to sell; by 1938—just 13 years after P&W was formed—the R-1340 Wasp had long since become a 600-hp engine; the R-985 Wasp Junior filled the 450-hp needs, and the R-1690 Hornet was in production at 850-hp, while the new R-1830 Twin Wasp and the R-2800 Double Wasp, at 1200- and 2000-hp respectively, had completed their tests and were just entering production.

Meanwhile, at Wright Aeronautical, the two men who had contributed the most to air-cooled aircraft engine development—Sam Heron and Ed T. Jones—had been lured from the Air Corps' experimental and development center at McCook Field (later, Wright Field, and today Wright-Patterson AFB, Ohio) by Charles Lawrance at Wright Aeronautical where they gave the J-4 Whirlwind their new cylinder and valve system to bring forth the famed J-5 Whirlwind. The J-6 series quickly followed, ranging in power from 165- to 300-hp, along with the 750-hp R-1820 Cyclone.

Wright Aeronautical was merged with the Curtiss Aeroplane and Motor Company in 1929 by wheeler-dealer financier Clement M. Keys (who had controlled Curtiss since the early '20s) to form the Curtiss-Wright Aircraft Corporation. In 1931, when Curtiss-Wright decided to abandon liquid-cooled aircraft engine development (despite the success of its D-12 and Conqueror engines during the '20s) to concentrate on the Wright air-cooled radials, the Air Corps was forced to look elsewhere for the 1000-hp V-12 it was sure it would need within a decade.

The Air Corps favored the in-line V-12s because they presented a much smaller frontal area (and therefore less drag) than the big radials, and because cooling problems were yet to be solved with the high-horsepower radials above 15,000 ft. So the Air Corps went to General Motors' miniscule (less than 30 employees) Allison Division where a new V-12 of 1710 cubic inch displacement and a planned rating of 750-hp was in its early stages of development under a Navy contract to supply engines for the Navy's huge airships, *Akron* and *Macon*.

The Air Corps was mostly jawboning, because it had almost no money to spend. It bought a dozen Allison V-1710s between 1932 and mid-1934 which were shipped to Wright Field where Air Corps enginemen under the direction of Opie Chenoweth tried to uprate them to 1000 hp with no success. Not until March 1937, after Allison's Ron Hazen, Charles McDowall and Robert Atkinson had almost completely redesigned the V-1710, did it at last pass a type test at 1000-hp. This was, by the way, just a few months after the Rolls Royce Merlin passed its type test at 990-hp. Both engines were rated for 87 octane fuel. The V-1710 required pure Prestone as a coolant and weighed 1280 lbs. The 1335 lb Merlin was cooled with a water-Prestone mix.

During WWII, Allison would produce almost 70,000 V-1710s, the last ones rated at 1600-hp. Production would continue into 1947, after a final order to equip the P-82 Twin Mustang, but none ever propelled a Navy dirigible. Both the *Akron* and *Macon* were destroyed in crashes before the Allisons meant for them could be delivered.

Navy Airships *Akron* and *Macon*

Adm. William Moffett (he wasn't the kind of man one called "Billy") never lost faith in the great rigid airships as patrol and reconnaissance vehicles

Fig. 4-8. Trio of Curtiss F9C-2 Sparrowhawks. Engine cowlings were red, white and blue. Engines were Wright R-975s of 420 hp which gave the Sparrowhawks a top speed of 176 mph. (USN)

Fig. 4-9. Army's Keystone LB-7 bomber of the late '20s was powered with two P&W Hornet engines of 525 hp each. A total of 210 Keystones (crews called them "Keystone Comedies") with different engine installations were procured following the Mitchell trial. (USAF)

Fig. 4-10. Great Lakes G-1 torpedo bomber of 1929 was typical of the heavy biplanes procured by the Navy during the '20s for that mission. (Charles W. Meyers collection)

for the fleet. The Germans had used Zeppelins as strategic bombers in WWI with limited success, but the record of the huge airships subsequent to that time was not very good. The Italian-built *Roma* had crashed during test flights in the United States in 1922; the Navy's ZR-2, built in Britain as the R.38, also crashed on a test flight, and the Goodyear-built ZR-1 *Shenandoah* was lost in a storm in 1925. Only the German-built ZR-3 *Los Angeles*, in U.S. Navy service since 1924, appeared to be headed for a long and useful life (it was finally decommissioned in 1932 as an economy measure), but was inadequate for the sea duty Moffett envisioned since it was actually a WWI design. The Hoover Administration had, in 1928, approved purchase of two airships, the ZRS-4 and ZRS-5, which were much larger than the *Los Angeles* and which were specifically designed for extended service at sea.

The two new airships, to be christened *Akron* and *Macon*, were nearly identical. The first to be completed was the *Akron*, which was 785 ft in length, 133 ft in diameter, 146 ft in height. It contained 6.5 million cu/ft of helium. Her eight engines furnished a total of 4480-hp, and she could carry a useful load of 160,000 lbs at speeds up to 84 mph. Her engines were placed inside the great hull; her propellers—which could be turned in different directions for forward, reverse, or even upward thrust—were mounted outside at the end of extended driveshafts. Also inside the hull was hangar and maintenance space for five small scout-fighter planes which could be launched and returned to the airship in flight by means of a retractable trapeze. Six Curtiss F9C-2 Sparrowhawks (plus two prototypes) were built for the *Akron* and *Macon*, with more planes to be ordered as needed.

The *Akron* was placed in service in October, 1931, with Lt. Cmdr. C.E. Rosendahl as her captain, and for a year and a half she seemed well on her way to the vindication of Moffett's support, her 10,000-mile range allowing her to roam the seas for many days without refuelling. But then the *Akron* was lost (unnecessarily, most believed) on 4 April 1933, just two months after the *Macon* was christened.

The *Akron* crashed in a storm off the New Jersey Coast while flying at a very low altitude when her helmsman apparently raised her nose too

Fig. 4-11. Maj. Joe R. Reed and his crew chief inspect damage to Douglas O-2H observation plane after the Liberty engine failed at low altitude. (Joe R. Reed collection)

Fig. 4-12. The U.S. Marine Corps' Curtiss OC-2 Falcon of 1930 was Wasp-powered, had a top speed of 155 mph. (USN)

abruptly and allowed the rear of the airship to strike the water. The great aerial machine broke up, and 73 of the 76 men aboard her lost their lives, including Adm. Moffett.

The *Macon* entered service in June 1933, two months after the *Akron's* loss, and received the *Akron's* Sparrowhawks, since none of the planes were aboard the *Akron* when it went down. At sea, the planes' landing gears were removed and belly tanks added to give the small scout-fighters greater range. The lack of a landing gear didn't matter, since the only place the planes could "land" was on the extended trapeze of their mother airship.

This combination—an airship of great range, plus four (usually) scouting planes fanning out to patrol all points of the compass—provided the Navy with eyes over many thousands of square miles of ocean. If the *Macon* had survived it is quite possible that other, similar airships would have been built, because they easily offered the most effective and economical means of guarding the sea approaches to America's coasts. No nation was in a better position to exploit these aerial behemoths because the United States possessed the world's only known deposits of non-flammable helium prior to WWII. Germany, the master builder of these machines, was forced to use highly-flammable hydrogen in her airships.

The *Macon* was lost to a fatal flaw in her structure. Her vertical tail atop the rear of the airship was improperly attached to the hull, and this critical component failed in flight during marginal weather off the California Coast near Big Sur on 12 February 1935. Miraculously, all but two of the 81 aboard survived the ensuing crash.

Many in the Navy believed then (and still do) that the airship program should have continued; but without Adm. Moffett's leadership, the U.S. Navy's lighter-than-air vehicles were henceforth limited to the relatively small, non-rigid "blimps," primarily used during WWII to hunt enemy submarines in U.S. coastal waters.

Transition: The Biplane Era Passes

Despite the impoverished status of the U.S. Army Air Corps during the '20s and much of the '30s, and despite the lack of promotion and the low pay, the Air Corps attracted—and often held—some very able men. It seems remarkable today that any of them should have remained in the service. Following Billy Mitchell's court martial, those officers with any rank who were known to share Mitchell's views were shown by the Army's General Staff how foolish that could be. All were exiled to lesser commands: Majors H.H. "Hap" Arnold, Carl Spaatz, Lewis Brereton and Gerald Brandt; Cols. Hugh Knerr and Frank Andrews; Lt. Cols. George Kenney and Joe McNarney all suffered career setbacks. Maj. Arnold, for example, was relieved of his post in Washington, D.C. and sent to Marshall Field where his command consisted of four tired DH-4s and 13 men. Perhaps these blatant punishments merely strengthened the resolve of such men. In any case, they all hung tough—if temporarily silenced—perhaps aware that the time would come when the nation would sorely need their counsel.

During the late '20s and early '30s, significant progress was made in aircraft and aircraft engine development, mostly due to the new and expanding markets in civil aviation. The demand for more efficient airliners and a booming market for private airplanes, along with the appearance of truly reliable engines in all power ranges, encouraged the airframe builders to push ahead with fresh ideas. By

Fig. 4-13. Curtiss F6C-4 Hawk of VF-9M. This craft was plane number two of Fighting Nine. (USN)

Fig. 4-14. Boeing P-12C Army fighter was powered with P&W R-1340-9 Wasp of 525 hp and had a top speed of 178 mph. Army took delivery of 366 of the P-12 series, 1929-1932 inclusive. Navy version was the F4B series. (USAF)

Fig. 4-15. Curtiss F11C-2 Goshawk was fitted with the Wright R-1820 Cyclone of 715 hp; had a top speed of 205 mph. The Navy bought 27 of this model during the early '30s and later redesignated it the BFC-2 (bomber-fighter). (USN)

1931, John K. "Jack" Northrop was building the first of his all-metal stressed-skin airplanes in which the metal skin carried much of the load, resulting in a lighter internal structure, and the small but talent-ridden National Advisory Committee for Aeronautics (NACA, forerunner of NASA) developed a wide array of new airfoils and provided much other useful aerodynamic data to industry with its wind tunnel work at Langley Field, VA, including engine cowling shapes for the air-cooled radials that not only greatly reduced drag but also improved engine cooling.

These advances produced the first "modern" airliner in 1933, the Boeing 247 for United Air Lines—an all-metal, low-wing, twin-engine craft with retractable landing gear. It was limited only by its small size (10 passengers). Donald Douglas rectified that with the first of his famed DC series airliners, built for TWA, the following year. It was the DC-1, which quickly (1936) evolved into the DC-3, known as the C-47 in the Air Corps and the R4D in Navy service.

Prior to 1936, the military services normally purchased airplanes in batches of 25 or 30 at a time. The Army took delivery of only 247 Curtiss Hawk biplane fighters ("pursuits") between October 1925 when the first was delivered, and April 1932, when it accepted the last one. During the biplane era, the Army favored Curtiss fighters, Douglas observation planes, and Martin or Keystone bombers. The Navy favored Boeing fighters and Douglas torpedo planes. The U.S. Marines usually received castoff Navy airplanes.

The Marines were fortunate to have any airplanes at all, and probably wouldn't have had it not been for a series of incidents in Haiti and Nicaragua where the Marines were sent to restore order and protect what was then seen as America's best interests when rebel guerillas threatened those governments.

Fig. 4-16. The Curtiss P-6E Hawk was the last biplane fighter purchased by the Air Corps. Its Curtiss V-1570 Conqueror V-12 engine produced 600 hp and gave the P-6E a top speed of 193 mph. The Air Corps took delivery of 45 P-6Es in early 1932, paying $12,362 each for them, plus an additional $10,000 each for engines, propellers and guns.

Fig. 4-17. The *USS Lexington* as it appeared during the early '30s. The "Lady Lex" and its sister carrier *Saratoga* were commissioned in the late fall of 1927. Both were converted cruisers of 36,000 tons, and both carried 72 aircraft. (Joe R. Reed collection)

Marine Fighting Squadron Nine was also instrumental in saving Marine aviation during this period. Aware that a move was afoot to eliminate Marine aviation, Fighting Nine organized an aerial exhibition team of seven pilots who flew precision aerobatics in close formation just as today's Blue Angels do. They called themselves the *Rojas Diablos* ("Red Devils") and, performing at county fairs and other civil celebrations, gained a great deal of favorable publicity and goodwill for the Corps in general and Marine Air in particular.

Fighting Nine did it all on a shoestring, and with dedicated mechanics who kept their aging biplane fighters in service often by fabricating their own spare parts. On one occasion these crews built an airplane from the salvaged remains of several others and gave it a fictious serial number. That later caused a great flap in Marine Headquarters where there was no record of the plane's acquisition. Headquarters finally decided that the airplane did not exist and that settled the matter. (For other Fighting Nine exploits, see Jess Barrow's *WWII: Marine Fighting Squadron Nine*, TAB Book No. 2289).

A New Generation of Aircraft

After the Navy received its first aircraft carrier, the *Langley*, in 1922, only two more were added to the Fleet during the next dozen years, the *Saratoga* and *Lexington*, converted battle cruisers that entered service in the fall of 1927. But then four more were commissioned prior to WWII: *Ranger* in 1934, *Yorktown* in 1937, *Enterprise* in 1938, and *Wasp* in 1940. President Roosevelt, always attentive to Navy needs, originally funded *Yorktown* and *Enterprise* through a provision of his National Recovery Act (NRA; "recovery" from the Great Depression), and although the Supreme Court later held the NRA to be unconstitutional, Roosevelt had no trouble getting the money from Congress to pay for them, as well as the *Wasp*. The Congress seldom argued with FDR because of his immense popular support.

The United States should have possessed at least twice that number of aircraft carriers, enough to support a two-ocean Navy, but this is a judgment made in hindsight. No one in the Navy Department at that time fully realized the role the aircraft carrier would play in the future defense of the country. The carrier was still a theoretical weapon, actually untried in battle.

Our point is, however, that the Navy was relatively better funded during the '30s than was the Army, and especially the Army Air Corps. Roosevelt did not overtly oppose the Air Corps, he simply ignored it as long as possible.

Unfortunately, the Army General Staff, headed by the temperamental Gen. Malin Craig during the critical late '30s, *was* overtly opposed to a modern air force and made certain that the Air Corps remained totally subservient to the presumed needs of ground commanders, while admitting no offensive role for Army aviation—a position shared by most congressmen. The idea of a strategic bombing force was heresy, and any air officer who presumed to disagree with this doctrine was summarily transferred to the boondocks and reduced to his permanent rank. When Gen. George C. Marshall replaced Craig as Chief of Staff in 1939, Marshall rescued the "Billy Mitchell Crowd" and returned all of them to positions of high responsibility. Hap Arnold was, after a lengthy penance, promoted to Brig. Gen. and appointed Chief of the Air Corps in 1938, although that post had been diluted in 1935 with formation of the "General Headquarters Air Force" at Langley Field, which was supposed to be on an equal level with that of the Air Corps Chief. The GHQ Air Force controlled the Air Corps combat arm, while the AC Chief was responsible for training and supply. This confusing arrangement split whatever authority the top air officers possessed under Malin Craig.

Meanwhile, able Army air officers did as well as they could under the hostile Malin Craig and, in 1936, as the Congress became mildly alarmed at Hitler's occupation of the Rhineland, Italy's invasion of Ethiopia, civil war in Spain, and Japan's continuing aggressions in China, money was appropriated for 77 new Seversky P-35 fighter planes for the Air Corps.

Fig. 4-18. A BF2C-1 Hawk flown by Lt. Cmdr. J.D. Barnwr of VB-5B operating from the *USS Ranger* in 1935. The BF2C-1 had a top speed of 225 mph; power was the 770-hp Wright R-1820-04. Navy bought 27 of this type in 1934. (USN)

Fig. 4-19. The carriers *Yorktown* and *Enterprise* were christened during 1936 and each received a squadron of Curtiss SBC-3 Helldivers. The SBC series remained in production until 1941. (Merle C. Olmsted collection)

Fig. 4-20. Douglas O-46A observation plane, 90 of which were delivered to the Air Corps in 1935-1936, was a pretty airplane but already obsolescent when it appeared. (USAF)

A year later, Germany, Italy and Japan signed an anti-Comintern pact, Hitler formally renounced the Versailles Treaty, the Japanese sank a U.S. gunboat on the Yangtze River, and money was found for 210 new Curtiss P-36 fighters for the Air Corps. It was the largest single order for Army airplanes since WWI. At the same time, Wright Field issued a specification to the nation's struggling airplane industry asking for proposals for a 2000-hp fighter airplane.

That specification was a bit far out and Wright Field knew it. No 2000-hp aircraft engine existed in 1937, and the Air Corps had no money either in hand or promised to buy such planes. But all concerned knew that the gestation periods for new military aircraft was growing much longer as the planes became more complicated and that engines, especially, required several years to develop. It wasn't simply a matter of increasing the size of existing engines to obtain more power. Better fuels were needed for higher compression ratios, and improved metals had to be formulated to withstand the greater pressures and higher operating temperatures. As aircraft speeds increased, a host of new aerodynamic questions arose. Next to nothing was known about compressibility, a phenomenon that some engineers believed—and others did not—would be encountered as planes approached the speed of sound. (Lockheed was to soon face the problem, which was indeed real).

Barely solvent Lockheed, a small company which had produced only 277 airplanes since its organization 11 years before, responded to the Air Corps' specification with exciting plans for a fighter plane fitted with a pair of 1000-hp Allison V-1710 engines (then still in development). Lockheed's proposed airplane would, if built, demand answers to questions which had not yet been asked. On

Fig. 4-21. A new era in U.S. fighter airplane design began in 1934 when Don Berlin designed the Curtiss P-36. Pictured is the wooden mock-up.

Fig. 4-22. Prototype P-36 first flew in April 1935, and was penalized by use of the Wright R-1670 engine, a decided failure. Berlin had no choice but to try this engine since he worked for Curtiss-Wright. (Donovan R. Berlin)

Fig. 4-23. The Air Corps asked Curtiss to install the new P&W R-1830 Twin Wasp in the P-36 and the happy result was an order for 210 such machines in June 1937, the largest U.S. fighter plane order since WWI. (Donovan R. Berlin)

Fig. 4-24. In March 1938, P-36 designer Don Berlin suggested to the Air Corps Material Division at Wright Field that the P-36 be fitted with the new Allison V-1710 engine. That resulted in the P-40, and a contract for 524 of those machines in April 1939. Deliveries to the Air Corps began in June 1940, and eventually totalled 13,763, including Tomahawks and Kittyhawks to Britain and the Commonwealth countries. (USAF)

The Navy took delivery of 503 Brewster F2A Buffalo fighters beginning in December 1937, but those were interim craft with a number of weaknesses, and were replaced by the Grumman F4F Wildcat for fleet duty. A total of 1978 Wildcats were built for the Navy (plus 431 for Britain) beginning in 1938. The famed Chance Vought F4U Corsair was contracted that same year, designed for the P&W R-2800 2000-hp radial engine which was in its early stages of development at the time. The first Corsair would fly in 1940, and 7829 would eventually be built for the Navy and Marines.

Actually, all of the American-designed 400 mph fighters appeared as test models at about the same time, with the XP-38 leading the pack in 1939. All the rest followed in 1940, except the XP-51, which was originally built for the British and first flew in 1941. None of these craft was developed and available for combat when Pearl Harbor was attacked. It's true that the P-38 Lightning was thrown

paper it was a 400-mph airplane, at least 100 mph faster than the Curtiss P-36s which would begin entering service a year later, and it would certainly force the state-of-the-art beyond present limits.

But Wright Field (apparently Opie Chenoweth, head of the Air Corps Technical Service Command) liked the Lockheed proposal, which was actually the work of young Clarence "Kelly" Johnson, a recent University of Michigan graduate. Gen. Oscar Westover, who endured for three years under Malin Craig as Chief of Air Corps, approved a contract for one experimental model of the new fighter which was designed the XP-38. It was officially described as a "defensive interceptor" in order to get it past Craig and the Congress.

The Navy, too, was looking to the need for faster and better airplanes and let contracts as early as November 1935 for experimental fighters, the Grumman XF4F-1 and the Brewster XF2A-1. At that time, the Navy had 867 pilots, the Marines 110. Those figures were up to 1068 and 180 respectively when WWII began in Europe.

Fig. 4-25. Lt. Col. Benjamin S. Kelsey (later, General) was the test pilot and Air Corps project officer for the P-38 program. When this photo was taken he was recovering from a broken ankle received when he parachuted from a YP-38 after pulling its tail off in a dive. (USAF)

Fig. 4-26. The Boeing Model 299, a daring project by the Boeing Company, first flew in 1935 and evolved into the famed B-17 series of WWII. A total of 12,726 were built, although only 134 were built or on order early in 1941. (USAF)

into combat in mid-1942, but it was not combat-ready until the P-38J-25 version came off the production lines in 1944. During the early, desperate months of the war for the United States, the Navy's F4F Wildcat and the Army's P-40 carried the burden.

The P-40 was simply a re-engined P-36. Originally powered with the P&W R-1830 of 1050-hp, the P-36 had a speed of 310 mph and outstanding maneuverability. It was as good as any fighter in the world when it entered squadron service in 1938. By then, however, its designer, Donovan Berlin, Chief Engineer at Curtiss-Wright, was recommending that it be fitted with the 1090-hp Allison V-1710-19, and that resulted in the 365 mph P-40, which first flew in October 1938. P-40 deliveries to the Army began in mid-1940, and 13,737 were eventually built, many for America's allies during WWII.

The Republic P-47 Thunderbolt, more often referred to as the "Jug" by those who flew and serviced her, was a brute of a fighter plane—rugged, powerful and fast. Its prototype also appeared in 1940, and it would be the principal U.S. fighter over Europe when the Luftwaffe offered the most resistance. Therefore, America's top aces in the European Theater of Operations (ETO) were Jug jockeys. The several versions of the P-47 had top speeds ranging from 425 to above 450 mph. Power came from the 2000-hp P&W R-2800 which, with water injection, could produce 2300-hp for short periods.

On the face of it, the P-38 Lightning should have been at least as fast as the P-47, and it probably would have been had it possessed the Thunderbolt's wing. The P-38, however, was a load-carrier—it could deliver a bomb load equal to that of a medium bomber—and it could outclimb just about anything. With a top speed of 405 to 420 mph, depending upon model, it was probably fast enough, and its firepower was truly awesome. Once it received a redesigned intercooler system and automatic controls for its turbosuperchargers, maneuvering flaps, and dive brakes, all of which finally came together in mid-1944 (but not until more than half of the 10,036 Lightnings had been built), did the P-38 come into its own. The late models were fearsome machines indeed, arguably the best all-around fighter-bomber of the war. Its long range and two engines made it the hands-down favorite of fighter pilots in the Southwest Pacific, that "extra fan" providing a large margin of security for long overwater missions.

The P-38's wing, while a great asset in one way, proved a liability in another, and that was quickly discovered when Maj. Signa Gilkie took one of the first service test YP-38s above 30,000 ft and entered a dive. As the airspeed built above 500 mph the airplane's tail began to buffett severely. As the dive continued the machine became progressively nose-heavy, increasing its dive angle to near vertical, while the control yoke oscillated stiffly and defied Gilkie's utmost efforts to move it. He managed to recover by use of his elevator trim tab after the aircraft entered denser air below 18,000 ft.

Wind tunnel tests at Cal Tech established that the tail flutter was the result of turbulent airflow created by the sharp juncture at wing and fuselage, and that was eliminated by a wing fillet that smoothed out the airflow over the tail.

But not until October 1942, 16 months later, when a scale model of the P-38 was tested in the Ames Laboratory high-speed wind tunnel, was the loss of control in 500 mph dives explained. The P-38's wing was entering compressibility. The airflow around the wing was travelling more than 40 percent faster than the airplane itself, and was reaching Mach One (the speed of sound) and creating a shock wave when the aircraft reached an airspeed of slightly over two-thirds Mach, or Mach .67 to be exact. (Most other WWII advanced fighters could be pushed into aerodynamic compressibility, but not as early. The British Spitfire, for example, encountered compressibility at .82 Mach.)

A new wing was out of the question for the P-38; American fighter planes were desperately needed in every theater of war and production was all-important. There was no time to design and test a thinner wing. Therefore, Lockheed engineers devised a "bolt-on" dive brake that tended to limit the P-38's speed in a dive to just short of compressibility in dives of 60 degrees or less.

Col. Ben Kelsey, the Army's fighter airplane project officer, personally tested this modification and approved it in February 1943—but Lockheed was never able to satisfactorily explain why it was not incorporated into the P-38 production lines until mid-1944.

As mentioned, the other high-speed fighters also experienced this phenomenon. At least two P-47s lost their tails to it in test flights, and both

Fig. 4-27. When the U.S. was plunged into WWII all sorts of civil aircraft were drafted. The famed Beech Staggerwing (Model 17) became the UC-43 in Army dress, and was used as a "command transport." (Beech Aircraft Corp.)

Fig. 4-28. General of the Army George C. Marshall (L) and Army Air Forces Chief, Gen. Henry H. Arnold. Insignia on Arnold's jacket pocket is Aviator's wings, earned prior to WWI. (USAF).

Col. (later general) Kelsey and Lockheed test pilot Ralph Virden pulled the tails off P-38s recovering from high-altitude dives. Virden was killed; Kelsey successfully parachuted. The problem was not solved until after WWII when true transonic airplanes were developed.

Had President Roosevelt and his congressional leaders been properly responsive to the nation's security needs during the '30s, American pilots would not have fought for a year and a half in obsolescent and undeveloped airplanes. (Indeed, they may not have had to fight at all.) Of equal significance is the fact that if the aircraft and other key industries in the United States not had sizable arms orders from France and Britain as early as 1937, we would have been plunged into war with far less.

A $25 million order from the British for medium bombers allowed Lockheed to begin plant expansion in mid-1938 (Lockheed was building a handful of small airliners for Japan at the time) and that in turn would make P-38 production possible. In March 1940, the British ordered 667 P-38s, and that got the P-38 production line moving months before the USAAF ordered that airplane in quantity. French orders for 730 Curtiss P-36s in 1939 and 1940 similarly aided Curtiss-Wright. Martin and Douglas also sold airplanes to America's future allies prior to 1940, and all this, including a British order for 1000 P-40s, prompted the U.S. aircraft engine builders along with the airframe makers to expand their production facilities.

True, in 1938 President Roosevelt dramatically called upon the U.S. aircraft industry to produce 10,000 planes per year—and develop a capacity for twice that number—while Britain's Prime Minister Chamberlin was in Munich to sell out Czechoslovakia to Hitler's insatiable appetite in a bid for time. And less than two years later, in the summer of 1940, Roosevelt would up his appeal to 50,000 planes per year as his Secretary of War, Henry L. Stimson, was noting that "Airpower had decided the fate of nations . . ." By that time Poland was gone; Norway, Denmark, Belgium and the Netherlands had fallen to the Nazi conqueror; France was defeated, and the British stood alone, somehow both pathetic and magnificent in their awful peril.

But while Roosevelt was making these ringing pronouncements, he and his Congress were doing little to actually build U.S. airpower or the aircraft industry in the United States. Whatever expansion the aircraft factories accomplished during this period was done with private capital, which in turn was based upon their orders in hand. Not until the myopic U.S. Congress at last enacted the Lend-Lease Bill (HR 1776) on 11 March 1941—just nine months before the attack on Pearl Harbor—did the U.S. aircraft industry receive federal funds for plant expansion.

Meanwhile, after General Marshall took charge of the Army in 1939 (the first non-West Pointer to be Chief of Staff since 1914), the weak and poorly-equipped Air Corps was steadily strengthened with as much speed as could be mustered against congressional opposition. The congressional majority, obviously with Roosevelt's tacit approval, remained adamantly opposed to a U.S. strategic bombing force right up to the minute that they stared disaster in the face, and Chief of Air Corps, Gen. Arnold, had employed a deception or two in order to keep Boeing's B-17 program alive and to procure less than 100 B-17s by 7 December 1941.

Under Gen. Arnold, the divided authority of Air Corps command came to an end, and on 20 June 1941, with Gen. Marshall's strong support, the Army Air Corps became the United States Army Air Forces (USAAF), Lt. Gen. Henry H. Arnold commanding. On 9 March 1942 Gen. Marshall completely reorganized the War Department, and the Army Air Forces received virtually complete control of the development of its special weapon—the airplane. Administering its own affairs, it also came to exercise considerable influence over the Army's conduct of the war in general.

The hour was late and the enemy was upon us, but somehow, our society has always seemed to produce the kind of people we need the most and, with our survival as a free nation at stake, President Roosevelt seemed to possess the ability to recognize them when they were most needed. He passed over 34 higher ranking officers to select George Marshall as the Army's top commander. As events would prove, he never made a better decision.

Chapter 5

WWII: The Desperate Months

Sunday, 7 December 1941, dawned clear and beautiful over Hawaii with the mists, as always, scudding low among the peaks of Oahu's Koolau Range. On a lonely hill overlooking Oahu's north coast, Sgt. Joe Lockhard and Pvt. George Elliott were manning a primitive radar set, scanning the empty Pacific. They were bored and anxious for their relief crew to arrive.

It was exactly two minutes past seven a.m. when Lockhard called to his companion, "Hey, George. Come look at this." He made a note with his pencil. "I make it 136 miles."

"What is it?"

"I don't know. But it's our job to report it."

Lockhard cranked the field phone and, after some delay, reached the watch officer at Fort Shafter, a young lieutenant. He made his report, adding that the scope seemed to indicate a large fleet of airplanes, some 130 miles away, approaching Oahu from slightly east of north.

The lieutenant acknowledged the message and hung up. Nothing to get excited about. Twelve B-17s were due about 8:00 or 8:30 from San Francisco.

The lieutenant was right; two flights of AAF B-17s were due from the mainland. He was also wrong; what Lockhard and Elliott had observed on their scope was indeed something to get excited about. It represented the radio echos from 352 Japanese airplanes from six aircraft carriers: 171 Val dive bombers, 102 Kate attack bombers, and 79 Zero fighters. At 7:55 am, approximately 45 minutes after Lockhard's alert was logged at Fort Shafter, that deadly aerial armada began raining destruction on Pearl Harbor.

No warning was ever sounded. The attacking force achieved complete surprise, partly because the Japanese ambassador and a special envoy continued to negotiate settlement of U.S.-Japanese differences until, literally, the last minute. This pair of Japanese officials was actually in Secretary of State Cordell Hull's office with a note from their government when Hull was informed of the attack.

The military's primary failure at Pearl Harbor

was the failure of reconnaissance, which should have been the Navy's responsibility. With a large part of the Navy's ships at anchor in Pearl Harbor, the sea approaches to the great base were essentially unguarded. Although the PBY series of long-distance patrol planes had been available since the mid-'30s, the Navy had not seen fit to procure them in sufficient number to provide a viable early warning system for vital installations vulnerable to attack by enemy fleets. And prior to WWII the U.S. was completely without another form of reconnaissance which might be classified as a "super long-range warning system," a worldwide intelligence-gathering organization which could have given the President and his advisors critical data concerning the military and political composition of Japan as well as her probable intentions.

It was, of course, the question of Japan's intentions that figured most prominently in America's vulnerability. Britain's Prime Minister, Winston Churchill said (*The Second World War*, Houghton Mifflin Co., 1948), "All the great Americans around the President and in his confidence felt as acutely as I did the awful danger that Japan would attack British or Dutch possessions in the Far East and would carefully avoid the United States . . ." And Gen. Hap Arnold said in his memoirs, "Like most officers in the War Department, I was under the impression that, if a Japanese attack occurred, it would be made first against the Philippines and then would be carried down the east coast of Asia to Singapore, to the Islands of Borneo, Java and Sumatra." Obviously, it never occurred to Roosevelt, Churchill, or any of their advisors, that the Japanese could misjudge us as badly as we misjudged them.

With this erroneous position permeating the thinking at the top, there should be small wonder that the Army and Navy commanders in Hawaii were lulled into similar attitudes. Both were sacked after the debacle at Pearl, however.

The Japanese Kate bombers, most of them armed with torpedos, concentrated on the Navy ships at anchor around Ford Island, while the Vals struck at Navy, Marine, and Army airfields and other key installations. The Zeros were free to strafe targets of opportunity since they encountered virtually no U.S. fighter opposition. Eight Army fighters (six P-36As and two P-40s) managed to take off during the attack, and accounted for 10 enemy bombers between them. Lt. George Welch, in a P-40, shot down four. Army and Navy antiaircraft gunners shot down another 18 of the enemy—plus one P-36.

Fig. 5-1. Army fighters in Hawaii at the time of the Japanese attack included 99 P-40Bs and Cs, along with 36 P-36As, in the 15th and 18th Pursuit Groups. (USAF)

Fig. 5-2. A P-36 may well have scored the first air victory for the U.S. in WWII. Six managed to get airborne and engage the enemy during the Pearl Harbor attack. Two P-40s also joined the fight. All but 27 P-40s were destroyed on the ground.

The attack ended at approximately 0945 hours. The departing Japanese left behind 2400 American dead, 1500 wounded, four battleships sunk, 14 ships heavily damaged, and 233 U.S. warplanes destroyed—plus the certainty that they had aroused the sleeping giant.

The surprise attack on Pearl Harbor united the American people in an outraged determination to fight more effectively than anything the President could have said or done. An hour earlier, the U.S. Congress would have rejected war. But after the news reached Washington (about 1325 hours, or 1:25 pm due to the time difference), and was flashed to a stunned public, even the isolationists were breaking out their flags and calling for vengeance against this enemy who had so greviously wounded us "without provocation."

President Roosevelt called Sunday, the 7th of December 1941, ". . . a date which will live in infamy," and the U.S. Congress responded with

Fig. 5-3. A Japanese Navy Zero fighter leaves the deck of its carrier early on the morning of 7 December 1941 for the surprise attack on Pearl Harbor and other targets on Oahu. (USN)

roars of anger. A formal declaration of war against Japan came on 8 December 1941, and when Japan's Axis partners, Germany and Italy, followed with declarations of war against the United States, the nation was embarked upon an all-out, two-front war.

The Philippines Lost

Nine and a half hours after word of the Pearl Harbor attack reached the Philippines, the Japanese treated confused U.S. forces there to a repeat performance. Again, despite those hours of warning, all U.S. aircraft were caught on the ground at Clark Field, near Manila. The Navy's Asiatic Fleet under Rear Adm. Thomas C. Hart—if three cruisers, 13 old destroyers, six motor torpedo boats and 29 submarines could be regarded as a "fleet"—was at

Fig. 5-4. Japanese Kate torpedo bomber takes off for the strike against U.S. ships anchored in Pearl Harbor. (USN)

Fig. 5-5. This captured photo, taken from a Japanese Kate, was snapped at the exact instant the first torpedo struck the battleship *Oklahoma*. The *Oklahoma* is third from left, with the *West Virginia* anchored alongside. (USN)

sea. (Official Air Force records do not agree as to the time of the attack in the Philippines. Maj. (ret) Al Fernandez, who was on the flight line at Clark when the first bombs fell, told this author the time was 1220 hours and, or course, 8 December since the Philippines are east of the International Date Line, though six hours earlier on the clock. Lt. Gen. (ret) Joseph Moore, who flew one of the three P-40s which got into the air to engage the enemy, told us it was "about 1130 hours." Official Japanese records give it as 1330 hours Tokyo time, which would have been 1230 hours Manila time.)

In overall command in the Far East was Lt. Gen. Douglas MacArthur, and just what he did with the hours of warning he was given is not easily explained. Adm. Hart's radio man picked up the Navy signal from Pearl Harbor 34 minutes after the attack there began, the same signal that was received in Washington D.C., and Hart ordered that it immediately be repeated to MacArthur's headquarters in Manila, as well as to all British and Dutch forces in the area.

Fig. 5-6. The *Arizona* explodes, partly hiding the *Oklahoma*, as the *California* burns in background. (USN)

It is clear that MacArthur and his staff were fully functioning no later than 0400 hours, and Air

Fig. 5-7. Curtiss P-40s, destroyed on the ground by strafing enemy planes, were bulldozed into pile of scrap during clean-up at Wheeler Field in the days following the attack. (USN)

Fig. 5-8. The Douglas B-18 Bolo, a DC-2 with bomber fuselage, was the "economy bomber" on hand in Hawaii and the Philippines when war came; it was essentially useless. (USAF)

Force records show that he "alerted" all his air units at 0430 hours. But there is no record of further orders prior to the noontime attacks on Clark and Iba Airfields. There is also no explanation as to why Navy Patrol Wing 10 at Cavite and the 17 B-17s at Clark Field were not dispatched at dawn to reconnoiter, particularly in the direction of Formosa, from which a Japanese air attack must (and did) come. MacArthur certainly knew that the President and the Chiefs of Staff all expected that the Philippines would be an early target if war came.

Air Force Gen. Lewis Brereton, who had assumed command of the Far East Air Force (FEAF) only the day before, was at MacArthur's headquarters at 0500 hours seeking permission to send his 17 B-17s against the Japanese airfields on Formosa, but MacArthur was too busy to see his air commander, and MacArthur's Chief of Staff, Gen. Southerland, told Brereton that "Americans must not fire the first shot in this part of the world." That remarkable order may or may not have been changed before noon. Later statements from those involved do not agree on that question. It should be noted that, although MacArthur had been in Manila since the previous summer, he had no reliable telephone network between his headquarters and his units in the field. The air raid warning system consisted of a radar set at Iba Field, which was out of commission, and a number of designated ground observers along the Luzon coasts. Not one report from a ground observer reached the air units before the enemy arrived. Meanwhile, MacArthur's radioed dispatch to the President late that morning read: "Every possible defense measure is being undertaken. My message is one of serenity and confidence." MacArthur, too, was ready to fight WWI again.

On 8 December 1941, the FEAF consisted of the USAAF 19th Bomb Group, equipped with 34 B-17s (half of which were on the big island of Mindanao, 500 miles to the south of Manila); the 6th Philippine Pursuit Squadron, with 11 obsolete Boeing P-26s, and the four-squadron 24th Pursuit Group (PG), which had 72 Flyable Curtiss P-40s and 35 flyable Seversky P-35s, plus 35 P-40s and 11 P-35s in maintenance or grounded for lack of parts. Some other obsolete aircraft were at Clark Field, but they were of no practical use. The 24th PG's four squadrons, the 3rd, 17th, 29th and 21st, were scattered at Iba, Nichols, Clark, and Del Carmen Fields respectively.

The pilots of the 29th Pursuit Squadron (PS) sat in their P-40 fighters all morning awaiting orders that never came. Then, high in the western sky, someone saw a line of specks, which rapidly resolved into a large number of planes, flying line-abreast, and slanting down toward Clark Field.

Capt. (later, general) Joe Moore and Lts. Randy Keator and Eddie Gilmore were the only ones to get off the ground to meet the attacking force. Four P-40s immediately behind them were destroyed while on their takeoff runs, while fourteen others were destroyed or crippled by strafing Zeros before ever reaching the runway. Moore, Keator, and Gilmore shot down five of the enemy before faulty ammunition silenced their guns.

A few minutes after Clark Field was hit, Iba Field, across the mountains, was struck by other enemy raiders, losing 13 of its 15 P-40s. Moore's squadron lost 18 of its 23 P-40s.

After the attack, the fighter squadrons dispersed to small dirt airstrips and pooled their remaining aircraft, and at the end of a week there was but 24 P-40s left. All but one of the B-17 bombers had been destroyed on the ground at Clark. A few P-35s remained, but they were no match for the

Zeros and were not flown in combat. All air combat over the Philippines during the ensuing 90 days was ridiculously one-sided. The invader never appeared with less than 30 Zeros, and the Americans never met them with more than six P-40s. Often, the pilots of the 24th PG attacked with two, sometimes four-plane elements.

Spare parts were cannibalized from wrecks, oil was strained through makeshift filters and reused, tailwheel tires were stuffed with rags, and some P-40s seemed to have more bullethole patches than original skin. The ammo problem was never solved; fully a third of it was defective, and aircraft gun oil congealed into a molasses-like varnish in cold air at high altitudes. No mail, no supplies, no help ever reached the Philippines after the war started there. Food, medicine, and eventually ammunition was in extremely short supply, but the American and Filipino forces held out.

The main Japanese invasion, following preliminary landings, began on 22 December 1941. The attack centered on Luzon, the northernmost and largest island of the archipelago, where all but a small fraction of the defending forces were concentrated. The main landings were made on the beaches of Lingayen Gulf in the northwest and Lamon Bay in the southeast, and on 23 December, MacArthur ordered a general withdrawal into the mountainous Bataan Peninsula, across Manila Bay from the capitol city. Manila itself was occupied by the Japanese without resistance. The 15,000 American troops and 45,000 sketchily-trained Filipinos had their food rations cut in half by mid-January, and their air cover had dwindled to nine P-40s, while airmen without planes to fly or service took up rifles and joined the infantrymen in foxholes.

This gallant contingent of American men and women (a number of Army nurses were with the troops), without hope of relief or rescue, called themselves the "Battling Bastards of Bataan" ("no momma, no poppa, no Uncle Sam"). With Filipino patriots, they pinned down two divisions of the enemy's best assault troops and greatly upset the Japanese timetable of conquest.

By April, the defenders were subsisting on about 15 ounces of food daily, mostly rice supplemented by lizard meat, and thousands succumbed to dysentery, dengue, malaria and scurvy. The P-40s flew as long as it was possible to get one into the air, and one can guess at the mood of those airmen as revealed in a grimly humorous message relayed by an American submarine: "Dear President Roosevelt. Please send us another P-40. The one we have is full of holes."

Actually, they had two P-40s when the end came. On 8 April, Gen. Jonathan Wainwright, left in command after MacArthur's escape (by order of the President) to Australia a month earlier, retreated to the caves of Corregidor Island in Manila Bay with

Fig. 5-9. Lt. Boyd D. Wagner, flying a P-40E, became America's first WWII ace when he shot down six enemy aircraft over the Philippines on 12 and 13 December 1941. (USAF)

most of the surviving Americans, and sadly ordered the remaining defenders of Bataan to surrender. Incredibly, the Americans on Corregidor held out another month before they, too, were forced to surrender, their food and ammunition exhausted. More than most Americans, they paid the price for 20 years of what Billy Mitchell described as " . . . incompetency . . . almost treasonable administration . . . and the delusion of the American Public."

Coral Sea and Midway

The chief goal of American deployment to the Pacific during most of 1942, following the initial reinforcement of Hawaii and the Panama Canal, was to build up a base in Australia and secure the chain of islands leading to it. As early as January, a task force of division size was hastily sent to New Caledonia, and for a few weeks an effort, doomed to failure, was made to stem the enemy's invasion of Java. Thereafter, the buildup had as its first object the defense of Australia itself because, at the end of January, the Japanese had occupied Rabaul on New Britain Island, thus posing an immediate threat to Port Moresby, the weakly-held Australian base in southeastern New Guinea at Australia's doorstep. Two U.S. divisions went to Australia in March and April as construction of air bases was rushed to completion on the steppingstone islands along the ocean routes to Australia and New Zealand. After the western anchor of this chain, New Caledonia, was secured, Army and Marine garrisons and reinforcements were sent to various other islands along the line, culminating with the arrival of American troops in the Fiji Islands in June 1942.

These moves came none too soon because during the spring, the Japanese, after occupying Rabul, pushed into the southern Solomons, within easy striking distance of the American bases on Espiritu Santo and New Caledonia. They also occupied the northeastern coast of New Guinea, just across the narrow (but mountainous) Papuan peninsula from Port Moresby, where the Americans and

Fig. 5-10. The P-40E was deployed in the Philippines when the Japanese struck, along with some P-40Bs and Seversky P-35s. The P-40E (pictured) had a slightly narrower fuselage than earlier models, shorter landing gear legs, larger radiator scoop, and six wing guns. (USAF)

Fig. 5-11. The *Lexington* was lost in the Battle of the Coral Sea. Crew abandons ship as escorts stand by. (USN)

Australians were preparing bases and airfields.

The stage was thus set for a major test of strength in the Pacific: American forces thinly spread along an immense arc from Hawaii to Australia; the Japanese securely in possession of the vast areas north and west of that arc, prepared to strike in force at any point.

Nevertheless, as tenuous as this deployment may have appeared, the security of Australia and New Zealand was essential. Later, as American arms grew stronger, this southern semi-circle could be matched with a string of steppingstone bases across the Central Pacific and, with MacArthur proceeding up the east coast of New Guinea to retake the Philippines, the giant jaws of the pincer would be closed and all enemy forces within cut off from supply, reinforcement, or retreat.

All that would take time, American lives, and a great deal of America's treasure, but it did, during those early, desperate days, provide the blueprint for victory. There can be little doubt that the Joint Chiefs planned well in the Pacific war with Japan. Adm. Ernest J. King, Commander-in-Chief of the U.S. Fleet (appointed immediately after Pearl Harbor; another excellent choice made by President Roosevelt), clearly dominated most of those decisions. Adm. King was 62 in 1942, a 1901 Naval Academy graduate—fourth in his class—who spent most of his career at sea until 1927 when he qualified as a naval aviator. He became chief of the Navy's Bureau of Aeronautics in 1933, and was regarded as an "airplane admiral" thereafter.

The first test of the American military posture in the Pacific came in May, when the Japanese made an attempt from the sea to take Port Moresby. That precipitated the great aircraft carrier battle of the Coral Sea. The battle itself was indecisive, but it constituted a strategic victory for the Americans because the enemy was forced to abandon his planned invasion of Port Moresby. Thereupon the Japanese struck eastward, hoping to complete the destruction of the U.S. Pacific Fleet and to seize Midway—a bid for clear naval supremacy in the Pacific.

We should mark the boldness of the U.S. Navy as it ventured forth to fight in the Southwest Pacific when it was the inferior force and in hostile waters. Early in May 1942, two small task forces that had earlier made surprise raids against the enemy's troop buildup on New Guinea's northeast coast

Fig. 5-12. V./Adm. Frank Fletcher's Task Force 17 fought the Battle of the Coral Sea, and joined Adm. Spurance' Task Force 16 for the Battle of Midway. (USN)

joined forces south of the Louisiades and moved northward to intercept the Japanese invasion fleet bound for Port Moresby.

The American units were Task Force 17 under Rear Adm. F. J. Fletcher, who had the carrier *Yorktown* and her escorts, and Task Force 11, consisting of the carrier *Lexington* and her support vessels, commanded by Rear Adm. A.W. Fitch. On 7 May, this combined force, strengthened by the addition of Australian cruisers and destroyers, sent its aircraft against the enemy force and sank the Japanese light carrier *Shoho* during a furious air battle, although some enemy planes were able to sink a U.S. destroyer and tanker. Darkness brought a lull in which both sides lost track of one another, but on the following day Japanese aircraft set fires aboard the *Lexington* which destroyed her, and severely damaged *Yorktown*, while U.S. Navy pilots seriously damaged the enemy's fleet carrier *Shokaku* and shot down most of her planes. The Japanese invasion force, with its air cover gone, had no choice but to flee.

The "Lady Lex" was a poor trade for the *Shoho*, but Moresby—and Australia—had been saved from invasion and all that that portended.

The Battle of the Coral Sea was unique in another way: For the first time in history, a great sea battle had been fought *solely* in the air, the opposing ships never within sight or gunrange of one another. There would be many more such battles.

Less than a month later, the enemy, still confident, was ready to take Midway and deliver a knockout blow to the U.S. Pacific Fleet. It would, in the bargain, occupy Attu and Kiska in the Aleutians, and bomb the U.S. Navy base at Dutch Harbor, Alaska. All this *should* have worked out as planned. It did not because the commander of the U.S. Pacific Fleet, Adm. Chester W. Nimitz, was aware of the enemy's intentions.

Details are unavailable even today, because U.S. intelligence people are loath to talk much about codes, but we do know that U.S. Navy cryptographers in the Office of Naval Intelligence had broken the Japanese diplomatic code prior to Pearl Harbor, and since that code belonged to the same family of codes employed by the Imperial Japanese Navy, Adm. Nimitz was reading portions of the Japanese Navy's radioed messages. That is what allowed Nimitz to plan the ambush of an overwhelmingly powerful enemy force at Midway. Nimitz knew a little of Yamamoto's plan, and correctly guessed the rest of it.

Adm. Yamamoto had reason to feel confident. With the *Lexington* gone, the *Saratoga* and *Yorktown* under repair, and the *Ranger* and *Wasp* in the Atlantic, the Americans should have no more than two carriers, *Enterprise* and *Hornet*, in the Pacific (the ancient *Langley* had long since been downgraded to tender status), while Yamamoto would have an armada of truly awesome proportions. He would send two aircraft carriers and their phalanx of supporting ships northward to attack the U.S. Naval base at Dutch Harbor, Alaska, and to occupy the Aleutian Islands of Attu and Kiska. Con-

Fig. 5-13. Navy F4F Wildcat fighters prepare to take off from the carrier *Enterprise*, 12 May 1942. (USN)

Fig. 5-14. Rare photo, dated 4 June 1942, one of the *Yorktown's* SBDs just prior to takeoff during the Battle of Midway. A handful of these aircraft were about to become the most significant planes in U.S. Naval history. (USN)

Fig. 5-15. Vice Admiral Raymond A. Spruance was junior to Fletcher at Midway, but after Fletcher lost the *Yorktown* he signaled that Spruance was to deploy his ships as Spruance saw fit. (USN)

Pearl to complete a two-month repair job on the *Yorktown* in a matter of days, sent three heavy and three light battle cruisers, with ten destroyers, to harass the enemy's Aleutian Invasion Force, and assembled two task forces with which he hoped to dry-gulch Nagumo. All were gone from Pearl Harbor by 28 May—*before* the enemy subs arrived to attempt interception.

Task Force 16, commanded by Rear Adm. Raymond A. Spruance, was made up of the carriers *Enterprise* and *Hornet*, six cruisers and nine destroyers; Task Force 17 consisted of the carrier *Yorktown*, two cruisers and five destroyers, commanded by R./Adm. Frank J. Fletcher (the senior commander over both forces). These two forces sailed to a point—Adm. Nimitz called it "Point Luck"—350 miles northeast of Midway, where they were to figuratively "lie in the bushes" and wait for Nagumo's powerful strike force.

Fletcher and Spruance reached Point Luck on 2 June and settled down to wait, Nimitz having deduced that the enemy intended to strike sometime between the 4th and 6th of June. In the meantime, Navy PBY Catalina long-range patrol planes from Midway were searching for the Japanese fleet, although they were limited by a large storm front

currently, far to the south, would be his Midway Invasion Force, containing one carrier, troop transports, and escorting vessels. Between these two would be his Midway Strike Force One under Adm. Chuichi Nagumo, consisting of four aircraft carriers (*Akagi, Kaga, Hiryu* and *Soryu*), two battleships, three battle cruisers, and 12 destroyers. Finally, Yamamoto himself would loiter about 300 miles behind Nagumo with one carrier, three battleships and a host of escorts, serving as a reserve or mop-up force. Meticulous planner Yamamoto also dispatched submarines to act as pickets in Hawaiian waters; their job was to attack the U.S. fleet as it (presumably) charged out of Pearl Harbor in response to the attack on Alaskan territory.

Meanwhile, Adm. Nimitz was doing some planning of his own. He inspired repair crews at

Fig. 5-16. U.S. Navy aces in their F4F-4 Wildcats just after Midway are Lt. Cmdr. John Thatch in No. 1 and Lt. Edward "Butch" O'Hare in No. 13.

Fig. 5-17. This F4F-4 on Henderson Field, Guadalcanal, 9 February 1943, has 19 aerial victory symbols on its fuselage, although several pilots had flown this craft to achieve that total for lucky No. 2. (USN)

which was advancing from the northwest. The U.S. commanders knew that Yamamoto would very likely take advantage of the rain and low clouds to make his approach undetected. (Radar was a new invention at the time and of limited value.)

Early on the morning of 3 June Yamamoto's Aleutian Invasion Force made a successful attack on Dutch Harbor, and later landed unopposed on Kiska and Attu in the Aleutians. Weather conditions were so poor that a number of Japanese pilots were lost when they failed to find their carriers after the strike—a problem shared by the U.S. task force in the area.

Also on 3 June, at about 0900 hours, Yamamoto's Midway Invasion Force, approaching Midway from slightly south of west, was discovered by a Catalina patrol plane some 700 miles from its destination. Army and Marine aircraft based on Midway unsuccessfully attacked this force during the late afternoon and evening hours while, out at Point Luck, Adm. Fletcher listened to their radio chatter and decided that was not the prize he sought. He could ask no questions because his command was maintaining strict radio silence. As night fell, he and Spruance moved to a point about 200 miles north and slightly east of Midway, with about ten miles separating the two task forces. With the enemy invasion force nearing its objective, his heavy guns were certain to come charging out of the fog and rain by daylight.

Fletcher was right. Under scattered clouds ahead of the weather front, Nagumo began launching bombers and fighters from his four carriers for the attack on Midway at 0430 hours on 4 June. And just an hour later, at 0536 hours, a pair of Catalinas found Nagumo's force and immediately radioed its position, course, and speed.

At that moment, the advantage passed to Fletcher and Spruance, because Nagumo was totally unaware of their presence.

Between 0700 and 1000 hours, Midway-based planes struck at Nagumo's force but were driven back with serious losses. Then, 41 TBD Devastator torpedo planes from *Enterprise, Yorktown* and *Hornet* went in at wavetop level, but the enemy ships' massed defensive firepower, plus that of their Zero combat air patrols, was impenetrable. The Devastators achieved no meaningful hits and only four returned to the *Enterprise*, two to *Yorktown*, and none to *Hornet, Hornet's* Torpedo Squadron Eight being completely wiped out.

But those crews had not been sacrificed in vain, because their determined attacks had drawn Nagumo's Zeros down to the surface and left the defending fighters low on fuel and ammunition. As the few surviving torpedo planes left the scene, high above—unmolested at 20,000 ft—*Yorktown's* 17 SBD Dauntless dive bombers, led by Lt. Cmdr. Maxwell F. Leslie, were peeling off and taking dead aim on the Japanese carrier *Kaga*. It was 1022 hours and time had run out for Nagumo.

A minute and a half after Leslie's 17 planes began their dives, Lt. Cmdr. Clarence W. Mc-Clusky, leading 37 Dauntlesses from the *Enterprise*, arrived to select two more fat targets: Nagumo's own flagship, the carrier *Akagi*, and the smaller carrier *Soryu*.

Thus it was that, within the space of a few hundred heartbeats, the Imperial Japanese Navy suffered a blow from which it never recovered. By 1029 hours, the 51 Dauntlesses from *Yorktown* and *Enterprise* were reforming in a ragged, exuberant formation for the flight back to Point Luck, leaving behind three enemy aircraft carriers aflame and sinking.

Nagumo's fourth carrier, the *Hiryu*, had a short reprieve because the *Hornet's* air group failed to immediately locate it after the enemy fleet changed course following the initial attacks. They would sink the *Hiryu* later in the day, but not before its planes severely damaged the *Yorktown*.

By the time the Japanese realized that they were fighting three U.S. carriers, their strike force had none. Yamamoto ordered a full-speed withdrawal (including, of course, the Midway Invasion Force far to the south).

Fig. 5-18. A P-40F of the 44th FS, 18th FG, on the fighter strip at Henderson Field, Guadalcanal, June 1943. The F model P-40 was powered with a Packard-built Rolls-Royce Merlin. (USMC)

Fig. 5-19. Grumman TBF Avenger comes aboard the escort carrier *Santee* during operations off Guadalcanal, January 1943. (USN)

The *Yorktown* was listing at too great an angle for her flight deck to be used, so her planes returned to *Enterprise* and *Hornet*. Adm. Fletcher transferred his flag to an escorting cruiser, the *Astoria*, and the *Yorktown's* crew was ordered to abandon ship after it appeared that she would capsize. Fletcher then signaled to Spruance, ordering him to proceed as he saw fit, and that the remaining ships of Task Force 17 would follow.

Spruance pursued the fleeing Japanese for two days, and on the 6th launched two final air strikes against them, sinking the heavy cruiser *Mikuma* and heavily damaging the cruiser *Mogami*. Then, with some of his escort vessels running low on fuel, Spruance reluctantly turned back.

But the enemy managed to strike a final blow. Early the next morning, 7 June 1942, Japanese submarine I-168, commanded by Lt. Cmdr. Yahachi Tanabe, put two torpedos into the crewless *Yorktown* and sent her to the bottom as she was being towed toward Pearl Harbor by the minesweeper *Vireo*. Tanabe also sank the escorting destroyer *Hammann*. Thus, alone among Yamamoto's entire sea armada, submarine I-168 could return to Japan claiming victory over an American ship at Midway.

After the Battle of Midway, strategic initiative in the Pacific belonged to the U.S. Navy. In addition to his carriers and battle cruisers, the enemy lost 258 airplanes and many of his best pilots. U.S. losses were 40 planes from Midway, and 92 aircraft from three carriers, plus the *Yorktown* and *Hammann*. Few if any Japanese airmen were rescued, although a number of U.S. Navy pilots were plucked from the sea by roving destroyers. After Midway, both the U.S. and Japan had six aircraft carriers remaining, but America would increasingly add carriers to the U.S. fleet, while Japan (actually fighting a defensive war following the defeat at Midway) was unable to replace her lost aircraft carriers and highly trained carrier pilots. Japan's far-flung oceanic empire could be maintained only as long as the Imperial Japanese Navy dominated the Pacific. That dominance was lost at the moment when U.S. Naval Aviator Maxwell Leslie peeled off in his Dauntless and centered his gunsight on the broad deck of the Japanese carrier *Kaga*.

New Guinea and the Solomons

Neither America's leaders nor the American people knew it at the time—and if they had it would not have mattered after the surprise attack on Pearl Harbor—but Japan entered WWII with limited aims and with the intention of fighting a limited war. Its objective was to secure the natural resources Japan lacked (oil, tin, rubber, etc.) in Southeast Asia and much of China, and to establish what Japan's Premier Tojo described as the "Greater East Asia Co-Prosperity Sphere." In other words, Japan would swiftly grab what she wanted, then stand firm behind a solid defensive position and negotiate a peace that would leave her in possession of most of her conquests.

Had she followed the course that President Roosevelt and his advisors expected, she might well have gotten away with it. On the eve of Pearl Harbor, there was a lot of sentiment in the United States against involvement in the war in Europe or a war with Japan. But Japan's decision to "neutralize" the U.S. Navy by a surprise attack unified a divided people, aroused America to wage a total war, and denied the Japanese any chance of conducting the war on their own terms.

After Midway, Japan's war planners had to modify their master plan considerably, and with the mobility of their carrier striking forces curtailed, concentrated on strengthening their existing defensive perimeter. They were far from defeat, and in fact were not ready to negotiate. According to statements made by Japan's military leaders at war's end, they expected the United States to grow weary of attempting to breach those defenses, after which Japan would consider the terms of a negotiated peace.

Meanwhile, the U.S. Joint Chiefs naturally turned to the elimination of the threat to their tenuously held bases in the Southwest Pacific, the lifeline to Australia. On 2 July 1942, they decided to begin a series of operations that would destroy the Japanese stronghold at Rabaul and establish Allied control of the Bismarck Archipelago.

The campaign would have three tasks: (1) Forces of the South Pacific Area (under V./Adm. Robert Ghormley, later commanded by Adm. William "Bull" Halsey) would seize base sites in the southern Solomons; (2) South Pacific forces would advance up the ladder of the Solomons while Southwest Pacific forces (under Gen. Douglas MacArthur) would move up the north coast of New Guinea; (3) The forces of the two theaters would converge on Rabaul and clear the rest of the Bismarck Archipelago. Adm. Nimitz, overall commander of the Pacific Ocean Areas—including the North, Central, and South Pacific—would run the Solomons operations, while Gen. MacArthur would be responsible for the Southwest Pacific. Gen. Marshall and Adm. King would referee the anticipated differences between the hard-bitten Nimitz and the flamboyant MacArthur (although they did not state it quite that way).

MacArthur's air support would be provided by the USAAF Fifth Air Force, born from the ashes of the Far East Air Force in the Philippines, and commanded by Gen. George Kenney. (The former FEAF commander, the fiesty Gen. Lewis Brereton,

Fig. 5-20. Lockheed F-5A reconnaissance version of the P-38, with cameras rather than guns in its nose. Bars were added to the star insignia in July 1943. (USAF)

Fig. 5-21. Fifth Air Force's field-modified medium bombers were so successful skip-bombing and strafing in the Battle of the Bismark Sea that North American was inspired to build the B-25G and H Mitchells armed with 75mm field cannon. Beside cannon, B-25H (shown) could also bring ten forward-firing .50-calibor machine guns to bear on strafing target.

was in India forming the USAAF 10th Af.)

Air support in the Solomons would be provided by Navy and Marine fliers, plus a handful of Army P-39s and P-40s, until formation of the USAAF 13th AF early in 1943.

The offensive began on 7 August 1942 when the 1st Marine Division landed on Guadalcanal and nearby islands in the southern Solomons. The enemy reacted vigorously, and six times during the next four months challenged the U.S. Navy in a series of sharp battles, while air fighting was almost a daily occurrence.

During the first days of bitter fighting on Guadalcanal, the Navy, Marine, and USAAF aircraft, commanded by Rear Adm. J.S. McCain, operated from bases on New Caledonia and in the New Hebrides, with some initial assistance from the air groups of *Saratoga*, *Enterprise*, and *Wasp*. The carriers, operating in confined waters, withdrew from direct support on 9 August. By 20 August, the Marines had pushed a stubborn enemy, a few feet at a time, beyond the airstrip and Marine Fighting Squadron 233 and Scout Bombing Squadron 232 moved in. There were plenty of enemy soldiers in the surrounding rain forest, and would be for months, but the fliers took care of their missions and depended upon the "Gyrenes" to protect the airstrip. This was Henderson Field, known to the airmen there by its code name, "Cactus One." A week later, the *Enterprise* brought a deckload of P-40s, and in the weeks to follow other Air Force and Marine air units arrived.

Fig. 5-22. The Eastern Aircraft Division of General Motors built Wildcats under the designations FM-1 and FM-2. The FM-2 was easy to recognize with its tall rudder. The British received more than a thousand Wildcats. (USN)

During Christmas Week, Marines, strengthened by Army troops, took over the area known by Army troops, took over the area known as "Lunga Beach" on Guadalcanal and it became Fighter One Base, with Marine Fighting Squadron 214 (VME-214, Pappy Boyington's "Black Sheep") at one end of the strip, and the P-40-equipped 44th FS of the 18th FG* at the other. Contrary to Hollywood's portrayal of the Black Sheep, there were no Army nurses on Fighter Base One and no liquor. There were Spam, dehydrated potatoes, mosquitos, and dysentery in abundance.

Guadacanal was not declared secured until 9 February 1943. In the meantime, in addition to the fierce fighting on the island, six major sea battles were fought in the area. *Saratoga's* air groups sank the Japanese light carrier *Ryujo* during the Battle of the Eastern Solomons, 23-25 August; *Enterprise* was damaged by enemy carrier-based bombers during that battle and forced to retire. Then the *Saratoga* took a submarine torpedo on 31 August

---

*In May, 1942, all USAAF Pursuit Groups became "Fighter Groups," and Pursuit Squadrons became "Fighter Squadrons." Normally, a Fighter Group consisted of three squadrons of 35 aircraft per squadron—on paper, at least. In combat areas, groups were often under-strength.

and went to Australia for repairs, and the *Wasp* was sunk by a submarine on 15 September while escorting a troop convoy to Guadalcanal. During October, the *Hornet*, in Task Force 17, repeatedly sent her planes against enemy targets on Guadalcanal and, with *Enterprise*, fought in the Battle of Santa Cruz (26-27 October) in which she was sunk by Japanese dive bombers. In the final carrier actions of the campaign, *Enterprise*, severely damaged during the Battle of Santa Cruz (the enemy threw four carriers into that battle, two of which were put out of action but not sunk), went to Noumea, New Caledonia for repairs, and was back in action by 15 November.

In the long, proud history of the U.S. Marine Corps, no pages stand out more vividly than those containing the record of the prolonged Battle for Guadalcanal. That campaign alone should provide a shining beacon of inspiration for every man and woman who has worn that uniform since. On the ground and in the air, the Marines spearheaded the bloodiest fighting, and the Marine air groups alone accounted for 427 enemy planes destroyed in combat.

The advance from Guadalcanal began 21 February 1943, in the Russells, sixty miles to the northeast. Although there were no noteworthy naval engagements for a time, aerial fighting continued unabated. Enemy air attacks on Guadalcanal, particularly on Henderson Field, did not let up until June, and on the 16th April the island was subjected to one of the most devastating air strikes of the campaign. The Japanese sent 160 bombers and fighters which were intercepted by more than 100 American fighters from the Army, Navy and Marine Corps. The enemy lost 107 planes; the Americans, six.

By the end of 1943, Adm. Nimitz was ready to begin his final assault on Rabaul, and the drive up the Solomons ended with occupation of the Green Islands—just 120 miles from Rabaul—on 15 February 1944. As Adm. Arleigh Burke put it, "Behind lay bloody Guadalcanal—an epitaph, and enduring symbol of American bravery and sacrifice."

In January 1943, the USAAF 13th Air Force was formed around the 347th FG, which had been operating over Guadalcanal and adjacent waters since the previous October. The 347th contained one squadron each of P-40s, P-39s, and P-38s. The 13th AF gradually accumulated a hodgepodge of B-17s, B-25s, and other aircraft, including the 8th and 18th FGs equipped with P-38 Lightnings, and the 5th, 42nd, and 307th Bomb Groups (BG) flying B-24 Liberators and B-25 Mitchells. While the bombers went to Rabaul and attacked enemy shipping in the area, the fighters of the 13th AF opposed enemy raids over the Solomons and the advancing ground forces. Australian P-40s (Kittyhawks) joined in this effort and guarded the "back door" in the southern Solomons and New Caledonia.

Meanwhile, Gen. Kenney's 5th AF on New Guinea was being built up around the 49th, 24th, and 35th FGs, which were equipped with whatever fighter planes Kenney could lay hands on. Early in 1943, Kenney had a total of 330 fighters, of which 80 were P-38s and 72 were the decidedly inferior P-39s. The rest were P-40s, including seven Royal New Zealand Air Force squadrons and eight Royal Australian Air Force squadrons, plus one Dutch squadron. (British and Commonwealth squadrons contained 9-12 aircraft.) Kenny's bomber force would grow from the relative handful of B-17s, A-20s and B-25s of the 7th, 19th, 3rd and 22nd BGs possessed early in 1943 to a total of 11 bomb groups a year later; an eventual total of five USAAF fighter groups after the 475th and 58th FGs were added. Gen. Paul "Squeeze" Wurtsmith was the 5th AF's fighter commander.

The 5th AF, flying from airstrips in the Port Moresby area, made all the difference in the Battle of the Bismark Sea. In fact, that battle was fought primarily between enemy warships and Kenney's airplanes. On 1 March 1943 the Japanese sent a 16-ship convoy from Rabaul toward Lae on New Guinea's north coast to beef up their base there with an additional 6000 troops and thereby keep MacArthur contained in southern New Guinea. But F-5 Lightnings (the recce version of the P-38, fitted with cameras in place of guns) of the 17th Photo Squadron (PhS) discovered the convoy en route. On 2 March, in poor weather, 28 B-17s, escorted by 16 P-38s, sank one of the troop transports in Huon Gulf and shot down two enemy fighters. On the following day, skip-bombing and strafing, 28 Lightnings, with a mixed formation of 5th AF A-20s, B-25s, and some Australian Beaufighters, sent two destroyers and three transports to the bottom. U.S. Navy PT Boats accounted for the rest of the transports. Of the 16-ship convey, only four destroyers survived, rescuing perhaps half of the enemy soldiers and beating a retreat to Rabaul in deteriorating weather.

It was not a large battle by WWII standards, but taken together with victory in the Solomons and devastating air strikes against the Japanese airfields on New Guinea's north coast which destroyed 200 enemy planes on the ground (made possible by use of a secret jungle airstrip built by U.S. Army engineers only a few miles from the enemy strongholds), the 5th AF over New Guinea, and the 13th

Fig. 5-23. Japanese Mitsubishi G4MI Betty Bomber. P-38s of 347th FG bushwhacked Betty carrying Admiral Yamamoto, costing Japan her best military mind. (USAF)

AF over the Solomons, gained control of the air—with the help, of course, of the Marine Corsair units moving up through the Solomons. That greatly facilitated American strategy in the Pacific.

That strategy was predicated upon three lines of advance: Across the Central Pacific, the USAAF 7th AF in support of Naval units via the Gilberts, Marshalls, Marianas, Carolines and Palaus toward the Philippines; in the Southwest Pacific the 5th AF covering (and often leading) MacArthur's march up the north coast of New Guinea toward the Philippines; and the South Pacific line of advance up through the Solomons with the 13th AF, plus Navy, Marine and RAAF squadrons, to encircle and neutralize Rabaul, which was as important to Japan as was Pearl Harbor to the U.S. as a Pacific base.

During the first two weeks of April 1943, Adm. Yamamoto moved most of his carrier air groups onto Rabaul for Operation *I-go*, and all-out attempt to regain control of the air over New Guinea and the Solomons, and in mid-month struck at Port Moresby and Milne Bay with 150-plane raids. But Yamamoto's great aerial offensive was abruptly terminated by a flight of 14 P-38s from the 347th FG on Guadalcanal. On 18 April these Lightnings were dispatched by Adm. Bull Halsey (Nimitz' deputy in the South Pacific area) to shoot down a certain Japanese Betty bomber due to arrive at an ememy airfield on Bougainville at a given time.

Halsey's information came from the Japanese themselves, by way of the Navy's decoding experts, and the prize was a big one: Adm. Isoruku Yamamoto would be aboard that bomber.

The P-38s flew a long, roundabout route, staying well out to sea to avoid detection. Counting on Adm. Yamamoto's reputation for punctuality, they carefully timed their arrival over Bougainville to coincide with that of their quarry.

Yamamoto was on time. So were the P-38s. The admiral's plane went down aflame under the guns of Capt. Thomas Lanphier, while the remaining Lightnings shot down a second Betty and engaged the escorting six Zeros. One P-38, flown by Lt. Ray Hine, was lost in the fight.

But the enemy's Operation *I-go* was called off. Japan had lost her greatest military strategist.

Chapter 6

The War in Europe

Four days after the surprise Japanese attack on Pearl Harbor, Germany and Italy declared war on the United States, effectively settling any question there may have been in the public mind as to whether or not America would also have to fight in Europe.

President Roosevelt, his military leaders, and perhaps many Americans had accepted that fact long before. As early as 1939 the President had looked the other way as American-built warplanes were pushed by hand across the border into Canada for delivery to England, a practice that supposedly got around U.S. neutrality laws. On the eve of France's defeat in June 1940, the President directed the transfer of large stocks of Army WWI weapons, and ammunition and aircraft to both France and Great Britain; after France fell these munitions helped to replace Britain's losses in the evacuation of its forces from the Continent at Dunkerque. More aid to Britain was forthcoming in September when the United States traded 50 over-age destroyers for offshore Atlantic bases. The American position was clear by March 1941, when the Congress passed the Lend-Lease Act, sweeping away the pretense of neutrality and by openly avowing that America would become an "arsenal of democracy" against aggression.

Actually, these acts constituted a measure of self defense, the fundamental purpose being to help contain the military might of the Axis powers—Germany, Italy and Japan—until the U.S. could build its own shaky defenses.

American military preparations and actions during the remaining months of 1941 prior to the Japanese attack were steadily toward U.S. participation in the war against Germany. In April, the President authorized an active naval patrol of the western half of the Atlantic Ocean. In May, the United States assumed responsibility for the operation of military air routes across the North Atlantic via Greenland, and across the South Atlantic via Brazil. In May, Roosevelt also proclaimed an unlimited national emergency and ordered the Army and Navy to prepare an expeditionary force to be sent to the Azores to block any German advance into the South Atlantic.

A few days before the Germans invaded the Soviet Union (22 June 1941), the President sent U.S. Marines and the 33rd FS to guard Iceland. The 33rd, which belonged to the 8th FG, flew its P-40s off the deck of the aircraft carrier *Wasp* to Reykjavik with orders to attack any Axis aircraft or ship found within 50 miles of shore. By October the U.S. Navy was fully engaged in ship convoy duties in the western part of the Atlantic, and Navy ships, with some assistance from Army aircraft, were joining with British and Canadian forces in warring against German submarines. During the third week in October, the new U.S. Navy destroyer *Kearny* was torpedoed in the North Atlantic and President Roosevelt declared in indignation, "We have wished to avoid shooting, but the shooting has started, and history has recorded who fired the first shot . . . All that will matter is who fired the last shot!" Actually, the *Kearny* was joining British warships in an attack on a German U-boat when she was hit.

In November Congress voted to repeal prohibition against the arming of American merchant ships and their entry into combat zones, and the stage was set (as Prime Minister Churchill noted on 9 November) for "constant fighting in the Atlantic between American and German ships."

Apparently, all of the overt American moves in 1941 toward involvement in the war against Germany were acceptable to the majority of the American people, with only a small though vociferous minority criticizing the President for the nation's

Fig. 6-1. The P-40s of the 33rd FS, 8th FG, were sent by President Roosevelt to Iceland in August 1941 to forestall the possibility of German seizure of that strategically located island. (USAF)

Fig. 6-2. Carrier *Ranger* bound for North Africa with replacement P-40Ls (Merlin powered) as escorting destroyer drops depth charges over suspected enemy submarine. (NASM)

departures from neutrality. America, along with the British and Dutch, had also embargoed oil shipments to Japan and imposed other trade sanctions on the Nipponese for their international misbehavior, and no one questioned the propriety of that. (Those embargos forced Japan to do *something*, even if it was wrong, because she had no oil or certain other strategic materials of her own, and the American/British/Dutch position left her with no face-saving way out, because resumption of normal trade was tied to the condition that Japan get out of China and Indochina and, in effect, renounce her treaties with Germany and Italy. Premier Tojo and his warlords never considered that alternative.)

North Africa and Italy

Once the nation was committed to war, every American, from the President to the humblest citizen, seemed to possess the same attitude toward it: a strong resolve for quick, direct, and total action. The trouble was that during 1942 the strength of our arms did not match the strength of our will.

Nevertheless, after the Battle of Midway the U.S. Navy, weak and exhausted though it was, was completely confident that it would soon own the Pacific Ocean, and (although the Joint Chiefs were against it) President Roosevelt confidently placed his finger on a map of the North African coast and told them that, since the Allies were not yet ready to invade Hitler's Europe, we would invade North Africa instead, and then move up through Italy to attack Europe's "soft underbelly."

The invasion of North Africa, Operation *Torch*, was Churchill's idea, prompted by the fact that Germany's brilliant Field Marshal Erwin Rommel, the "Desert Fox," was then chasing the British 8th Army across Libya and threatening Britain's supply of Middle East oil. Also, with the Germans and their Italian allies in possession of that narrow but strategic strip of the North African littoral between Tunisia and Egypt—the Mediterranean on the north and impassable desert to the south—they denied use of the Mediterranean to Allied shipping and largely diluted the value of the Suez Canal.

Torch was scheduled for 8 November, and just five days before that Gen. Bernard Montgomery's British 8th Army broke out of its defensive position at El Alamein in Egypt (Rommel's Afrika Korps had been stopped just 70 miles short of Alexandria), and was pursuing Rommel westward into Libya. By that time, most of the 400-ship invasion force was at sea, including the U.S. Navy Task Group 34.2 under Rear Adm. E.D. McWhorter with the fleet carrier *Ranger* and the escort carriers *Sangamon, Suwannee*, and *Santee* to provide air cover for the landings. The escort carrier *Chenango* was also along, her deck containing the 33rd FG's 78 P-40s. The 1st and 14th FG's P-38's were waiting at Land's End, England, and would stage through Gibralter after the invasion was underway.

The invasion came off as scheduled, before daylight on the morning of 8 November 1942, with American troops put ashore near Casablanca in French Morocco and in Algeria near the ports of Oran and Algiers. The French fought for their German masters for three days before throwing down their arms; during that time Allied air support for the invasion came from McWhorter's carriers, bolstered by Royal Air Force (RAF) Spitfires from Malta.

On the 10th, airfields near Oran were taken and the 33rd's Warhawks immediately moved in, while P-38s of the 1st and 14th FGs began operation the following day from Tafaraoui, Algiers. These USAAF groups were part of Gen. James Doolittle's newly created 12th AF, which also included the 301st, 310th, 97th, 47th, 98th, 319th, 320th, and 17th BGs flying B-17s, B-24s, B-25s, A-20s, and B-26s. The 31st FG, equipped with British Spitfires, also went into action over North Africa within a week.

The only trouble with Doolittle's 12th AF was

Fig. 6-3. This Bf.109G of JG 27 was shot down during the Tunisian Campaign. Powered with the Daimler-Benz DB 605 of 1475 hp, it had a speed of 403 mph at 21,325 ft. Armament was two 7.9 mm machine guns and a 20mm cannon, the latter firing through the prop spinner. (USAF)

that *Torch* commander Gen. Dwight D. Eisenhower soon had its 800 airplanes (300 fighters, 300 bombers, and support aircraft such as C-47s) spread over 600 miles of desert to serve the presumed needs of the ground commanders, which in both deployment and mission denied the American fighter pilots the opportunity to do their job as it should be done, i.e., *first* gain control of the air.

The 12th AF—and the troops on the ground depending upon it—paid heavily for Eisenhower's on-the-job training until "Ike," aware that he was doing something wrong, sent to England for Gen. Carl "Tooey" Spaatz (probably America's most able air commander) to tell him what it was. Jimmy Doolittle probably had the answer, but lacked Eisenhower's trust.

Doolittle had been a lieutenant colonel just six months before, and eighteen months before that, a civilian. He had left the Air Corps in 1930, after 12 years' service, and returned in 1940. Then, in April, 1942, he led 12 B-25 Mitchells off the deck of the carrier *Hornet* for the celebrated raid on Tokyo. Twelve medium bombers loaded with fuel—they were launched more than 800 miles at sea—could not deliver sufficient bomb tonnage to greatly dam-

Fig. 6-4. A P-40F Warhawk of the 64th FS, 57th FG, 9th AF, which fought through Egypt, Libya and Tunisia attached to the Desert Air Force. The 57th later fought in Italy. (NASM)

age the enemy, but the Tokyo raid did provide Americans, civilians and servicemen alike, with a tremendous morale boost at a time when all war news was bad. All of the B-25s, and some of their crews, were lost after running out of fuel over China in bad weather, but Doolittle and his surviving

Fig. 6-5. The Junkers Ju.87 Stuka, German dive bomber, was designed for close air support of the mechanized German Army in Europe, but was easy prey for Allied fighters in North Africa. (NASM)

crews returned to the United States as heros, and Doolittle was promoted to the rank of brigadier general by a grateful President. As commander of the 12th AF, Doolittle wore two stars. Later, as boss of the 15th and 8th AFs in turn, he was a lieutenant general—a *lot* of rank and responsibility for a reserve officer.

Gen. Eisenhower faced several unanticipated problems in Northwest Africa in addition to strong Luftwaffe action. The Germans reacted to the invasion with unexpected speed and began an airlift of troops into Tunisia from across the Mediterranean just one day after the American troops were landed ashore. Initially slowed by the confused French resistance, and then confronted by seasoned German forces, while depending upon a supply line that reached all the way back to the United States, Eisenhower found his drive toward Tunis slowed until it became bogged in the mud of seasonal rains. He had expected to be in Tunis by Christmas, but Rommel was retreating from the opposite direction across Libya in good order and would, in late January 1943, halt his westward retreat at the Mareth Line, a series of old French fortifications near the southern border of Tunisia, which the British 8th Army would find difficult to penetrate. Meanwhile, 100,000 German and Italian troops commanded by Gen. Juergen von Arnim blocked Eisenhower's forces in northwest Tunisia. The Allied plan to defeat both von Arnim and Rommel by squeezing them between the American and British armies east of Tunis having failed, Eisenhower had no option but to assume defensive positions in the harsh Tunisian mountains until he could accumulate enough strength to attack in conjunction with a renewed strike by Gen. Montgomery against the Mareth Line.

In the meantime, the 12th AF was being frittered away in a seemingly endless series of scattered, uncoordinated actions. Gen. Spaatz changed

Fig. 6-6. The P-38J model (foreground) with intercooler radiators beneath the engines was a greatly improved machine, but did not enter combat until the war in the MTO had moved into Italy. Photo-recon F-5B in background. (USAF)

Fig. 6-7. The Focke-Wulf 190 was a formidable enemy, probably the best German fighter of the war. Its 1760-hp BMW twin-row radial gave it a speed of 395 mph at 17,000 ft. Shown here is an FW 190A-8 carrying aft fuselage "defense of the Reich" bands seen in last days of the war.

Fig. 6-8. The Martin B-26 Marauder medium bomber had a reputation as a "widow maker," but crews swore by it. The 9th AF contained eight Marauder groups. (USAF)

Fig. 6-9. Chancellor of Germany Adolf Hitler, and Reichsmarschall Herman Goering, boss of the Luftwaffe. (USIA)

Air Chief Marshal Tedder's Commonwealth Desert Air Force, with complete control of the air, had lead Montgomery's 8th Army all the way from El Alamein in Egypt, because Montgomery as well as Montgomery's superior, Gen. Sir Harold Alexander, Commander-in-Chief, Middle East, understood the proper use of airpower and utilized it wisely, i.e., they listened to Tedder.

Tedder's Desert Air Force mostly consisted of RAF and SAAF (South African Air Force) squadrons flying Hurricanes, Spitfires, and Kittyhawks, along with some Beaufighters and Wellington bombers, plus the small U.S. 9th AF which had been formed in Egypt the previous August by Gen. Lewis Brereton.

Brereton had four Warhawk groups, the 57th, 79th, 324th and 325th FGs; two medium bomb groups, the 12th and 322nd; and two B-24 heavy bomb groups, the 98th and 376th. None possessed its normal complement of aircraft, and Brereton had equipped his understrength bomber groups partly by shanghaiing some B-24s and their crews when they stopped in Egypt for fuel en route to India.

By early March 1943, all Allied airpower in the theater was operating under a single command and run by air officers and the situation in North Africa quickly improved for the Allies. Rommel, badly in need of fuel for his panzers, made an unexpected thrust in the Tunisian mountains against Eisenhower's forces in an attempt to capture NAAF airfield gasoline supplies. The Desert Fox gained Kasserine Pass and took 2000 American prisoners, but failed to reach the fuel he needed. He would undoubtedly have preferred not to have the prisoners because his only supplies came by airlift across the Mediterranean from Italy and Sicily and he was having trouble enough feeding his own troops.

On 7 April, the British 8th Army linked up with Eisenhower's forces in north-central Tunisia after skirting the Mareth Line. The two armies, which had started out nearly 1700 miles apart six months earlier, at last closed the pincer to surround Rommel and back him against the sea in northern Tunisia.

The German commander would hold out there until 13 May 1943 by which time, lacking the means

that. He told Ike that all his air units must be commanded by *air* officers; that the chain of command for all air operations must be through air officers all the way to the top; that the U.S. fighter groups must concentrate on defeating the Luftwaffe and taking control of the air. Then, and only then, could the Army move with its communications and supply lines intact and with effective, dependable direct air support, with the Air Force free to destroy the enemy's vital communications and transport, whether it be by ship or by air across the Mediterranean.

Eisenhower gave Spaatz a free hand to reorganize U.S. airpower in northwest Africa. Spaatz, coordinating with Britain's Air Chief Marshal Tedder (Montgomery's air boss), formed the Northwest African Air Forces (NAAF) around the U.S. 12th AF, with himself in command, and then placed it in the new Mediterranean Air Command with Tedder's Desert Air Force, and with Tedder in overall command.

to further resist, Rommel escaped to Italy and surrendered his 270,000 German and Italian troops. Allied airpower had swept the Luftwaffe from the air and severed Rommel's aerial supply lines across the Mediterranean.

The main blow was struck by 46 American Warhawks and 12 RAF Spitfires in a single action on 18 April, Palm Sunday, and that battle has been known ever since as the "Palm Sunday Massacre." Throughout that day, NAAF and Desert Air Force fighters had patrolled the Mediterranean off the Tunisian coast watching for the German transport planes but found nothing. Then, at 1650 hours it was the turn of the 57th FG's three squadrons, the 64th, 65th, and 66th, who could put up only 34 P-40s, so they were joined by 12 more P-40s from the 324th FG's 314th Squadron.

The Warhawks stayed low, flying abreast in four-plane formations, stair-stepped from 4000 ft to 12,000 ft. The dozen Spits were at 15,000 ft, just below an overcast, watching for enemy fighters.

For an hour, they saw nothing but an empty sea. Then suddenly someone saw the enemy's aerial convoy. The three-engined Junkers Ju. 52s were painted in green and blue camouflage that blended with the water below and were flying just a few feet about the surface. There were 30 of them, then, 60, then nearly a hundred. The Warhawks attacked in pairs.

It truly was a massacre. Some of the 30 or so Bf. 109 Messerschmitt and Macchi C.202 Italian fighters escorting the transports got past the covering Spits above, but the exultant P-40 pilots turned into them and dominated that confrontation as well.

Fig. 6-10. Crew members inspect battle damage to the tail of their B-25 Mitchell medium bomber of the 12th AF in Italy. Mission was to Yugoslavia. (USAF)

Fig. 6-11. Flight of 9th AF P-38s, returning from a mission against German targets, make the approach to their base at low altitude. Northrop P-61 Black Widows are just visible at lower left. (USAF)

At low altitudes, the P-40 gave up nothing to the Messerschmitts or Macchis.

It was all over within ten minutes, and the P-40s, low on fuel and ammunition, turned for home. Six of their number and one Spitfire had gone down, but the enemy's very lifeline in North Africa had been cut. The official score was 58 Ju.52 transports, 14 Mc202 and four Bf.109 fighters destroyed, although there was little doubt that other Ju.52s, badly damaged, had gone down into the sea unnoticed during the confusion of battle. Three pilots of the 57th FG became "instant" aces that evening: Lts. Richard E. Duffey and Arthur B. Cleveland each got five Ju.52s, and Lt. McArthur Powers shot down four Ju.52s and one Messerschmitt.

The enemy made several more desperate attempts to run the Allied aerial blockade during the following week, with about 20 transport planes each time, and each time suffered disaster. A final attempt, at night, was met by night Beaufighters of the Desert Air Force.

The enemy was allowed no respite. The combined Mediterranean Air Command, ever more fat and sassy with battle experience and receiving new U.S. air groups (including the Lightning-equipped 82nd FG and the P-40-equipped all-black 99th FS), mounted a three-week air offensive against the heavily-fortified Italian island of Pantelleria which lay about 50 miles off the Tunisian coast. Pantelleria surrendered on 11 June—the first bit of enemy territory in history to be taken with airpower alone.

Later that summer, when the Warhawk pilots of the 325th FG (the "Checkertails") felt that they had sufficiently discouraged the Italian defenders

Fig. 6-12. North American's Mustang, designed around the Allison V-1710, became a true thoroughbred when re-engined with the Rolls-Royce Merlin, built under license in the U.S. by Packard. This early P-51B shows unusual markings: RAF camouflage, serial, and fin flash with red-bordered (mid-1943) U.S. "star and bar." (USAF)

on the island of Sardinia, they dropped a note, addressed to the commanding general, suggesting that he surrender the island to the 325th FG. That undoubtedly amused Tedder and Spaatz when they heard about it, but they were forced to pass the word that any such negotiations would be handled at a higher level.

After Pantelleria fell, Sicily was next, a campaign that lasted less than a month after the NAAF destroyed nearly 1000 Axis aircraft, most of them on the ground. During the invasion by 160,000 troops of the U.S. 7th Army and British 8th Army, the Allied air cover extended well into Italy; by 13 July 1943, elements of Tedder's Mediterranean Air Command were making themselves at home on Sicilian airfields. Three weeks later, the Germans

Fig. 6-13. Definitive version of the Mustang was the bubble-canopied P-51D, seen here in service with the 8th AF's 20th FG. This early "D" lacks the later-standard dorsal fin. Note the 108-gallon drop tanks, which allowed the Mustangs to escort the 8th's "heavies" to even the most distant targets. (Merle Olmstead collection)

retreated across the Strait of Messina into Italy, and the Allies could look across those scant three and a half miles of water to the tip of Italy, toward what President Roosevelt had called "Europe's soft underbelly."

The Italian Campaign

It did not prove to be very soft. Although, with invasion imminent, the Italians disposed of their dictator, Benito Mussolini, and signed a separate peace with the Allies, they remained virtual prisoners in their own country which was occupied by 26 German divisions. And the Germans intended to fight for every inch of Italy.

On 3 September 1943 British forces under Montgomery landed in extreme southern Italy, and the U.S. 5th Army under Lt. Gen. Mark Clark followed with an assault on the beaches near Salerno, a point selected because it represented the northern limit of effective Allied air support operating from airfields in Sicily. The ground-based aircraft of the Mediterranean Air Command—mostly the 9th and 12th U.S. Air Forces—provided all air support because all U.S. Navy carriers were in the Pacific.

The Italian Campaign would drag out for 19 months, the Germans (under Field Marshal Albert Kesselring) at last surrendering on 2 May 1945, just five days before the war ended in Europe with the German surrender at Eisenhower's headquarters in Reims, France.

Less generally acclaimed than other phases of WWII, the campaign in Italy nevertheless had a vital part in the overall conduct of the war. At the crucial time of the Normandy landings, 25 Allied divisions in Italy were tying down 26 German divisions that might well have upset the balance in France. As a result of this campaign, the Allies obtained airfields useful for the strategic bombing of Germany and the Balkans. Conquest of the Italian peninsula further guaranteed the safety of Allied shipping in the Mediterranean.

Gen. John Cannon's, 12th AF, operating from captured airfields around Naples and Salerno, was a tactical air force, its air groups primarily consisting of fighters and medium bombers. The newly-formed 15th AF contained B-17 and B-24 heavy bombers, along with P-47 fighters and three P-38 groups transferred from the 12th AF, and filled a

Fig. 6-14. Enemy flak severed the oil line of this Republic P-47 Thunderbolt of the 12th AF, so Lt. Edwin King returned to base thoroughly bathed in oil. He was strafing gun positions near Brascia, Italy. (USAF)

Fig. 6-15. The Messerschmitt Bf.109F had a top speed of 382 mph at 17,000 ft, and was considered by many Luftwaffe fighter pilots to be the best of the 109 series. The more powerful 109Gs and Ks which followed gained weight and lost maneuverability.

strategic role under Gen. Nathan Twining. The 9th AF, which had fought from Egypt to Tunisia with Tedder, joined the 8th AF in England for the air offensive against Germany. Also to England went Gens. Eisenhower, Spaatz and Doolittle, with Air Marshal Tedder, to prepare for the cross-channel invasion, and Gen. Ira Eaker replaced Tedder as the top air commander in the Mediterranean Theater of Operations (MTO).

Gen. Eaker had approximately 1200 fighter airplanes in Italy: seven fighter groups in the 12th AF and five fighter groups in the 15th AF, plus 16 squadrons of RAF, RAAF, and SAAF fighters. The RAF squadrons were mostly equipped with Spitfires, while the Australians and South Africans went to Italy from North Africa with Kittyhawks. About half of the 12th AF fighters were Warhawks at first, but all were re-equipped with Thunderbolts (and, eventually, Mustangs). The 15th AF had three Lightning groups (plus one photo-recce F-5 group), two Thunderbolt and one Spitfire group (31st FG). While the Thunderbolt and Spit groups switched to Mustangs late in the war, the Lightning groups in the MTO kept their P-38s.

Eaker also had 10 medium bomber and light bomber groups in the 12th AF, two flying A-36s (Allison-powered dive bomber Mustangs), four equipped with B-25 Mitchells, and three with B-26 Marauders. The 15th AF, by mid-1944, contained no less than 21 heavy bomber groups (the 15th was bombing Germany from its bases in Italy by then). Six of these groups flew B-17 Flying Fortresses, and 15 groups had B-24 Liberators.

The 325th FG, which fought with the 12th AF in North Africa and was transferred to the 15th AF in Italy, flew P-40s, P-47s and P-51s in turn, and provides us with an interesting statistic: They destroyed 3.6 enemy aircraft for each P-40 lost in combat, 3.9 for each P-47, and 3.2 for each P-51. If *that* doesn't start some arguments, nothing will.

Throughout the winter of 1943-44 the Germans occupied strong defensive positions anchored on the towering peaks around the town of Cassino, about 90 miles south of Rome. On 22 January 1944, American and British troops landed at Anzio, 60 miles behind the enemy's "Winter Line," but the Germans kept this force pinned down on its beachhead, and but for constant Allied air strikes this force could not have survived. The Winter Line was not breached until May 1944, after the 12th AF had methodically destroyed all rail and highway routes of supply to the Germans.

The enemy withdrew to the Apennines in northern Italy and stubbornly remained there until, again, with his lines of supply severed by Allied airpower, half-starved, the bereft of the means to further resist, he surrendered just a few days before the war ended in Europe.

Throughout the final year of the war in Europe, the 15th AF in Italy coordinated its mass attacks on Germany with those of the U.S. 8th AF in England, and the 15th's P-38s, because of their long range, always escorted their "Big Friends."

A typical mission was that of 2 April 1944 when 450 B-17s and B-24s of the 15th AF went to Steyr, Austria, to bomb a ball bearing plant and aircraft factory. The 82nd FG furnished initial escort; while still miles from the target, the bombers were attacked by 50 Bf.109s, FW.190s, and Macchi C.202s. The Lightnings fought them off, downing three of the Messerschmitts, and although there was another formation of enemy fighters circling above, the P-38s refused to take the bait and stayed with the bombers.

Fifteen minutes later, at 1045 hours and right on time, the 325th FG's Thunderbolts arrived to relieve the P-38s and to take the Big Friends on to the target area. During the next 45 minutes, the 325th Checkertails warded off an attack on the bombers by 21 Messerschmitts. Then, at 1130 hours, 46 P-38s from the 1st FG arrived, their assignment being to protect the bombers in the target area. But the P-47s, with fuel running low, were scarcely out of sight before the bomber formation was attacked by 70 enemy fighters. That could have resulted in a sticky situation, because there were not enough P-38s on the scene to handle the Messerschmitts and Focke-Wulfs. At that point, any western movie fan could have almost heard the sound of a U.S. Cavalry bugle in the distance, because the 14th FG charged into the melee with 37 more P-38s. With more than 80 Lightnings fighting together, only six enemy fighters were able to get through to the bomber stream, two of which went down under the guns of the bomber crews.

The Luftwaffe tried again shortly after 1200 hours as the bombers began coming off their targets and turning for home. Forty twin-engine Messerschmitt *Zerstorers* (110s and 210s), armed with rockets, struck at the bombers in head-on attacks flying four abreast. The P-38s quickly broke up these formations and, in a 20-minute running battle, destroyed 18 of them.

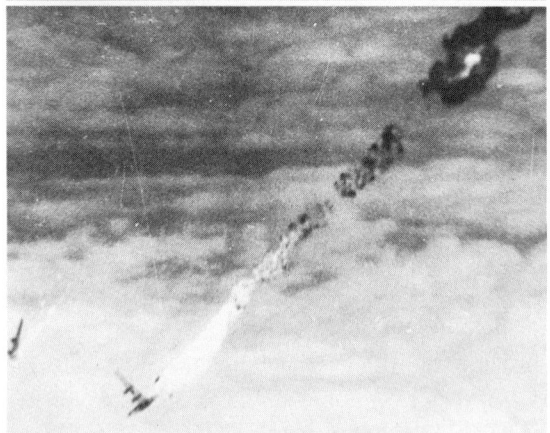

Fig. 6-16. A B-24 Liberator of the 15th AF is hit by flak while attacking the marshalling yards at Munich, Germany. (USAF)

Fig. 6-17. "... into the valley of the shadow..." B-17s of the 91st BG, 8th AF, leave the coast of England 27,500 ft below headed for Germany, 4 January 1944. (USAF)

The 14th FG stayed with the bombers until relieved by a P-47 group just south of Klagenfurt. Later, back at base with no losses of their own to count, the 14th's pilots had a good laugh to drain away the tension when one of them, Lt. Robert Siedman, observed: "I'll bet Hitler would be real mad if he knew that a little Jewish boy had shot down three of his pilots today."

During the early summer of 1944, nine Allied divisions and many 12th and 15th AF units were withdrawn to prepare for the invasion of Southern France which would follow on 15 August against thinly held German positions and almost no Luftwaffe opposition. German airpower had been swept from the skies over Italy, and the decimated Luftwaffe, fighting a desperate, defensive battle against the great Allied bomber offensive that was methodically destroying Germany's ability to make war (and as Eisenhower's armies swept across France following the cross channel invasion the previous June), had lost control of the air over Europe.

Assault on Fortress Europe

To the American ground forces gathered in England, the shooting war against Germany began with the cross-channel invasion of the Normandy Coast on 6 June 1944. To the U.S. air forces in the European Theater of Operations (ETO), it began long before that.

The buildup of the U.S. 8th AF in England was markedly slowed at the beginning when most of its handful of air groups were taken away by the 12th AF for the North African Campaign. During the summer of 1942, P-38s, B-17s and C-47s were flown across the North Atlantic with refueling stops in southern Greenland and Iceland. Another transatlantic air route was established across the South Atlantic to Africa's Gold Coast with a mid-ocean refuelling stop at tiny Ascencion Island. Many of these aircraft went to the 12th and 15th AFs. By early 1943, however, warplanes ferried across the North Atlantic remained with the 8th and 9th AFs in England, while the South Atlantic ferry route was used to deliver aircraft to the 10th and 14th AFs in the China-Burma-India (CBI) Theater of Operations.

President Roosevelt and Prime Minister Churchill agreed, at the Casablanca Conference in January 1943, that a combined bomber offensive against Germany was a necessary prelude to the cross-channel invasion. The primary aims were the destruction of the Luftwaffe (both in combat and by

Fig. 6-18. This 8th AF B-17, returning damaged from a mission over Germany, reached its base in England only to crash on landing with its brakes shot away; the crew escaped. (USAF)

Fig. 6-19. A 9th AF Douglas A-26 Invader hurtles earthward following a direct hit by German 88mm flak which blasted away one wing. (USAF)

bombing the enemy's aircraft factories) and Germany's sources of oil. The RAF would bomb by night and the USAAF would bomb by day—around the clock, when the two bomber commands possessed the machines to make that possible.

The biggest problem facing the 8th AF was uncertainty. Airpower had never been used in a massive, coordinated effort to destroy the industrial base—or key parts of that base—of a modern nation. Initially, Arnold and most of his air commanders believed that the U.S. heavy bombers were armed sufficiently (nine .50-cal guns) that, in large formations at least, they could protect themselves against concentrated attacks by enemy fighters. However, premature raids by two to three hundred B-24s and B-17s, in August 1943, against the Rumanian oil fields at Ploesti and the German ball bearing and aircraft factories at Regensburg and Schweinfurt, without fighter escort, proved the fallacy of that when the bomber forces sustained losses of near 20 percent.

At that time, fighter escort deep into Germany was not possible. The P-47s of the 8th and 9th AFs lacked the range to stay with the bombers beyond the German border.

By October 1943, the 8th AF possessed two groups of P-38s and while the Lightning had the potential of becoming a very effective long-range fighter, the P-38G and H versions that equipped the 55th and 20th FGs were not truly combat-ready aircraft—certainly not for the ETO. Their supercharger system demanded more attention from the pilot than he could reasonably be expected to give it during the heat of battle, resulting in a lot of blown engines; cockpit heating and windshield defrosting were completely inadequate for the altitudes and temperatures at which the air war over Europe was fought. These craft had no dive brakes, no maneuvering flaps or aileron boost. Not until August 1944 would the P-38J-25 be available in significant numbers, the first fully developed Lightning. It and subsequent versions would be the sweethearts of the AAF fighter pilots in the Southwest Pacific, but by that time most fighter groups in the ETO were being re-equipped with the P-51 Mustang, and all but one P-38 group disappeared over Europe.

Nevertheless, throughout the late winter and early spring of 1944, the period during which the

Fig. 6-20. A formation of B-17 Flying Fortresses and one of its 78th FG fighter escorts, a P-47 *Thunderbolt*, usually referred to as the "Jug" by its pilots. "Jug" pilots were largely responsible for the defeat of the Luftwaffe over Europe. (USAF)

Fig. 6-21. Scratch one Messerschmitt. This is how it looked to the gun camera of "Jug" pilot Capt. Floyd Brandt of the 19th Tactical Air Command as he participated in the protection of Patton's exposed southern flank. (USAF)

Luftwaffe was defeated, the P-38s did the job assigned to them. Air superiority in the ETO was largely won by the P-47 groups in aerial combat. There were 22 Thunderbolt groups in the 8th and 9th AFs, and seven P-38 groups by May 1944, and many of the P-47 groups were in action months before the P-38s arrived.

By late March 1944, Allied airpower was dominant over Europe (the Luftwaffe lost more than 800 fighters during February and March), and although the P-51 Mustang was probably the best air superiority fighter airplane of the war, it was not in action in large numbers until after the showdown battles with the Luftwaffe in February and March, 1944.

Throughout the winter and spring the P-38s took the bombers into Germany—Bremen, Frankfurt, Munster, Soligen, Berlin—after the P-47s had escorted the bombers across France. The intelligence summaries of these raids reveal that, more often than not, the German fighters did not attack the bombers while the P-38s were with them, attacking instead while the P-47s were in escort. There is no explanation for this, because the P-47 was certainly a more deadly adversary than the early P-38. Perhaps the Germans at that time didn't think so; one captured Luftwaffe pilot referred to the P-38s as "those forked-tail devils." In any case, the German fighter pilots were ordered to avoid combat with Allied fighters if possible and to concentrate on the bombers.

Overlord: The Cross-Channel Invasion

At 0145 hours on 6 June 1944, 9000 paratroopers of the U.S. 101st and 82nd Airborne Divisions

Fig. 6-22. A Focke-Wulf penetrates the fighter escort screen to attack a B-17 during a mission to Bremen, Germany, 29 November 1943. (USAF)

Fig. 6-23. *Little Warrior* takes a direct hit from flak over Quakenbruk, Germany 29 June 1944. Craft fell out of control a few seconds later. More Liberators were built during WWII than any other American airplane. (USAF)

Fig. 6-24. The concentrated fire of a P-47's eight .50-caliber guns spells doom for an enemy fighter. (USAF)

began jumping from more than 800 9th AF C-47 transports over France's Cherbourg Peninsula inland from the Normandy beaches. At the same time, some 200 RAF transports dropped 5000 British paratroopers, while 200 gliders followed with heavy weapons, guided to open fields by flare paths set up by the paratroopers. Concurrently, 8th and 9th AF bombers joined the U.S. Navy bombardment of the enemy's coastal defenses. At daybreak the first of the five divisions of U.S. and British troops began pouring ashore on the Normandy beaches. Behind them, the mightiest sea armada of all time—4000 ships, stretching back to the coasts of England—was bringing more men and guns. Overhead, 11,000 Allied airplanes, hastily painted the night before with special black and white "invasion stripes" (hopefully, to prevent friendly troops below from firing on them), provided an air umbrella against enemy air attack and fanned out across Normandy at treetop level to interdict enemy movement for miles behind the beachheads.

Fig. 6-25. America has possessed no greater air leader than Gen. Carl "Tooey" Spaatz, whose career began in 1916 and ended with his retirement in 1948. Today's independent United States Air Force was born under his command. (USAF)

Some 50,000 Allied soldiers were ashore in France before the day—"D-Day"—was over.

After D-Day, most U.S. tactical aircraft and many strategic bombers were diverted from the pure air offensive against Germany to give close air support to the advancing ground forces. The 8th and 9th AFs together possessed 2900 heavy bombers, 3000 fighters, and 400 medium bombers. If some U.S. infantrymen slogging through the mud sometimes wondered where the Air Force was, they should have been told that (1) it had been there *long* before, which was why they were advancing without fear of enemy air attack, and (2) it was presently miles ahead, systematically destroying enemy transportation, communications, troop concentrations, tank farms, and supply lines—in short, going for the enemy's vitals while the ground forces en-

Fig. 6-26. Flames envelop this 9th AF B-26 Marauder after a direct hit on its left engine by German antiaircraft gunners. (USAF)

Fig. 6-27. The Casablanca Conference, January 1943: President Roosevelt and Prime Minister Churchill (seated). Standing, left to right: Gen. Hap Arnold, Adm. Ernest J. King, Gen. George Marshall, Adm. Sir Dudley Pound, Gen. Sir Alan Brooke, and Air Chief Marshal Sir Charles Portal. (USAF)

gaged his extremities. Thus, the Allied armies swept across France in almost direct proportion to the effectiveness of their airpower. They were stopped or slowed, usually, for one of two reasons: (1) when their advance was so rapid that it outstripped their lines of supply, and (2) when weather screened off a sector from their eyes in the sky and allowed the Germans to concentrate sufficient strength for a counterattack.

Although the American tactical aircraft were being efficiently employed, one U.S. General, George ("Blood and Guts") Patton, Jr., a tough, bold old rooster, found a way to substitute it for a division or two of mobile ground troops. On 25 July, he sent his U.S. 3rd Army racing through a five-mile breach blasted in enemy defenses along the St. Lo-Periers Road by 8th and 9th AF planes, and dashed toward Germany depending entirely upon American fighters and medium bombers to protect his exposed southern flank. To most veteran ground commanders, such a move bordered upon madness, but the pilots—mostly from Gen. O.P. Weyland's 19th Tactical Air Command—bombed and strafed like demons (at altitudes that should have qualified them for Combat Infantryman Badges) and proved so effective that 20,000 German soldiers, attempting to turn Patton's flank, surrendered *directly* to the Air Force—without ever engaging the 3rd Army. Later, speaking of tactical air support for his armored divisions, Gen. Patton characterized the relationship as "love at first sight."

A week after D-Day, Hitler began sending his *Vergeltungswaffe* (vengeance weapons) against London. The first of these was the V-1, a small, unmanned and gyro-stabilized aircraft powered with a pulse-jet engine and carrying a ton of explosives. About 8000 of these flying bombs were sent against London and Antwerp, about half of which were shot down by Allied fighters and antiaircraft artillery before Allied bombers snuffed out V-1 production and destroyed their launching sites. By September 1944, the V-1 was no longer a threat. Hitler, however, had another and more terrible vengeance weapon, the V-2.

The V-2 was first fired against London and Paris on 8 September 1944. It was a short-range ballistic missile carrying slightly less than a ton of explosive, and it could have—like the German jet fighter—altered the course of the war in Europe had Hitler possessed enough of them soon enough, and employed them correctly. As it was, the 2500 V-1s, and perhaps 100 V-2s, that struck England killed almost 10,000 civilians and leveled more than 200,000 buildings.

Meanwhile, Allied strategic bombers sys-

Fig. 6-28. This B-17 somehow moved directly beneath another as the upper aircraft released its bombs over Berlin. Bomb at lower left struck the stabilizer of the Fortress with this result and the plane fell away out of control. (USAF)

Fig. 6-29. This shot-up 358th FG P-47, painted with "invasion stripes," nosed up during landing. Crew chief rushes to aid pilot as other control blaze from the ruptured drop tank and medics stand by. (USAF)

Fig. 6-30. Consolidated (today, General Dynamics) B-24 Liberator releases bombs over Bielefeld, Germany, 24 February 1945. (USAF)

tematically eliminated the enemy's oil industry. By the spring of 1945, gasoline production in Germany and German-occupied territory had dropped to seven percent of the normal capacity and the Nazi war machine became almost immobile. The mechanized German Army was afoot; panzer units had to hoard fuel for weeks in order to make a single move. New fighter airplanes for the Luftwaffe, produced with supreme effort but in surprisingly large numbers in underground plants, were grounded with empty tanks—and there destroyed by low-flying Allied fighters.

Allied ground forces, moving swiftly beneath skies totally controlled by their own aircraft, swept over the Reich to meet Russian forces at the Elbe River on 25 April 1945. Five days later, Adolph Hitler committed suicide amid the rubble of Berlin. A few days after that, on 7 May 1945, a prostrate Germany, her cities in ruin, surrendered to the

Fig. 6-31. A formation of B-24s bound for Ingolstadt, Germany, 1 March 1945. (USAF)

Fig. 6-32. Troop-laden gliders, two towed behind each C-47 of the 439th Troop Carrier Group, carry reinforcements to the U.S. 9th Army for the historic crossing of the Rhine River, 24 March 1945. (USAF)

Allies' Supreme Commander, ETO, Gen. Dwight D. Eisenhower.

When the end came in the ETO, America had about 13,000 combat airplanes in that theater. The Western Allies had dropped 2,770,540 tons of bombs on the continent, of which 1,500,000 tons fell from U.S. bombers, largely during the final ten months of that conflict.

Many air commanders today believe that the Allies forfeited a chance at a relatively cheap victory in the ETO during the spring and early summer of 1944, and that invasion of Europe was not necessary. Allied airpower, they point out, was free to destroy all German industry, including Germany's ability to feed her people, after defeat of the Luftwaffe.

They are probably right; Gen. Von Rundstedt, Commander-in-Chief of German Armed Forces in Western Europe, said after the war, "Three factors defeated us in the West where I was in command. First, the unheard-of superiority of your air force, which made all movement in daytime impossible. Second, the lack of motor fuel—oil and gas—so that the panzers and even the remaining Luftwaffe were unable to move. Third, the systematic destruction of all railway communications so that it was impossible to bring one single railroad train across the Rhine. This made impossible the reshuffling of troops and robbed us of all mobility."

A negotiated peace with Germany in the summer of 1944 would undoubtedly have left Germany intact, and the Soviets no farther west than the Polish border, a not unattractive thought today. It would have required the Germans to punish their own war criminals, another attractive thought. But could we, at that time, have accepted that? Probably not. The Nazi excesses were simply too horrible, and in a sense all Germany shared their guilt.

Chapter 7

Victory and the Unreal Wars

The Second World War demanded that Americans fight in some strange and unlikely places. U.S. troops understood England, France, Italy, and even the German enemy—they are people much like ourselves, with cities and trains and homes and dogs. Even North Africa had towns. But the Aleutians were a different story. So, too, were the airstrips of northern Assam, the awesome Himalayas, China. There, as in the rain forests of the Solomons and New Guinea, the young American in uniform was prone to demand: "What am I doing in this stinking hole? Tojo can *have* it as far as I'm concerned!" But our fighting men have always griped (often with good reason) and then have gone ahead and performed their assigned missions, often magnificently.

The Aleutian Campaign

Nowhere did the American serviceman have a better right to gripe than in the bleak Aleutians. Of all the unreal, "lesser" wars contained in WWII, it was, perhaps, the "unrealest." Americans had to be there to prevent the Japanese from grabbing bases from which the enemy could strike at the North American Continent. But the Japanese were not the primary enemy in that cold, mist-shrouded and desolate land—the weather was the most dangerous foe to the pilots of the 11th AF who had to fly in it. Navigating through the icy mists was likened to "flying inside a bottle of milk," and violent winds could sweep the lifeless tundra with unsuspected suddenness. Distances were great—the Aleutian chain arcs across the extreme North Pacific from the Alaskan Peninsula to within a few miles of Soviet territory. Japan is closer to them than Seattle.

At the time of the attack on Pearl Harbor, the U.S. had a dozen old Douglas B-18 Bolo bombers and 20 even older P-26 fighters in Alaska. Not until a month before the Battle of Midway (and the Japanese occupation of Kiska and Attu in the western tip of the Aleutians) did the first P-39s and P-40s arrive at Otter Point and Cold Bay on Umnak Island to protect the U.S. Navy base at Dutch Harbor. Later that summer, a squadron of P-38s would arrive and the 343rd FG would be organized, each of its three squadrons flying a different aircraft. The 407th BG, equipped with B-24s, made up the balance of the 11th AF's combat units.

When the Japanese attacked Dutch Harbor (Chapter 5) in a diversionary thrust immediately preceding the Battle of Midway, the P-40s shot down six of the enemy's carrier-based planes, but thereafter aerial combat over the Aleutians was extremely rare. The Japanese never had more than two or three squadrons of Rufes (a floatplane version of the Zero) and some Kawasaki Ki-97 flying boats in the Aleutians, and they were anything but aggressive. But airstrips were difficult to build on the spongy tundra, and since the enemy seemed content to merely remain where he was—a thousand miles from Umnak—new airstrips had to be built, because only the P-38 fighters could reach him, barely.

A new strip at Adak, 375 miles closer to Kiska, allowed the fighters to accompany the 407th's Liberators on raids against the enemy bases. Due to the lack of enemy air opposition, the P-38s carried bombs, and due to the Aleutian weather, tucked in close to the bombers and followed their lead. (The Army's WWII fighter pilots, being hastily trained, were not particularly noted for their navigational and instrument flying skills.)

Throughout the winter and early spring of 1943 (though it's hard to tell the difference in the Aleutians) the 11th AF flew bombing and strafing missions to Kiska and Attu. Then, on 11 May, a small U.S. Navy task force operating with the Es-

Fig. 7-1. Warhawks of the 11th AF prepare for a patrol on a typical mist-shrouded day in the Aleutians. (USAF)

Fig. 7-2. Lightning pilots of the 343rd FG at Adak are briefed during the battle for Attu. (USAF)

cort Carrier *Nassau* put the U.S. Army 7th Division ashore at Attu and the 2300 enemy troops on the island were soon overwhelmed. Navy and Marine aircraft from the *Nassau* added their muscle to that of the 11th AF in providing close air support for the men of the 7th Division fighting in the snow-covered mountains of Attu.

Two months later, American troops invaded Kiska, only to find that the Japanese had already slipped away in the fog.

The 343rd FG, completely equipped with P-38s, moved westward to the island of Shemya, where its hapless pilots and support people were doomed to stand guard for the rest of the war, fighting the weather and boredom in a "stinking hole" that each would gladly give to the Japanese if only he could be sent somewhere else to fight. The U.S. Navy also set up an air station on Attu, from which planes of Fleet Air Wing 4 henceforth patrolled the North Pacific.

Over the Hump with the AVG and the 14th AF

The American Volunteer Group (AVG), more popularly known as the "Flying Tigers," is not easy to accurately describe. It was organized under the direction of Claire Lee Chennault, a retired U.S. Air Corps captain who had been in China since 1937 attempting to train and lead Chinese pilots against the Japanese invader. The AVG's personnel was recruited and its aircraft purchased through the Central Aircraft Manufacturing Company in Burma—actually, an assembly plant for Curtiss-Wright fighters (fixed-gear versions of the P-36 up to that time) sold to China by wheeler-dealer William D. Pawley. (Pawley did not actually work for Curtiss-Wright. He may be more accurately described as an international promoter who collected

Fig. 7-3. The P-40 of AVG pilot Charles Older, a Marine reserve officer who achieved 10½ kills with the Flying Tigers. Older later ran his score to 22½ as a Lt. Col with the 14th AF, and today is a Los Angeles Superior Court Judge. (Tom Haywood)

Fig. 7-4. Robert "Duke" Hedman's airplane. Chinese insignia is painted over the original RAF roundel on wing. The AVG P-40s actually were Curtiss H81-A2 Tomahawks ordered by Britain. (Tom Haywood)

records reveal that the 100 P-40s needed to equip the AVG were billed "to China" three months earlier. (That transaction is a fascinating one because C-W billed Madame Chiang Kai-shek's "China Defense Supplies," a duly registered Maryland corporation, for only 87 airplanes, although 100 were actually delivered. Those machines were H81-A2 Tomahawks built for the RAF, essentially the same as the USAAF P-40B.)

The AVG's three squadrons flew from improvised airstrips near Rangoon, Burma and Kunming, China, their primary mission being to protect Generalissimo Chiang Kai-shek's supply routes through Burma. The Chinese Nationalist leader had been fighting the Japanese invader for years, and was the only force standing between advancing

Fig. 7-5. Col. David "Tex" Hill, a Flying Tiger double ace and ex-Navy dive bomber pilot, also transferred to the 23rd FG, 14th AF, and ended the war with 18¼ official victories in P-40s. (USAF)

highly-placed friends, thought big, and had the guts to back his schemes with action.)

The AVG flew under the flag of China, and their airplanes carried Chinese insignias. The pilots and most of the supporting personnel were American civilians. That made them, by definition, *mercenaries*. But that is an oversimplification. Almost all were reservists in the USAAF, the U.S. Navy or Marines. Most of them believed that war with Japan was imminent. So they were patriots and adventurers, and their reasons for agreeing to go to China to fight the Japanese months before Pearl Harbor were as varied as the men themselves. Their story belongs here because the U.S. 14th AF in China grew from the AVG, and because, after the Tigers were disbanded in mid-1942 and the U.S. 23rd FG was born in their place, most of them returned to duty with their respective branches of service.

The release of U.S. military reservists for combat under a foreign flag—an active combatant—was probably about as legal as pushing American warplanes across the border into Canada, but President Roosevelt signed an executive order, without publicity, on 15 April 1941 permitting Pawley's representatives to recruit the 350 pilots and support personnel—an act that had clearly been agreed upon earlier because Curtiss-Wright billing

Nipponese and weakly-held British positions in Burma and India.

Contrary to popular belief, the AVG did not enter combat until *after* the attack on Pearl Harbor, their first air battle coming on 10 December 1941. But during the winter of 1941-42, the "Flying Tigers" (apparently named by a *Life* magazine correspondent) provided the American public with the only heartening news to come out of the war during those months. During their first ten weeks of combat the AVG shot down 217 Japanese planes and claimed another 43 as probables while losing 16 P-40s and four pilots.

The Tigers, including Papa Tiger Chennault, earned all the acclaim they received. Never at any time did they have more than 55 flyable P-40s (the enemy had over 600 combat aircraft in the area); they had no spare parts, an uncertain supply of fuel, faulty ammunition, poor food and worse housing. Since they were civilians, they were somewhat on the undisciplined side—23 quit and went home as the result of an argument with Chennault over mission assignments, and Chennault "dishonorably discharged" a few others, including Greg "Pappy" Boyington. On the ground they were individualists, typical young Americans, with names such as Laughlin, Dupouy, McGarry, Schiller, Rossi, and the usual complement of Smiths. In the air they were as deadly a team of fighter pilots as has ever been assembled.

The AVG was disbanded on 4 July 1942, with the USAAF 23rd FG born in its place. At that time, 87 pilots and 164 support personnel remained of the original 350. During its 30 weeks of combat, the

Fig. 7-6. The Chinese built bamboo and paper P-40s that served as decoys for Japanese raiders of the Flying Tigers' field at Kunming. (NASM)

Fig. 7-7. Generalissimo Chiang Kai-Shek and Maj./Gen. Claire Chennault after the AVG was disbanded and the 23rd FG born in its place as part of the new China Air Task Force, later the 14th AF. (USAF)

AVG had 297 confirmed air victories and 240 unconfirmed, plus 40 enemy aircraft destroyed on the ground. Four AVG pilots died in combat; three were taken prisoner by the Japanese. Only five pilots and 17 mechanics chose to remain in China and accept induction into the 23rd FG, although 55 volunteered an additional two weeks duty to help the 23rd get into operation. These, and the rest of the Tigers returned to the Navy, Marines, and to service elsewhere with the USAAF. The AVG produced 26 aces.

The Assam Trucking Company

In March 1942, while Americans and Filipinos were holding out on Bataan and the AVG was fighting over China, AAF Col. Caleb Haynes was dispatched across the South Atlantic in command of 15 bombers on a secret mission to bomb Tokyo from a base in China. Haynes got as far as Karachi, India when his mission was cancelled. Doolittle's raiders had struck Tokyo the day before from the carrier *Hornet*.

Gen. Lewis Brereton, who had taken his sur-

Fig. 7-8. Warhawks of the 23rd FG near their base at Chengkung, China late in 1943. (USAF)

viving B-17s from the Philippines to Australia, and had then been ordered to India to form the U.S. 10th AF from whatever he could scrounge, grabbed Haynes' B-17s and sent Haynes to Dinjan, in the Assam Valley, close to India's northeastern border with Burma. Haynes' new mission was to form the Assam-Burma-China Ferrying Command, a shoestring operation that would supply fuel and ammunition to the AVG in China. Haynes was given two C-47s and promised more. His pilots were several Air Force fliers with "midnight" order changes and some Pan American Airways personnel. These were the first "Hump" pilots, the forerunners of a legendary breed who would fly the awesome Himalayas in ever-increasing numbers to supply not only the Flying Tigers but the 23rd FG, Chiang Kai-shek's forces, and the 14th AF. The whole idea

Fig. 7-9. A Douglas C-54 transport (DC-4 in civilian dress) of the Air Transport Command landing at Kunming, China, after a flight over the Himalayas from northern India. (Don Downie)

was to allow the Nationalist Chinese to continue fighting after the enemy had cut their overland supply route, the torturous 800-mile Burma Road which had linked Kunming with Lashio and the road to Mandalay in Central Burma.

Aided by China's airline, China National Aviation Corporation (CNAC, established and partly owned by Pan Am), Col. Haynes had a trickle of supplies reaching the AVG and Chiang Kai-shek by early May 1942, although the capacities of his C-47s were limited by the need to climb above the 16,000 ft peaks of the Himalayas in Northern Burma.

But the additional airplanes promised did arrive—first, some 10th AF B-24 bombers hastily converted to cargo carriers, then came the Curtiss C-46 which, though untested, had been ordered into production by Gen. Arnold because of its great cargo capacity and the pressing need. By December 1942, the ABC Ferry Command became part of the newly-created (everything seemed to be newly-created during the desperate days) Air Transport Command (ATC), often referred to by the air crews in India as the "Assam Trucking Company." ABC Ferry Command was delivering 2500 tons of supplies to China per month by early 1943.

They accomplished this by flying from the broiling sun of Assam, over fetid jungle and enemy occupied territory, above the world's highest mountain range, to the improvised airstrips in China. Navigational aids were few and unreliable;

Fig. 7-10. Workhorse of the "Hump," the Curtiss C-46 Commando. (USAF)

Fig. 7-11. The war was also won on the production lines back home. The Curtiss plant at Buffalo, NY is pictured in mid-war producing P-40s and C-46s. (NASM)

Fig. 7-12. On the China side of the Himalayas there was always plenty of hand labor to fill bomb craters and keep the airstrips open. (Don Downie)

Fig. 7-13. Warhawks and Marauders share this base in New Guinea of the 5th AF. (USAF)

as often as not the flight was in or above cloud, clouds that were welcome when enemy fighters were about. Their life-giving cargos were delivered regularly despite the eight months of monsoon rains and the four months of violent winds that followed each year, despite dysentery and malaria and fitful rest beneath mosquito netting in oppressive heat. Under the direction of Gens. Hoag, "Black Bob" Hardin, and later, William Tunner, the Hump airlift, in defiance of all reason and common sense, was delivering 71000 tons of supplies monthly by mid-1945.

As the Japanese were at last pushed back in Burma by Allied troops under Lord Mountbatten (including a U.S. Army regiment known as "Merrill's Marauders"), the Hump routes moved south to lower terrain and Douglas C-54s took over much of the load, some of them belonging to the Navy Air Transport Service.

A total of 1314 airmen died flying the Hump while delivering more than three quarters of a million tons of cargo.

The CBI Fighters

The 10th AF in India was made up of just seven combat groups: the 7th BG with B-24s, the 12th and 341st BGs with B-25s, and the 33rd, 51st, 80th and 311th FGs, the first three of which were equipped with P-40s, while the 311th flew P-51s.

The veteran 33rd FG, (having fought in North Africa and Italy before going to India) finally ended up in China, flying P-47s with Chennault's 14th AF

Fig. 7-14. White-tailed Warhawks of the 44th FS on Munda Airstrip, late summer 1943. (USAF)

while the 51st FG, after a stint in India, also joined the 14th AF in China where it eventually received P-51s, though it had a fourth squadron attached to it (the 459th FS) flying P-38s. The 80th FG, based in Upper Assam, also had one squadron of P-38s.

While based in India, these fighter groups saw little aerial combat, but were kept busy bombing and strafing in an attempt to stop the Japanese advances in Burma. Not until Col. Phil Cochran (who had come to India with the 33rd FG) led a daring glider assault deep into Burma behind enemy lines to cut the enemy's supply lines, did the Allies break Japan's grip on Burma.

In China, Chennault, who had assumed the rank of colonel in the Chinese Air Force as leader of the AVG, became a Brig. Gen. in the USAAF when the AVG was disbanded, and was given command of the China Air Task Force (CATF), originally consisting of the 23rd FG and a group of B-25s commanded by Col. Caleb Haynes. Early in 1943, the CATF became the U.S. 14th AF, which steadily

Fig. 7-15. Bell P-39s and P-400s (the latter a P-39 fitted with a 20mm cannon, the former with a 37mm gun) served in all theaters but were decidedly inferior to all enemy opposition in the air. Bell's follow-on design, the P-63 shown here, used a laminar-flow wing. Most P-63s built went to Russia under Lend-Lease. (USAF)

Fig. 7-16. Gen. Arnold meets with military leaders in the CBI; from left: Arnold, Gen. Chennault, Gen. Joseph "Vinegar Joe" Stilwell, Gen. Sir John Dill, Gen. Clayton Bissell. Chennault was normally at odds with all but Arnold. (USAF)

grew in strength during the following two years as it received air units from the 10th AF, and as the ATC was increasingly able to supply it.

The 14th AF fought a makeshift war at the end of an incredibly long supply line. Until the final year of the war, the P-40 was its main fighter airplane, and the 23rd FG alone accounted for 941 enemy aircraft destroyed, although most of its missions were against ground targets.

Perhaps the best assessment of the 14th AF was offered at war's end by Gen. Takahashi, Chief of Staff of the Japanese Armies in North China: "But for the 14th Air Force, we could have gone anywhere we wished in China."

The Final Thrust

MacArthur's return to the Philippines was something the people back home could at last identify with impending victory. For almost three years Americans had died taking a series of Pacific islands that most had never heard of before, and the papers reported great sea battles in which only the enemy ever seemed to lose any ships. (Censorship was something else the American people endured during WWII, but it was counterproductive in the sense that the people quickly lost confidence in official military bulletins and most felt that they never really knew how the war was going.) But here, finally, was the kind of evidence of success that everyone understood.

Militarily, the retaking of the Philippines held far more than psychological significance. It provided a major base of operations both for ships and land-based aircraft. Adm. Nimitz' Central Pacific forces, which included the 7th AF and the recently-created 20th AF, had moved 4000 miles across the Pacific, taking bases from Tarawa through the Gilberts and Marshalls to the Marianas, while MacArthur (whose command contained a high percentage of Australians and New Zealanders) had fought 1300 tough miles from Port Moresby to Hollandia on New Guinea's north coast and beyond to the island bases of Wakde and Biak. Adm. Halsey

Fig. 7-17. Capt. Albert "Ajax" Baumler became the first ace of Chennault's new China Air Task Force. (USAF)

Fig. 7-18. By early March 1945, Manila Bay was open to Allied shipping and Gen. Douglas MacArthur and Filipino statesman/soldier Carlos Romulo (standing) made a symbolic return aboard a U.S. Navy PT boat. (USAF)

had moved northward through the Solomons to neutralize the great enemy base at Rabaul. With Rabaul encircled and cut off from supply, it was left to "whither on the vine" after its air units were destroyed, invasion by Allied troops being unnecessary.

As the two forces under MacArthur and Nimitz came together southeast of Mindanao, with MacArthur on the island of Morotai and four strong U.S. Navy task groups operating from the Palaus, Yap, and Ulithi, their power was merged for the invasion of the Philippines at Leyte on 20 October 1944.

The 13th and 5th AFs were combined into the reborn Far East Air Forces (FEAF), and these fliers, together with land-based Marine air and carrier-based Navy air units, soon took possession of the air over the Philippines and led the allied

Fig. 7-19. Grumman F6F Hellcat escorts TBFs and SBDs from the new *Yorktown* in the Philippine Campaign, October 1944. (USN)

129

Fig. 7-20. Warhawks of the 80th FG at Nagahuli Airstrip in Upper Assam, India, 1944. (USAF)

Fig. 7-21. PBY-5A Catalina patrol plane drops depth charge over enemy submarine in Philippine waters. (USN)

Fig. 7-22. The 51st FG in India had a different idea for painting their P-40 air scoops. (USAF)

invasion of Luzon at Lingayen Gulf on 9 January 1945. Manila was liberated a month later.

Meanwhile, the Imperial Japanese Navy was decisively defeated attempting to turn back the Leyte landings. The Battle of Leyte Gulf, actually a series of actions from 10 through 29 October 1944, cost the enemy 1046 aircraft destroyed by carrier-based U.S. Navy planes alone, along with 26 major combatant ships, including three battleships, three heavy cruisers, and four aircraft carriers, the *Zuikaku, Chiyoda, Zuiho* and *Chitose*. The U.S. Navy lost the escort carriers *Gambier Bay* and *St. Lo*, the latter to Kamikaze attack. Kamikazes also damaged the carriers *Intrepid, Franklin,* and *Belleau Wood*.

The Kamikaze attacks would continue as the U.S. Navy operated close to the Japanese home islands, and although the censored press reports at the time minimized their effect, the truth is that this desperation tactic accounted for at least half of all U.S. Navy ships damaged and a fifth of those sunk throughout the war, most of the attacks coming during the final 10 months of the Pacific War. The Kamikazes also struck at important shore installations. Had the war not ended as it did, another 7-9,000 Kamikazes were waiting for the expected invasion of Japan.

While Allied troops were mopping up in the Philippines, U.S. Navy Task Group 52, with 12 carriers, under Rear Adm. C.T. Durgin, and TG 58, containing 17 carriers and commanded by Vice Adm. Marc Mitschner, accompanies by two Marine divisions to landings on Iwo Jima 19 February 1945, where the Marines faced 23,000 Japanese in exceptionally strong defensive positions. Iwo Jima was not secured until 16 March and at the cost of 4590 Marine dead, plus the loss of the escort carrier *Bismark Sea*, sunk by Kamikazes, along with serious damage to the *Saratoga*.

Fig. 7-23. Fire rages on the forward deck of the *Saratoga* after hit by Kamikaze off Iwo Jima 21 February 1945. (USN)

Fig. 7-24. Marine F4U-1 Corsair takes off from the carrier *Essex* for a strike against Formosa. (USN)

Fig. 7-25. The TBM torpedo bomber was the Grumman design (TBF) built by the Eastern Aircraft Division of General Motors. TBM above is aboard the carrier *Bunker Hill* during the Battle of the Philippine Sea. (USN)

Sea, sunk by Kamikazes, along with serious damage to the *Saratoga*.

The price paid for Iwo Jima was said to be justified by its location, since it gave the U.S. airfields halfway between Japan and the 20th AF's B-29 bases in the Marianas, and was later claimed to have saved no less than 2400 B-29s and their crews which would not have made it to the Marianas after missions to Japan. But that would seem to be an overstatement since fewer than 1200 B-29s went to the Pacific before the war ended.

The B-29 air offensive against Japan began in mid-1944 when the 58th Bomb Wing of the 20th Bomber Command (the 20th and 21st Bomber Commands were part of the new 20th AF which operated directly under the Joint Chiefs as a Global Air Force) began operations from Chengtu in west central China. But that was a premature effort which served mostly to prove that meaningful num-

Fig. 7-26. The U.S. Navy's leading ace in WWII was Cmdr. David Campbell, shown here in his F6F Hellcat aboard the *Essex*. (USN)

Fig. 7-27. Landing signal officer brings a Hellcat aboard the *Essex*. (USN)

bers of Superfortresses could not be supported by the ATC airlift over the Hump. By October, however, bases taken from the enemy in the Marianas were ready to handle the B-29s and the Superforts were concentrated there on five big airfields, two each on Guam and Tinian and one on Saipan.

The air assault against Japan was resumed in November 1944, but too many B-29s were lost to enemy defensive fighters and to fuel starvation on return to base, while results of the raids were disappointing. High level precision bombing was

Fig. 7-28. The Northrop P-61 Black Widow night fighter appeared late in the war but saw extensive action with Air Force units over the Philippines and subsequent battles; 9th AF also used the type late in the European war. (USAF)

Fig. 7-29. The Chance Vought F4U-4 Corsair, powered with the P&W R-2800-18W Double Wasp of 2325-hp, had a maximum speed of 424 mph at 23,000 ft. The reason the Marines got such a fine fighter first was because the Navy didn't clear the Corsair for carrier operations until April 1944. The Marines, however, regularly flew Corsairs from land bases throughout the war. (USN)

Fig. 7-30. This kamikaze, although burning from hits by Navy gunners, held determinedly to its final attack, smashing onto the deck of the *Essex* during the Philippine campaign. (USN)

not markedly affecting the production of the thousands of small shops that made parts and sub-assemblies for the Japanese war machine.

In January 1945, Gen. Curtis E. LeMay was sent to take command of the B-29 wings in the Marianas and was informed by Arnold that the Joint Chiefs expected the same kind of job that LeMay had done over Europe as a bomber commander where he had earned the sobriquet "Iron Pants."

By early March, LeMay had all his problems sorted out. He ordered his planes loaded with incendiary bombs, stripped of guns and ammunition, and told his crews that they would raid Tokyo at night from an altitude of 7000 ft.

Most of the crews were incredulous. The pressurized B-29 with remote controlled guns was a high-altitude strategic bomber; ol' Iron Pants was

Fig. 7-31. The flight deck of the *Randolph* after a night kamikaze attack 12 March 1945. (USN)

Fig. 7-32. Sixty-one squadrons of B-29s Superfortresses were activated in the 20th AF by war's end. Superfort engines were Wright R-3350s of 2430 war emergency hp; cabin pressurization and remote control of the ten .50-caliber and one 20mm guns were innovations. (USAF)

asking them to take it over the enemy's capital unarmed at low altitude and at night! Still, if one thought about it, it just might work. The enemy certainly would not expect them at low altitude and their heavy anti-aircraft guns would be set up to fire high above them. Intelligence reports indicated that the enemy had relatively few night fighters, and if the B-29s carried no guns, that would eliminate the danger of firing upon one another in the darkness, additionally, the weight saved would lower fuel consumption for the trip home. The bold plan just might work.

It did. Almost 16 square miles of Tokyo were destroyed by fire that night by 323 Superforts. During the next ten days Nagoya, Osaka, and Kobe were struck with similar raids to add another 15 square miles of fire-blackened ruins to those cities. The cost was 21 B-29s lost in 1489 sorties (a sortie being one mission one airplane).

Late in March 1945, LeMay was ordered to temporarily halt the aerial destruction of Japan's major cities and to aid in the invasion of Ryukyu Islands and Okinawa, in which the B-29s were used as tactical aircraft, attacking enemy airfields and sewing mines in the Shimonoseki Straits.

Fig. 7-33. Gen. Curtis E. LeMay. (USAF)

Fig. 7-34. Corsairs of the 2nd Marine Air Wing over Okinawa. (USN)

Fig. 7-35 Near the end, defeated Japan could no longer challenge the B-29s, seen here passing Mt. Fujiyama, and LeMay announced in advance where they would strike in order to spare civilian lives. (USAF)

The Ryukyus were but 400 miles from Japan and the enemy resisted with everything he had. The American force of four Army and two Marine divisions, accompanied by Adm. Durgin's TG 52 and Adm. Mitschner's TG 58, along with AAF air units, were met by mass Kamikaze attacks—up to 400 at a time—despite American air superiority. During the 83 days of the Okinawan Campaign, Kamikazes sank 35 U.S. ships and damaged 288.

Okinawa was finally secured on 21 June 1945 at the price of 12,500 American lives and 763 aircraft. The enemy, fighting from a maze of tunnels and caves that were largely immune to air attack, lost 110,000 soldiers who refused to surrender.

The Okinawan Campaign was the last and most violent for the U.S. Navy. Mitschner's and Durgin's task groups, fighting with a smaller British task

Fig. 7-36. Symbolic of peace in the Pacific and the end of countless tragic days, these Curtiss SB2C Helldivers return to their carrier, cruising serenely in the South China Sea.

force containing four carriers, were constantly on station in the battle area, and most of their ships logged more than 60 days of consecutive combat duty. Nine U.S. aircraft carriers were damaged, some seriously, although none were sunk.

After Okinawa was taken, the Superforts of the 20th AF resumed their assault on Japan, and by the end of July had devastated more than 100 square miles of the enemy's six largest cities. With both USAAF and Navy/Marine fighters ranging at will over the enemy's homeland, B-29 losses dropped to near zero, and Gen. LeMay began announcing in advance where he would strike next in order to cut civilian casualties.

The enemy was defeated. His navy was gone, along with most of his merchant shipping. Allied airpower was free to destroy whatever it chose to attack in his island nation. True, he had thousands of Kamikazes (planes of all types, including trainers) held in reserve, and a well-equipped army prepared to resist invasion. But an army that cannot maneuver, that cannot be supplied or fed, cannot long exist. Gen. LeMay, who was unaware that the U.S. possessed an atomic device, recommended against the presumed invasion of Japan, telling his superiors that the enemy's unconditional surrender was only a matter of time—he judged it at "several weeks."

Iron Pants may have been right, but President Truman (who had assumed office on 12 April upon President Roosevelt's sudden death) was not willing to wait several weeks, because, he said, Americans were dying every day, and therefore, if he could shorten the war by *one hour*, it was his duty to do so.

At 0245 hours on 6 August 1945, the *Enola Gay*, a B-29 from the 509th Composite Group, 20th AF, took off from Tinian in the Marianas and headed for Hiroshima with an atomic bomb in its bays. The *Enola Gay* (named for the mother of the aircraft commander, Col. Paul Tibbets) loosed her terrible weapon above the Japanese city at 0816 hours, and four square miles of Hiroshima were obliterated. The number of human casualties was unknown at the time, but are given today as 78,150 dead, 13,083 missing, and 37,425 injured.

Three days later, the B-29 *Bock's Car* dropped the second A-bomb on Nagasaki, killing 73, 884 people, and Japan sued for peace.

On 2 September 1945, in Tokyo Bay, formal surrender documents were signed aboard the battleship *Missouri*. The U.S. Navy has yet to explain why the ceremony did not take place on an aircraft carrier, the *true* symbol of victory in the Pacific.

Chapter 8

Uneasy Peace, and Another War

World War II changed the world and the peace that followed was an uneasy one. For a brief period, America felt secure. The U.S. was the sole possessor of the atomic bomb and had the means to deliver it anywhere in the world. Surely, the threat of such massive retaliation would deter the most ambitious aggressor.

The potential aggressor was, of course, the Soviet Union. Few Americans ever doubted that. At the end of WWII, while the United States and its Allies demobilized (the U.S. Army went from 8,000,000 in 1945 to 684,000 by 1950), the Russians kept much of their military intact, and repeatedly demonstrated their allegiance to the communist canon which holds that "political power comes from the barrel of a gun."

Their national character was bared to the world by their acts immediately following Germany's surrender. In Poland, and in that part of Germany occupied by the Soviets, the only women who were not raped were those few who successfully hid for months. Everything of value was stolen. Millions of German "prisoners" disappeared into Soviet Siberia. Even the railway tracks were ripped up and shipped back to the Soviet Union. The terror and pillage that came in the wake of the Soviet army was little different than that practiced by the Mongol hordes of Genghis Khan 700 years earlier.

So the Free World knew its Godless enemy and watched in apprehension as the Soviet Union hammered its Iron Curtain around Eastern Europe. Poor President Roosevelt—sick and debilitated, just a month before his death, he had believed that he could deal with the Soviet dictator Stalin at the Yalta Conference. But the agreements made in good faith by FDR were to be regarded by the Soviets merely as positions of advantage from which to expand their communist dominion.

Berlin Big Lift

Among those agreements—which greatly affect us all to this day—was the supposedly *temporary* occupation of Germany by the Allies. The

Fig. 8-1. The USAF's first operational jet fighter was the 550-mph Lockheed F-80 Shooting Star which appeared in 1945. The F-80C, which entered service in 1948, had a thinner wing, allowing a higher critical Mach number. Two-seat versions became the T-33 jet trainer. (USAF)

Soviets were allowed to occupy East Germany and a portion of East Berlin (Berlin itself is 110 miles inside the Soviet sector). Britain, France and the United States occupied the remainder of Berlin and West Germany, and were guaranteed access to Berlin by rail, the *autobahn* (German express freeway), and three 20-mile wide air corridors.

By 1948, however, the Soviets possessed the secret of nuclear fission (by espionage), and were ready to test the will of the United States in Germany. It should have come as no surprise. From the start, the Soviets had refused to cooperate in Allied efforts to establish a new government that the Germans could run themselves and to begin rebuilding the German economy.

On 24 June 1948, the Russians stopped all surface transportation into the western sectors of Berlin, suspended parcel post service, and cut off electric power. They stopped barge traffic on the rivers, destroyed bridges, and tore up the tracks of the remaining railroad into the city from the west. Berlin was isolated.

Almost. The Soviets faced one problem with their blockade: Iron Pants LeMay happened to be the commander of the U.S. Air Force in Europe (USAFE). The Joint Chiefs under Truman also made some pretty good choices.

Within 48 hours, Gen. LeMay had all his C-47 transport planes (the Air Force version of the DC-3 airliner) flying milk, flour, medicines and coal into

Fig. 8-2. The Bell X-1A was a rocket-powered research aircraft; X-1 was the first airplane to exceed the speed of sound, 14 October 1947. (USAF)

the beleaguered city from Frankfurt, carefully staying within the prescribed air corridors. There was nothing the Russians could do about an airlift short of shooting down the unarmed transports, and that, of course, would have been a clear act of war.

The C-47s carried 80 tons of cargo to Berlin that first day. Meanwhile, orders went out around the world calling in Air Force C-54 four-engine transports for duty with Operation *Vittles*. Within a month a steady stream of U.S. and British transports were delivering 1500 tons of life-giving supplies to West Berlin daily. Then, after the new Military Air Transport Service (MATS)—successor to the wartime Air Transport Command and Naval Air Transport Service—took over the job with old "Hump" commander Gen. William Tunner running the show, the tonnage exceeded 5000 per day—including candy for Berlin's children.

During the 13 months the Berlin Airlift was in operation, MATS delivered 2,231,600 tons of essential cargos into that city, averaging 700 flights daily, to thwart the Soviet attempt to force the Western Allies out of Berlin. In so doing, MATS also administered a sound—and responsible—diplomatic/strategic defeat to the communist aggressor. The Soviets could find no face-saving way out. They simply lifted the blockade, and contented themselves with an ultimatum to Czechoslovakia which forced the Czechs into the Russian orbit, and announcement of the detonation of the first Soviet A-bomb.

Birth of the B-52

The fallout from the Berlin blockade was far more significant than the Russians could have foreseen when they recklessly imposed it. Among other things, it was indirectly responsible for America's B-52 global bomber program, plus a lot of rethinking of the U.S. defensive posture *vis a vis* Russia's newly-obvious expansionist policies.

Actually, Air Force brass had sent a new strategic bomber specification to the aircraft industry seeking proposals in mid-1946; they were looking down the 'pike 10 years, by which time it was reasonable to assume that the U.S. would need a fast, high-flying nuclear carrier of extra-long range. There was, however, significant opposition to the concept within the Air Force itself.

The Strategic Air Command (SAC) had been organized on 21 March 1946 with Gen. George Kenney as its first commander. At that time, Kenney was given 36,000 men, 18 bases and 600 aircraft—B-17s, B-29s and B-25s. The Air Force was ready to substantially restructure in anticipation of legislation that would separate it from the Army and make it an independent and co-equal branch of the U.S. military, the dream of Billy Mitchell and all other Army airmen since the First

Fig. 8-3. Lawrence Bell (L), who began his career as designer of the 1919 Martin GMB bomber and saw a Bell aircraft break the sound barrier only 28 years later, congratulates X-1A pilot Capt. (later General) Charles Yeager. (Bell Aerosystems)

Fig. 8-4. MATS C-54s (R5D in Navy dress) were the backbone of the Berlin Airlift which averaged 700 flights daily to keep the city alive—and from total Soviet control—for 13 months. (USAF)

World War. That act was passed by the Congress and signed by President Truman in mid-1947, becoming law on 18 September of that year. (The National Security Act of 1947 also created the CIA, another security measure long overdue.)

The early B-52 proposals from Boeing were for large propjets that lacked the performance envisioned by the Air Force. In any case, the B-52 concept had some strong opposition in the persons of Gen. George Kenney and Gen. Lauris Norstad, Deputy Chief of Staff for Operations. Kenney felt that the B-50 (essentially, the B-29 with bigger engines) would be a lot cheaper and that, therefore, he could have more of them. Also, the B-52, if it had the performance being asked for, would require technological advances that could take years to attain. There was no engine then available that would furnish the power such a machine would require.

Meanwhile, Convair wanted to go ahead with the mammoth B-36, a 1941 program that had been sidetracked by the war. The technology was available to build the B-36 at once, but Kenney and Norstad opposed the B-36 for the same reasons they were against the B-52. Assured of plenty of overseas bases, there was no reason the B-50 couldn't do the job.

In favor of the B-36 and the follow-on B-52 was Gen. "Tooey" Spaatz, Air Force Chief of Staff, but

Fig. 8-5. Convair B-36 (in background) had a span of 230 ft, six 3500-hp engines driving pusher props, and four turbojets of 5200 lbs thrust each. SAC had 33 squadrons of B-36s to enforce the peace until the B-52 began entering service in 1955. (USAF)

Fig. 8-6. This unlikely critter was the McDonnell XF-85 parasite fighter which was to be carried by the B-36 for protection against enemy fighters—one of those good ideas that didn't work out. (McDonnell-Douglas)

Fig. 8-7. Boeing XB-52 had pilot and copilot sitting in tandem in blister atop the nose. The first B-52 flight came on 15 April 1952. (The Boeing Company)

Spaatz knew he'd have a hard time getting money from Congress for them without the support of Kenney and Norstad. Then the Soviets blockaded Berlin and literally saved both new bomber programs.

One day after the blockade went into effect, Gen. Hoyt Vandenberg, just recently appointed Air Force Chief of Staff upon Spaatz' retirement, met with Air Force Secretary Stuart Symington and, with Kenney and Norstad in agreement, determined that a fleet of B-36s would be built to ensure the capability of a U.S. nuclear deterrent strike force until the B-52 could be brought along in the mid-'50s.

The Pratt & Whitney jet engine (the J-57) that made the B-52 possible was under development by late 1948, and the first B-52 prototype made its maiden flight on 15 April 1952. Deliveries of the B-52 Stratofortress to SAC began three years later.

The Air Force should be very proud of the B-52 program. It reflected high competence upon the several commands that planned and administered it. Boeing engineers, led by Edward Wells and Art Carlsen, produced an airplane that logically should not have appeared for another ten years. The Air Force knew exactly what it needed, and the senior officers stuck to their guns through many frustrations and the long gestation period required to get it.

A total of 744 B-52s were built during the plane's nine-year production run, the last being delivered to SAC in 1962. Throughout its service life, the B-52 Stratofortress has represented one critical leg of America's nuclear deterrent triad, along with the ICBMs and nuclear-armed submarines. In 1980, after 25 years as a first-line defender of the U.S. and the Free World, 300 B-52s continued in that role. In the absence of a new nuclear carrier to replace

Fig. 8-8. Drag chute deployed upon landing greatly aids in braking the 200,000-lb (488,000-lb fully loaded) Stratofortress to a safe stop. (The Boeing Company)

Fig. 8-9. Wings flex upward as B-52D takes off and outrigger wheels retract. Approximately 75 B-52Ds remain in service during the early '80s, along with the G and H models. (The Boeing Company)

Fig. 8-10. The B-52G and H versions are the prime nuclear carriers today, the Gs and Hs having a cut-down vertical tail. The G models are easy to differentiate from the Hs because the H model is equipped with turbofan engines and fatter engine pods than the G (above). (The Boeing Company)

them, they are expected by the Air Force to serve until the year 2000. The B-52s originally cost slightly less than $6 million each, and perhaps an equal amount has been spent on each of those still flying for updated electronics and weapons systems. Considering that this fleet of global bombers will contribute at least 40 years of service to the security of this nation, it is safe to say that seldom has the overburdened American taxpayer received so much for his hard-earned money.

The Korean War

If the Berlin blockade pushed the B-52 program off dead center, other threats to the Free World during the early '50s provided the impetus to keep it moving. By early 1949 it was obvious that a Chinese communist army, supported by the Soviets, would defeat Chiang Kai-shek's Nationalist forces and take possession of that vast land, while the Soviets had installed a former Russian army officer as premier in North Korea and supplied the North Koreans with arms and the belief that they should rule all of Korea.

At 0400 hours on 25 June 1950, 60,000 North Korean troops, spearheaded by 100 Russian-built tanks, swept across the 38th parallel (the border between North and South Korea) and drove rapidly southward, overrunning the South Korean capitol of Seoul four days later.

The South Koreans were, of course, unprepared for the invasion. U.S. occupation troops, who had supervised the withdrawal of the Japanese at the close of WWII, had stayed in South Korea only long enough to allow those gentle people to establish a government of their own under Korean statesman Syngman Rhee.

On the afternoon of the surprise invasion (it was 24 June in the U.S.), the United Nations Security Council met in emergency session to condemn the act, and President Truman ordered the 5th AF, which had planes in Japan and Okinawa, to evacuate U.S. citizens. Two days later, as the in-

Fig. 8-11. F-51 Mustangs were taken from mothballs and Air Guard units for service in Korea. Shown is an F-51 supplied to the Republic of Korea Air Force (ROKAF). (USAF)

Fig. 8-12. F-82 Twin Mustangs were basically stretched F-51H fuselages joined at a common wing center section and fitted with V-1710 Allison engines. F-82s pictured were radar-carrying night fighters. (USAF)

Fig. 8-13. Another retread: The T-6 Texans, armed with rockets, served as forward air control craft, spotting targets for the heavy ordnance carriers. The T-6 was an advanced trainer in WWII. (USAF)

Fig. 8-14. Lockheed F-94 Starfire saw service in Korea, primarily as a night fighter. The F-94 was a member of the F-80/T-33 family with thinner wing, afterburner, and nose-mounted search radar. (USAF)

vaders approached Seoul, Truman directed that U.S. Air Force and Navy planes give assistance to the South Koreans, and ordered Gen. MacArthur to take command of the troops being sent from 15 Free World nations (mostly the U.S.) to fight under the flag of the United Nations. President Truman termed the UN response a "police action."

Actually, that was an accurate description of the UN's intent, because the U.S. (and other countries which sent troops), had no objective except to

Fig. 8-15. The 670-mph North American F-86A Sabre appeared in 1949, and in December 1950 the USAF 4th Fighter Interceptor Wing went to Korea equipped with Sabres. Normal armament was six .50-caliber machine guns; later (H) versions sometimes replaced the machine guns with four 20mm cannons. (USAF)

Fig. 8-16. The Douglas A-26 Invader of WWII was redesignated B-26 in 1948 after the Martin B-26 Marauder was no longer in inventory. The Invader served in Europe and the Pacific in WWII, in Korea, and (shown here) in Vietnam. (USAF)

Fig. 8-17. The Black Sheep were back in Korea, operating off the escort carrier *Sicily*, and still flying Corsairs. Shown is a cannon-armed F40-4. (USN)

push the communists back across the 38th parallel and restore peace. Most also undoubtedly saw it as a test of the effectiveness of this new (1945) world organization in dealing with "brushfire" wars that could escalate into big wars.

U.S. airpower played a major role in the Korean War. American warplanes dominated the air and provided close air support that was the decisive factor in UN successes on the ground. There were four major offensives and counteroffensives in the Korean War: (1) The initial North Korean thrust which carried all the way to the southern end of the country by 15 September 1950, with the South Korean and UN troops backed into a pocket around Pusan; (2) A UN counteroffensive with an amphibious landing by the U.S. Marines at Inchon, just south of Seoul, which trapped half of the invader's army between the UN forces in the south and the Marines closing from Inchon. This done, the UN troops drove north across the 38th parallel, entered the North Korean capital of Pyongyang, and totally defeated the North Koreans as the drive reached the Yalu River, which separated North Korea from Manchuria. Then, the next day, on 3 November 1950, (3) Communist China entered the war by sending 300,000 troops across the Yalu and pushed the UN forces back below Seoul again by late January 1951. (4) The UN forces counterattacked

Fig. 8-18. This frosted Mustang crash-landed after being hit by enemy ground fire. Foamite controlled fire and the pilot was not injured. (USAF)

Fig. 8-19. Soviet MiG-15 was the standard fighter for the Soviet-bloc air forces during the '50s. In Korea, despite the fact that American pilots were not allowed to pursue the MiGs beyond the Yalu River, the F-86 pilots shot down 10 MiGs for every F-86 lost in combat. (Hudeck collection)

and once again advanced into North Korea, halting along a line that stabilized by November, averaging about 20 miles north of the 38th parallel. That would be the positions of the opposing forces when a truce was at last agreed upon on 27 July 1953.

Negotiations to end the fighting had been going on for two years when the agreement was finally reached. The unrepentant aggressors had stalled and seized upon any excuse to delay a settlement, apparently hoping to gain something from the war. But Dwight Eisenhower became President of the United States in January 1953; immediately after taking office, Ike sent a message to Moscow, Peiping, and Pyongyang saying that if satisfactory progress toward an armistice was not forthcoming, "... we intend to move decisively without inhibition in our use of weapons, and will no longer be responsible for confining hostilities to the Korean peninsula."

That was the kind of "negotiation" the communists understood, and it achieved the desired results.

Fig. 8-20. S./Sgt. Jerry Webb, B-29 tailgunner, points to a cannon hole close to his head after attack by MiGs. Sgt. Webb shot down one MiG, another gunner on this Superfort downed a second. The B-29's rudder controls were shot out, but it landed safely at its base on Okinawa. (USAF)

Fig. 8-21. ROKAF Mustangs operated under command of the 5th AF. Mustang #18 at left is flown by Major Dean Hess, ROKAF pilot training program commander. Hess was played by Rock Hudson in the biographical film *Battle Hymn*. (USAF)

At the outbreak of hostilities in Korea, the FEAF, made up of the 5th and 13th AFs, greatly reduced from WWII levels, had 535 operational aircraft, including 365 F-80 Shooting Star jet fighters and 32 F-82 Twin Mustangs. The Lockheed F-80 was America's first operational jet fighter, appearing in 1945, and was obsolescent by 1950 due to the pace of jet engine development and new lessons learned in the field of aerodynamics as jet and rocket-powered U.S. research aircraft attained ever-higher speeds. (USAF Capt. Charles Yeager had exceeded the speed of sound on 14 October 1947.) The North American F-82 was, literally, a "Twin Mustang," two stretched P-51H fuselages (F-51s after the USAF changed the Army's "P" for "pursuit" to "F" for "fighter" in 1948) joined together on a common wing centersection to make a single twin-engine aircraft. It was, however, fitted with Allison rather than Rolls-Royce engines.

A month after the war started, 764 National Guard F-51s were called to active duty, and 145 of them rushed to Korea aboard the carrier *Boxer*. World War II's illustrious 4th FG, now designated the 4th Fighter Interceptor Wing and equipped with F-86A Saberjets followed in December 1950 to take on the Chinese MiG-15s.

Actually, the United States was in the process of rebuilding the Air Force into a new all-jet air force to meet America's defense needs of the '50s.

Fig. 8-22. A North Korean YAK fighter shot down by an F-80 14 miles north of Suwon, 15 August 1950. (USAF)

At the end of WWII, the USAAF contained a whopping 218 air groups with nearly two and one quarter million men. Demobilization was so rapid and so thorough that the Army Air Forces were down to 52 groups on paper, with only two groups fully operational, by mid-1947. Many thousands of WWII combat aircraft—not a few of them brand new—were sold for scrap (movie flier Paul Mantz bought 500 war surplus airplanes for $50,000, sold the fuel in their tanks for $55,000, and still possessed the world's seventh largest "air force"), while a small percentage of the latest models were "mothballed" at Davis-Monthan Air Base near Tucson, Arizona, where the dry desert air contributed to their preservation.

However, the U.S. had trained more than a quarter of a million pilots during WWII and many remained in the National Guard or Air Force Reserve. These were the pilots called back to active duty to augment the relatively small FEAF in Korea; since most of the regulars were also WWII vets, the Air Force, Navy and Marine fliers over Korea were often called "retread tigers."

Retreads they may have been, but there is no substitute for experience, and the Americans' ten-to-one kill ratio over the North Koreans and Chinese pilots established that the old hands were quite as effective as the new breed. WWII aces became double aces in the skies over Korea, and the old saw which held that fighter pilots should be under 25 years of age was confounded by many a 30-plus retread at the controls of an F-86, F9F or F4U.

During the first enemy offensive, the F-80s and F-82s of the 5th AF shot down seven of 13 Russian-built YAK fighters and IL-10 attack planes attempting to shoot up Seoul's Kimpo Airfield, Lts. William Hudson and Charles Moran and Maj. James

Fig. 8-23. A Vultee (Stinson) L-5 liaison plane delivers mail to G.I.s at a forward gun position. The unarmed L-5s and Cessna L-19s performed many such unglamorous but essential duties in Korea. (USAF)

Fig. 8-24. Marine helicopters of HMR-161 carried 60,046 passengers, including almost 10,000 wounded. This front line evacuation of wounded by Marines and Army choppers proved not only lifesaving, but morale-building. (USMC)

Little being officially credited with the first U.S. air victories over Korea.

The North Koreans apparently had but 70 of the propeller-driven YAKs and 62 IL-10s. The 5th AF quickly destroyed them all, mostly on the ground. In November 1950, when the Chinese entered the war, they had approximately 500 Russian-built MiG-15 jet fighters, some apparently manned by Russian pilots.

On 3 July the U.S. Navy attack carrier *Valley Forge*, operating with the British carrier *Triumph* in the Yellow Sea, joined the FEAF aircraft in attacks on airfields and the enemy's lines of supply around Pyongyang. Navy Panther jets (F9Fs) of VF-51 shot down two YAK-9s. The two carriers worked with the Air Force to slow the communist advance. Late in the month, the attack carriers *Philippine Sea* and *Boxer* arrived, along with the escort carriers *Badoeng Strait* and *Sicily*. Eventually, the air groups from eleven U.S. aircraft carriers would operate in Korean waters, coordinating their air strikes with those of the FEAF aircraft in a ground support role, attacking enemy airfields, railroads, factories, oil refineries, and enemy troop concentrations. Marine Fighting Squadron 214, flying Corsairs from the deck of the *Sicily*, and VMF-323 aboard the *Badoeng*

Strait began operations over Korea on 3 August.

Although the Navy and Marines were unhappy over the fact that MacArthur and his air commander, Gen. George Stratemeyer, were bosses of all UN air units (what did the Army know about the logistics of maintaining a Navy task force in constant touch with hostile forces for three years?), Navy and Marine air nevertheless performed as usual. After the highly successful Inchon landing (MacArthur's idea, opposed by most of the Joint Chiefs), and the resulting defeat of the North Koreans, the U.S. Army commander, Gen. Walton Walker, declared that except for U.S. airpower, the UN troops could not have stayed in Korea—a self-evident fact, of course, but the kind of fact that ground commanders are often slow to acknowledge.

After the line of battle stabilized, just inside the North Korean Border in the fall of 1951, and the primary enemy was the Chinese Communists ("ChiComs"), the ground war became a series of small battles for advantageous outpost positions, artillery duels and reconnaissance patrols—while Navy and Air Force planes continuously struck at the enemy's supply lines and prevented a buildup of enemy forces—and the negotiators at Panmunjon argued fruitlessly over side issues such as the repatriation of one another's prisoners.

Meanwhile, Gen. MacArthur had been fired by President Truman on 11 April 1951. Gen. Matthew Ridgeway was sent to replace him after MacArthur made statements considered by the President to be at cross-purposes with the UN (and U.S.) policy in Korea. MacArthur wanted a naval blockade of the China coast, air attacks on China's war industries, and an invasion of China by Chiang Kai-shek's Nationalist Chinese forces from Taiwan. MacArthur said that he believed in meeting force with maximum counterforce, and that "... if we lose this war to communism in Asia the fall of Europe is

Fig. 8-25. Col. Francis S. Gabreski, Deputy Commander of the 5th AF's 4th Fighter Interceptor Wing and WWII 56th FG ace, was one of the "retreads" flying F-86s in Korea. (USAF)

Fig. 8-26. Lt/Col. Glen Eagleston, 4th Fighter Interceptor Wing's group commander, inspects damage to his Sabre after an air battle with MiGs. (USAF)

inevitable; win it and Europe most probably could avoid war . . . there is no substitute for victory . . ."

President Truman had no intention of going to war with Red China—all-out war, that is. He kept U.S. Navy and Air Force pilots on a tight leash, giving strict orders that they could not fly across the Yalu River even if in "hot pursuit" of enemy MiGs—a circumstance the ChiCom pilots soon learned to exploit—and no targets could be bombed north of the Yalu. The "police action" was not to

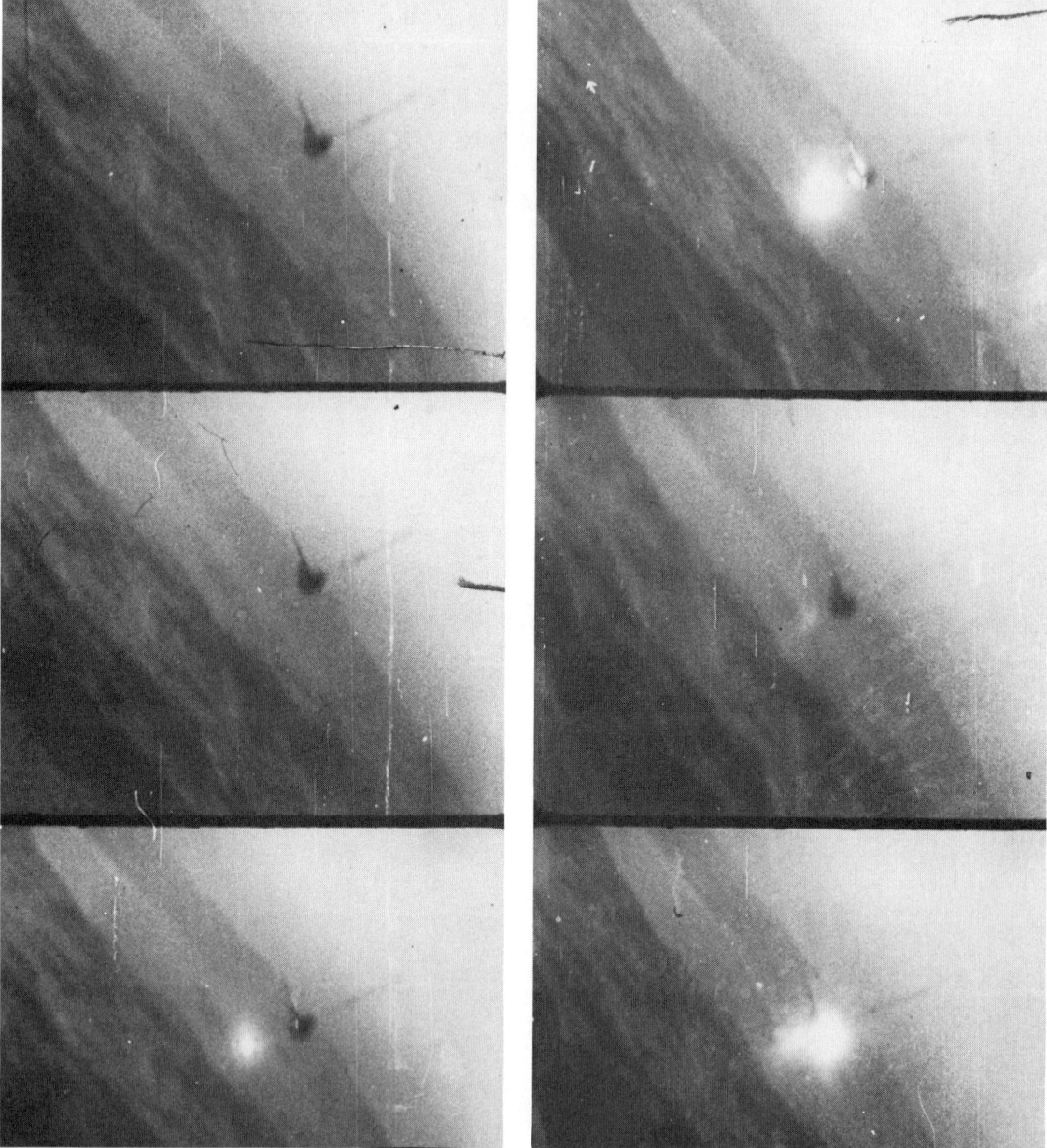

Fig. 8-27. These strips, taken from the gun cameras of an F-86, show the destruction of a MiG-15 during an air battle over Korea. (USAF)

Fig. 8-28. The Grumman F7F Tigercat was a 435-mph all-purpose fighter delivered to the Marines in 1945 and 1946. Most of the 364 produced were night fighter versions armed with four cannons and with a radar in the nose as shown. Engines were P&W R-2800s of 2100-hp each. (USN)

be carried into Chinese territory. Truman was undoubtedly right; it's better to talk than fight, even if it takes years for the talks to get anywhere. In any case, the American people would not have united behind such an action. They were, in fact, already showing signs of discontent with a war that was, for most, difficult to identify with America's best interest. Strangely, most Americans seemed to sympathize with MacArthur—there was a lot of controversy over his dismissal in the press and in Congress—although no one questioned the Commander-in-Chief's right to fire any general or admiral for cause. Civilian control of the military is essential in a free society, and is spelled out in the Constitution.

MacArthur's removal from command probably had no effect on subsequent events in Korea. UN field commanders had little latitude of action, particularly after the battle lines stabilized in November 1951.

When the final casualty report for the 37 months of fighting was prepared, total UN casualties reached over 550,000, including almost 95,000 dead. U.S. losses numbered 142,091, of whom 33,639 were killed, 103,284 wounded, and 5178 missing or captured. The bulk of these casualties occurred during the first year of the fighting. The estimate of enemy casualties, including prisoners, exceeded 1,500,000, of which 900,000 were Chinese.

The war's impact reached far beyond Korea. The primary result for the western bloc was a decided strengthening of the NATO alliance. Virtually without military power in June 1950, NATO would call on 50 divisions and strong air and naval contingents by 1953, a buildup directly attributable to the increased threat of general war seen in the outbreak of hostilities in Korea. The relative positions of West and East also had been affected during the war by the development of thermonuclear devices. The U.S. exploded its first such device in 1952, the USSR (Union of the Soviet Socialist Republics) in August 1953. The exact consequences of all these changes were incalculable; but it was certain that the cold war would continue and that both power blocs would face new challenges and new responses.

Chapter 9

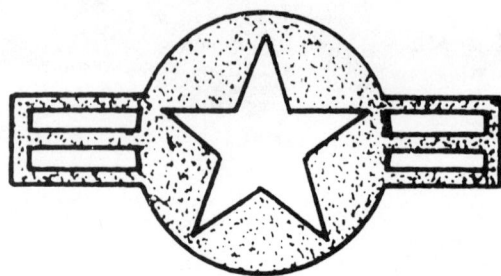

Johnson's War—and after

If it is true that those who fail to learn the lessons of history are doomed to relive it, Americans should demand that every congressman and every Presidential candidate be required to pass a comprehensive examination to establish that each possesses detailed knowledge of all the contributing factors that led to America's involvement in the Vietnam War.

Although U.S. involvement in Southeast Asian affairs actually began during the Truman Administration, the tragic bungling of America's role in the war that evolved there must be laid at the doorstep of the Johnson Administration. The indictment is especially severe because never before in history were U.S. military forces so totally misdirected on so grand a scale or the President's responsibility to the American people so incompetently performed.

The decisions faced by Lyndon B. Johnson regarding the American presence in South Vietnam when he was thrust into the Presidency by President Kennedy's assassination were basic and entirely manageable. Kennedy had increased the number of U.S. military advisors in South Vietnam from 700 to approximately 16,000. They were noncombatants, ordered not to participate in the fighting, their mission being to train the South Vietnamese Army. Therefore, the questions that President Johnson had to address were: (1) Assuming that the American assistance program to the South Vietnamese was both morally defensible and in the best interest of the United States, what should be the maximum limit of that assistance? And, (2) assuming that maximum assistance led to American involvement in hostilities, what should be U.S. policy in bringing the fighting to a quick end?

Airpower and the Flexible Response

Johnson's decision was to continue with the open-ended and heretofore untried theory of "flexible response" bequeathed by the Kennedy Administration.

The theory of flexible response sounded logical. It was a term coined by President Kennedy's Secretary of Defense Robert McNamara, a former

Fig. 9-1. Secretary of Defense in the Kennedy and Johnson Administrations Robert McNamara (R) championed the theory of flexible response which led to disaster in Vietnam, and through his "cost effective" approach to military spending and the concept of "commonality" in fighter airplane procurement, left the Pentagon in a shambles and America's ability to defend itself seriously degraded. With McNamara is Cyrus Vance, McNamara's deputy, who would later help implement President Carter's enervating defense policy. (USAF)

professor of economics at Harvard University and Ford Motor Company president, and it was born of the proposition that America needed a balanced combination of conventional forces available that would provide alternatives to deal with aggression other than the unhappy choice between massive nuclear retaliation or no retaliation at all.

Few would argue with that. However, the Kennedy/McNamara corollary was that, possessing a varied mix of forces, the amount of force used by the United States should always be commensurate with the threat. That was flexible response; that is what led President Johnson into a war in which the enemy could choose the kind of conflict best suited to his resources, could pick the areas of confrontation, and decide the level of the fighting. Vietnam was a war fought on the enemy's terms and at his convenience.

It was, of course, impossible to win such a war militarily, and since this enemy possessed a quasi-political organization trained in the arts of propaganda and terror, and effectively infiltrated it throughout the defended area, no stable political settlement was possible except in his favor.

President Johnson was well aware of the alternatives to flexible response. Gen. MacArthur had already stated the most obvious a decade years earlier in Korea: Meet force with *maximum* counterforce. If America must fight, do so to win and get it over with as quickly as possible.

Johnson had the means at his disposal to do just that *without* the use of nuclear weapons. The USAF and the Navy's air strike forces could have, in a matter of weeks, destroyed the enemy's ability to make war or feed his people, while few, if any, U.S. ground troops need be risked. North Vietnam was especially vulnerable to a massive strategic air offensive. The destruction of its Red River Dam complex alone would have denied to that country 90 percent of its domestic food supply. A sea blockade of the enemy's coasts, the aerial mining of his harbors, and aerial interdiction of his supply line from China would have severed his source of military and other war-essential materials. Meanwhile, his industries, transportation routes, electric generating plants and troop concentrations could have been pounded into the earth by SAC's B-52s. Johnson could have told the enemy exactly the same thing that President Eisenhower told the North Koreans, China and Russia in 1953.

Instead, Johnson decided to commit " . . . our American boys to a land war in Asia," an act he had promised, during the 1964 Presidential campaign, that he would never consider. He was unwilling to unleash American airpower, with no target restrictions, for fear that it would lead to nuclear war with the Soviets. He chose instead to fight a war that would not offend the enemy too much—an incredible stance for the world's most powerful nation (or the world's weakest, for that matter).

Fig. 9-2. Republic F-105 Thunderchiefs refuel from a KC-135 tanker on their way to tactical targets in North Vietnam, December 1965. Note that only two of the "Thuds" have received the new camouflage. (USAF)

The U.S. possessed a clear five-to-one nuclear advantage over the Soviets when President Eisenhower left office. Although that superiority had eroded some as a result of the Kennedy/McNamara adventure into "cost effectiveness" in the acquisition and maintenance of American arms, the Soviets did not have a numerically superior ICBM force in place until 1969 (1,054 American; 1,100 Russian).

To understand the U.S. presence in Vietnam, we must go back a bit. Prior to WWII, the French had ruled Vietnam, then called Indochina, which included Laos and Cambodia, for nearly 100 years. Even before that the country had been divided, the people of the north ruled from Hanoi, while the people in the south were ruled by emperors in Hue. The Japanese occupied Indochina during WWII. When the French returned after the war, President Truman felt that he had to aid the French in their "recolonization" partly because Truman saw the French presence there as a barrier to Soviet moves in that direction, and also because French cooperation in the formation of the North Atlantic Treaty Organization (NATO) was needed.

Meanwhile, a typical communist organization, originally formed in 1930 by Ho Chi Minh, and which had with no success opposed French rule in northern Indochina before WWII, grew in strength during that war by playing down its communist ideology while recruiting young people for the avowed purpose of ousting the Japanese. They called themselves the Viet Minh and, during the early '50s, with Soviet and Red Chinese money and arms, fought a guerilla war to expel the French, a task they accomplished in 1954 after the famed seige of the French garrison at Dienbienphu.

Following the French defeat in North Vietnam, a multination conference in Geneva produced the Geneva Accords that established conditions for a cease-fire in Indochina, provided for the independence of Laos, Cambodia, and Vietnam, while a political dividing line was drawn at the 17th parallel across Vietnam in recognition of the centuries-old differences between the people of the north and those of the south. Although the Geneva Accords called for free elections throughout Vietnam by July 1956, that provision, cleverly backed by the Soviets and Red China, embarrassed the U.S. because it resulted in President Eisenhower's refusal to sign the accords. The CIA had informed Secretary of State John Foster Dulles that the Viet Minh had terrorist agents in almost every South Vietnamese hamlet, and that the "free election" bit would be a

Fig. 9-3. The attack carrier *Forrestal* in the Gulf of Tonkin, 29 July 1967. (USN)

Fig. 9-4. CH-21 Shawnee ("Flying Banana"). These craft served in Korea and saw limited service in South Vietnam in that conflict. (U.S. Army)

Fig. 9-5. An Air Force F-4C Phantom, a Mach 2-plus fighter originally procured by the U.S. Navy in 1960 and added to Air Force inventory because of its outstanding performance. It was used extensively in Vietnam. (USAF)

farce until a stable government in the south could root out the northern infiltrators.

Aware that the Geneva Accords would do nothing to ensure the independence of Southeast Asian nations, the Free World nations had already met in Manila to form the Southeast Asia Treaty Organization (SEATO), and signed an agreement on 8 September 1954 pledging aid to any Southeast Asian country which asked for it if attacked. It was under terms of the SEATO pact that President Eisenhower sent some 400 U.S. military advisors and military equipment to South Vietnam when the French pulled out the last of their troops in 1956 in compliance with the Geneva Accords.

Ho Chi Minh counted upon the 1956 elections to give him all Vietnam, but a general of the South Vietnamese Army (ARVN), Duong Van Minh ("Big Minh") led a *coup d' etat* against the tottering Bao Dai government and repudiated the Geneva Accords.

Due to a revolt within his own ranks, Ho was not able to increase the terror campaign by his agents in the south until 1961. At that time, he announced the formation of the "National Liberation Front" (Viet Cong), and began escalating his war below the 17th parallel. The Viet Cong, organized around hardcore Red guerillas of the old Viet Minh, murdered 1719 and kidnapped 9688 South Vietnamese that year. About 6200 Viet Cong slipped into South Vietnam during 1961, and in much of the south the Viet Cong were sufficiently in control to levy taxes in rural regions. Even though ARVN troops might control many areas in daylight, it was generally accepted in much of the countryside that "the night belongs to the VC."

President Kennedy responded with more U.S. military advisors to help train and direct the ARVN's 200,000 men, and appeared less-than-surprised when the third corrupt and ineffective South Vietnamese government fell to still another

Fig. 9-6. With tail hook engaged, a Douglas A-4 Skyhawk of VA-12 returns to the attack carrier *Franklin Roosevelt* operating in the Gulf of Tonkin, 10 August 1966. (USN)

coup, which some believed was CIA-inspired.

That, then, was the Southeast Asian bucket of eels inherited by Lyndon Johnson when he assumed the Presidency in November 1963. By that time, the VC were boldy launching daylight attacks against ARVN forces, and U.S. advisors began to die: 42 in 1963, 118 in 1964.

Then on 2 August 1964 North Vietnamese torpedo boats attacked the U.S. Navy destroyer *Maddox* cruising in international waters in the Gulf of Tonkin. They were damaged and driven off by aircraft from the carrier *Ticonderoga*.

Two days later, at 2330 hours EST, Johnson told a nationwide TV audience that a second attack had occurred and that, as a result, retaliatory air strikes were underway.

There is no evidence that a second attack took place, but on 5 August, on orders from the President, 64 aircraft from the 7th Fleet carriers *Constellation* and *Ticonderoga* struck at motor torpedo boats and their supporting facilities at five points along the North Vietnamese coast and sank 25 boats along with their petroleum stores.

Fig. 9-7. An ordnanceman wheels Sparrow missiles to F-4 Phantoms aboard the U.S. 7th Fleet attack carrier *Midway* as the aircraft are prepared for a strike against Viet Cong positions in South Vietnam. (USN)

On that same day, Johnson used the "two" attacks on U.S. ships as his reason for asking Congressional support for " . . . all necessary action to protect our armed forces and to assist nations covered by the SEATO treaty." Congress gave him a signed, blank check. The exact wording of the Congressional resolution was: " . . . take all necessary steps, including the use of armed force, to assist any member or protocol state of the Southeast Asia Collective Defense Treaty requesting assistance in defense of its freedom." It was adopted by a vote of 416 to 0 in the House, 88 to 2 in the Senate. Johnson's War was to have a lot of sponsors.

When President Johnson obtained the Tonkin Gulf resolution, endorsing in advance whatever he decided to do in Vietnam, the Viet Cong had approximately 115,000 guerillas in the south; they had murdered an estimated 5587 and kidnapped an estimated 26504 South Vietnamese civilians.

With North Vietnam escalating the war (whether or not it was a "civil war" is an arguable point, because the people of Indochina had never been united), and the sketchily-trained and often poorly-motivated ARVN forces clearly unable to effectively oppose the enemy, it was obvious by 1965 that the U.S. would determine whether or not South Vietnam, Laos, Cambodia—and after that, perhaps, all Southeast Asia and peripheral nations—would fall to communism or mark the time and place where red aggression was contained in that part of the world.

Actually, an air offensive of sorts against North Vietnam was begun in March 1965, although it was limited to indecisive targets selected by the Joint

Fig. 9-8. Heavily-laden Grumman A-6 Intruder just prior to catapult launch from the attack carrier *Independence*. The A-6 electronics allow crew to "see" at night and through clouds for accurate bombing. (USN)

Fig. 9-9. An F-4B Phantom of VF-102 stretches out the arresting cable as it lands on the attack carrier *America*. (USN)

Fig. 9-10. North American F-100 *Super Sabre* was designed as an 800-mph superiority fighter. It appeared in 1954 and saw extensive use in Vietnam as a fighter-bomber. A total of 2294 were delivered to the Air Force. (USAF)

Fig. 9-11. The Northrop F-5A, a 1000-mph tactical fighter designed for use by NATO and Third World countries in an effort to achieve low-cost standardization. USAF proved F-5's combat worthiness in Vietnam in 1965 operation *Skoshi Tiger*, then abandoned the aircraft as a first-line combat type. A later version, the F-5E/F, is used by the Air Force and Navy in their "Aggressor" and "Top Gun" training programs to simulate Soviet MiG-21s. (USAF)

Chiefs, who in turn were fettered by the Johnson/McNamara policy of placing important strategic targets off limits. On 26 March, F-4 Phantoms from the 7th Fleet's carriers *Hancock* and *Coral Sea* struck at radar sites in the vicinity of Vinh Son, while Air Force F-100 Super Sabres and F-105 Thunderchiefs began a series of sustained attacks on bridges and the "Ho Chi Minh Trail," the collective name for the several routes of supply through eastern Laos used by the invader to funnel men and supplies into the south. The Air Force fighters were based in Thailand.

Air action was all the U.S. was capable of for a time, as the buildup of American combat ground forces did not begin until September 1965, with the arrival of the 1st Cavalry.

On 18 June, 27 B-52F Stratofortresses from Anderson Air Force Base on Guam, each carrying 27 750-lb "iron" bombs internally and 24 on external wing pylons, began a 10-month operation against Viet Cong troop concentrations in jungle hideouts in South Vietnam. The B-52 operations were code-named *Arc Light* while the overall air offensive was known as *Rolling Thunder*.

Two weeks earlier, the U.S. Marines had an airbase in operation at Chu Lai, 52 miles south of the major U.S. base at Danang, and the attack carrier *Independence* arrived in Subic Bay for duty with the 7th Fleet, making a total of five U.S. aircraft carriers operating off Vietnam. The nuclear-powered attack carrier *Enterprise* joined the action in December.

Within three years, U.S. military strength gradually built up in South Vietnam from less than

25,000 to over 500,000, including two Marine divisions. Regular ARVN forces meanwhile grew to over 340,000. South Korea sent 48,000 men; Australia, Thailand, New Zealand and the Philippines committed token forces. And despite nearly 180,000 communists killed and 70,000 captured during this period, the invader still managed to build his strength to nearly 240,000 men in the south, a feat accomplished by recruitment through terror and intimidation, and by sharply increasing the number of North Vietnamese regular army troops sent to VC units.

It was an unusual war by any standard. There were no front lines. The enemy could be anywhere and everywhere, and was often indistinguishable from the native population. The U.S. ground forces were spread around in fortified base camps from which they would strike out in search-and-destroy missions. On many such missions, particularly in the thick jungles of the highlands, companies and battalions would be far from any road and wholly dependent upon helicopters for resupply and evacuation. Most battles were fought at the platoon or company level. Ambush and counterambush were familiar tactics on both sides. The helicopter and good radio communications were the two essential ingredients that made it possible for the U.S. Army and Marines to engage in that kind of combat successfully, while the B-52s, Air Force and Navy fighters, despite the frustrating limitations placed upon them, limited the enemy's ability to fight and denied him the opportunity to concen-

Fig. 9-12. Douglas AD Skyraider series went into production in 1945. Its Wright R-3350 engine of 2700 hp gave it exceptional load-carrying ability. A total of 3180 were built in 28 different versions with production ending in 1957. U.S. Navy used the Skyraider until 1968. (USN)

Fig. 9-13. An A-4 Skyhawk approaches for landing on the attack carrier *Hancock* in the South China Sea. (USN)

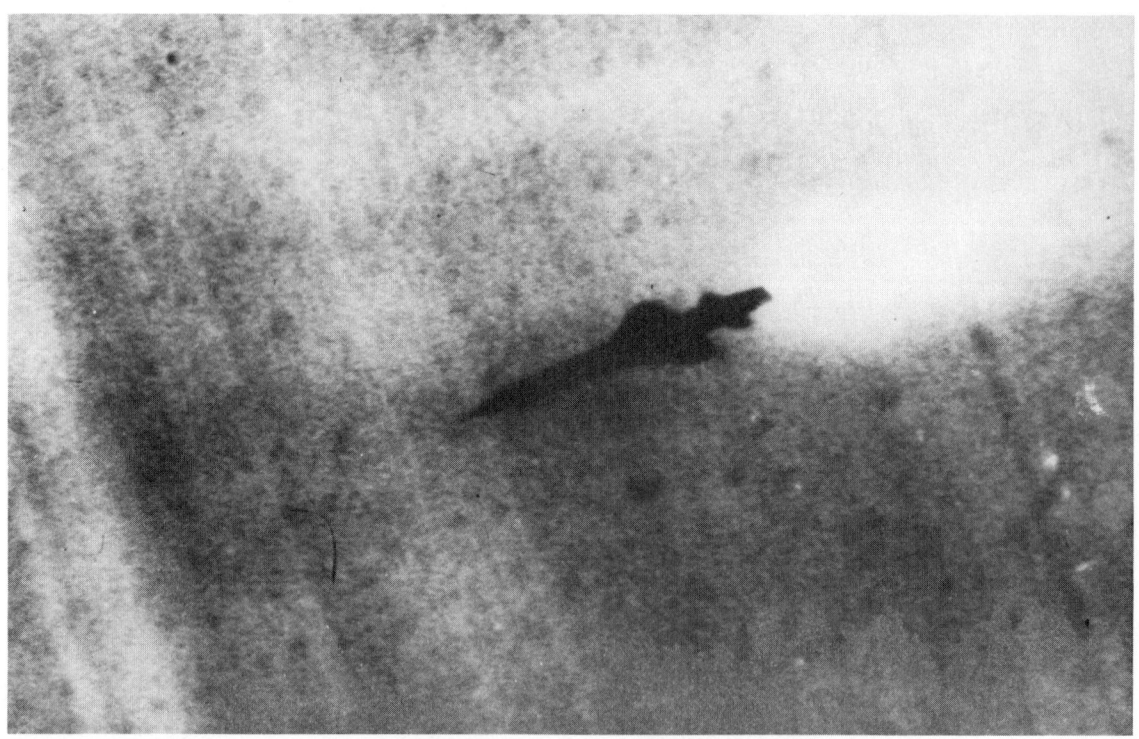

Fig. 9-14. A Soviet-made surface-to-air (SAM) missile was photographed by the pilot of an Air Force RF-101 Voodoo as it streaked by, missing its target, 20 June 1967. (USAF)

Fig. 9-15. A pair of F-105 Thunderchiefs with an F-100 Super Sabre en route to strike at Viet Cong positions. (USAF)

trate his resources for attacks in strength. Enemy air opposition was rare except over especially sensitive targets in the north.

The first helicopter to fly in large numbers in South Vietnam was the CH-21 Flying Banana, followed in 1963 by the faster and more versatile UH-1 Huey. The helicopter became the symbol of this new kind of war, a checkerboard campaign in which units might be picked up and set down swiftly almost anywhere from the forested highlands to the fertile, densely-populated river bottoms along the coast and the largely inundated rice paddies of the Mekong Delta region in the extreme south. As the enemy reacted by increasing his antiaircraft capability, the Huey Cobra appeared, a heavily armed gunship version of the UH-1.

The Huey Cobras were mostly employed in an attack role and were especially effective in close air support situations. Ground troops in radio contact with the Cobras could direct them with extreme accuracy to nearby targets. During street fighting in Hue, a U.S. Army platoon leader marvelled that "Those chopper guys would come in just a couple of feet over our heads and we could tell 'em, not which building we wanted hit, but which *doorway*. Man, *that's* close air support!"

Directing the war from Washington, the Johnson/McNamara planners, believing that the limited air strikes on North Vietnam had seriously hurt the enemy, decided that a major cutback in the air offensive could encourage the North Vietnamese to sit down in good faith at a meeting in Paris to negotiate a cease-fire.

It was true that Ho had been seriously hurt by the air attacks. By early 1968 all major railroad bridges in the north were down, petroleum storage

Fig. 9-16. Death of a MiG. An F-105's camera gun records this air victory over a Soviet-built MiG-17 near Hanoi. (USAF)

facilities were destroyed, war material could move southward only at night, and even then the trucks were in constant danger from U.S. night fighters. All consumer goods, including food, were strictly rationed, and 300,000 people (including many Chinese "volunteers") were fully employed repairing bomb damage to roads and rail tracks.

Therefore, President Johnson announced on 31 March 1968 that 80 percent of the area north of the 17th parallel (containing 90 percent of all North Vietnamese people) would be spared further attack by U.S. aircraft. Johnson had tried short bombing moratoriums during the previous two years, but this one was tied to the Paris negotiations.

But Ho Chi Minh had no reason to seriously negotiate with Johnson offering such a major concession, and all the Paris talks accomplished at that time was to provide Ho with a breathing spell while he rebuilt his shattered supply lines to the south.

Nevertheless, on 1 November 1968 (on the eve of the elections), Johnson halted all bombing of North Vietnam. He said at the time that Ho had agreed to some reciprocal measures of de-

Fig. 9-17. Army CH-37 helicopter delivers a field piece to a new firing position. (Sikorsky Aircraft)

Fig. 9-18. A fearsome foursome of F-105s over Vietnam. The *Thunderchief's* radar system allows it to attack enemy ground positions through clouds from any altitude. (USAF)

escalation. If Ho did so, there was never any evidence of it.

That was the situation when Richard M. Nixon took office in January 1969. The U.S. had half a million men in South Vietnam and American combat deaths were approaching the 33,000 mark, and although the Viet Cong and North Vietnamese People's Army had lost 500,000 men, they seemed prepared to lose that many more. Indeed, Ho declared that he was willing to fight for another 20 years if necessary.

Nixon, of course, was not. Nor were the American people. The average American found it difficult to understand a war with such confused beginnings, fought—seemingly endlessly—for no clearly defined purpose affecting America's vital interests, and offering no chance of victory.

A month after taking office, President Nixon, acting on the advice of his new Army commander in Vietnam, Gen. Creighton Abrams, secretly authorized B-52 strikes against enemy sanctuaries in Cambodia. He later extended that authorization to include Laos as well, since those "neutral" countries had from the beginning not only been used by the North Vietnamese as bases from which to conduct the war in South Vietnam, but eventually became victims of communist "wars of liberation" themselves.

But Nixon, too, had to learn that impressive "enemy body counts" reported by U.S. Army commanders was not a measure of progress in this strangest of wars. The enemy knew that time was on his side, and to him life was cheap.

By May 1972, a total of 200 B-52s were committed to the war in Southeast Asia, along with their KC-135 tankers (the "tanks" also served as aerial filling stations for the fighters), but Nixon ordered that no air strikes be made north of the 20th parallel. However, after the North Vietnamese walked out of another fruitless round of cease-fire talks in Paris on 13 December 1972, Nixon lifted that ban and authorized an air offensive against selected military targets in the Hanoi/Haiphong area. Navy A-6 Intruders, operating from carriers in the Gulf of Tonkin, and Air Force F-111s from Takhli Air Base in Thailand joined the B-52s in the round-the-clock all-weather offensive (*Linebacker II*) that came to be known as the "Eleven-Day War."

At 1451 hours on 18 December 1972, the first of 87 B-52s lifted off the runway on Guam bound for Hanoi. They would be joined by 42 more flying from U-Tapao Air Base in Thailand, along with some 400 fighters, including Marine F-4s escorting the KC-135 tankers.

Over their targets at 35,000 ft, the bombers were met by hundreds of surface-to-air SAM missiles and a few MiG-21 fighters; the F-111s and A-6s going in low faced the greatest concentration of antiaircraft artillery ever assembled. But losses were remarkably light, altogether: 15 B-52s and six F-111s, and with only a 36-hour pause for Christmas (during which time the North Vietnamese stri-

Fig. 9-19. The Army's Bell Huey helicopter became the symbol of the hit-and-run war in Vietnam, serving as ambulance, troop transport, gunship—name it, the *Huey* could do it. (Bob Dean)

Fig. 9-20. The Army's AH-1G Huey Cobra is a helicopter attack aircraft capable of carrying more than a ton of weaponry. It was also widely used during the last years of the war in Vietnam. (Bell Helicopter)

dently charged that the Americans were bombing schools and hospitals and spoiling all chance for a negotiated cease-fire), the air offensive continued, loosing over 20,000 tons of destruction on the enemy's transportation and oil facilities. On 30 December Hanoi wanted to talk again.

While the Eleven-Day War represented but a fraction of what an all-out strategic air offensive could have been, it was more than enough to force an agreement on cease-fire, effective 27 January 1973. Violations of the agreement by communist guerillas in Laos and Cambodia caused President Nixon to send the B-52s back into limited action until 15 August 1973, when the war in Southeast Asia ended—for the United States.

During the eight years the B-52 strategic bombers were in action over Southeast Asia, just six percent of their total missions were directed at decisive strategic targets.

Almost anyone who had read the *U.S. Strategic Bombing Survey*, commissioned by President Truman at the end of WWII, could have successfully planned a quick end to the Vietnam conflict in 1965. U.S. military leaders offered such a plan to President Johnson early that year, and fully explained it to the Senate Preparedness Investigating Subcommittee in mid-1967, but Johnson opted for the McNamara doctrine of flexible response, a policy not of action, but of *re*action (the "knee-jerk syndrome"). The total cost of that to America and the Free World has not yet been paid.

McNamara's Brand

Robert McNamara ran the U.S. Department of Defense just as he had the Ford Motor Company. His watchword was "cost effective," bureaucratic code for "get your money's worth," and in pursuit of his cost-effective programs, McNamara success-

Fig. 9-21. Many Hueys were fitted with the 7.62 mm Gatling gun mounted above a 2.75-in rocket launcher. Such aircraft were designated UH-1Bs and UH-1Cs. (U.S. Army)

Fig. 9-22. The AS-7A Corsair II light attack bomber was built by Vought and developed from the earlier F8U Crusader. The A-7 series entered squadron service in October 1966. (The Vought Corporation)

Fig. 9-23. The USAF also used Skyraiders over Vietnam and provided some to the South Vietnamése Air Force (VNAF). (USAF)

Fig. 9-24. A Kaman HH-43F Huskie rescue helicopter with fire bottle is first on the scene as an A-1E Skyraider crash-lands at Da Nang. (USAF)

Fig. 9-25. An A-4 Skyhawk approaches the flight deck of the *Ranger* in the South China Sea. (USN)

say you haven't had much practice," said the Queen.)

That airplane was then called the "TFX" for "Tactical Fighter, Experimental." It had been in the works for about 18 months when Mr. McNamara took charge of the Pentagon with John. F. Kennedy's inauguration as President in January 1961. The TFX was originally conceived as the Air Force's new 1700-mph long-range tactical fighter, and the idea went through the usual channels: Once Tactical Air Command (TAC) settled upon the performance parameters required of the new fighter it would need during the late '60s and '70s, permission to proceed with the project was obtained from Air Force Headquarters. Then, Air Force Systems Command took over to decide whether or not such a plane was feasible. Next, detailed specifications were drawn up to be sent to the aircraft manufacturers which, in turn, would produce plans showing

fully wrested control of weapons selection and the U.S. defense posture from the generals and admirals.

There was just one critical factor in the defense equation that McNamara's textbook efficiencies did *not* include: A dollars and cents appraisal of freedom itself.

In the name of fiscal responsibility, McNamara closed a number of airbases, cancelled the Skybolt air-to-air-missile program (which weakened NATO because it forced retirement of Britain's Vulcan bomber force), cancelled the B-70 supersonic strategic bomber program and the Nike-Zeus antiballistic missile which was planned to intercept Soviet ICBMs approaching targets in the United States. He expected to retire the B-52s, and planned to equip the Air Force and Navy with a single fighter airplane—one that would also serve as a *strategic bomber*. ("There's no use trying," Alice said, "One can't believe impossible things." "I dare

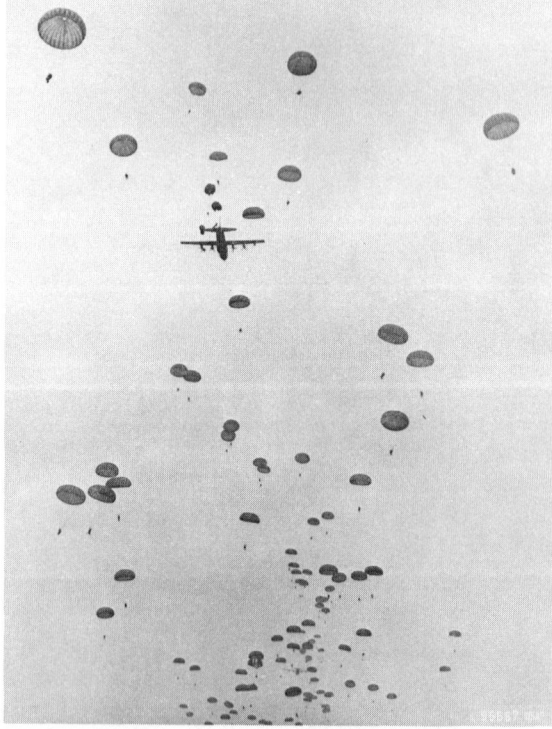

Fig. 9-26. USAF C-130 Hercules drops South Vietnamese paratroopers into Viet Cong stronghold southwest of Saigon. (USAF)

Fig. 9-27. An A-4 is launched from canted deck as F-4Bs prepare to follow from the main deck. (USN)

Fig. 9-28. A B-52D with black undersurfaces for service over Vietnam. The B-52s flew from Okinawa, Guam and Thailand, but target selection was made in Washington and meaningful strategic targets were largely off limits during the Johnson Administration. (The Boeing Company)

Fig. 9-29. Convair F-111, originally planned as a superior tactical fighter, was downgraded by McNamara's naive theory and the resulting airplane met none of the original design specifications. (General Dynamics)

Fig. 9-30. The F-111's terrain-following radar and other sophisticated systems are praised by its pilots, but the airplane itself, compromised by a multi-mission requirement, performs marginally in each role. As Gen. (ret) Eaker pointed out, it's not possible to mate a sports car and a four-ton truck. (General Dynamics)

Fig. 9-31. The Navy managed to prove that the F-111 was unsuited to navy needs and did without a new fighter until the political climate changed in Washington. Then it got the fighter it wanted, the F-14 Tomcat, seen here during initial tests early in 1974. (USN)

Fig. 9-32. The Convair F-106A is a 1500-mph USAF fighter with a service ceiling of 60,000 ft. It has been in operation since 1959 as a home defense weapon in the U.S. It is automatically directed to its targets by advanced ground radars. (F.H. Dean)

just how they would design and build such an airplane. Finally, with input from the several commands concerned. Air Force brass would get together to select the design they liked the best and, through the Secretary of the Air Force and Secretary of Defense, ask Congress to fund it. (Since 1974 the Air Force Test and Evaluation Center at Kirtland, AFB, N.M. evaluates the prototypes, and the Defense Systems Acquisition Review Council makes the decision as to whether or not the new hardware is recommended for acquisition to the Secretary of the Air Force.)

Meanwhile, the Navy, too, had a new fighter proposal in the mill, and therefore, when these proposals appeared on the desk of Defense Secretary McNamara, scarecly before he had time to warm his chair, McNamara made his incredible decision: The TFX would be redesigned, in *two* versions, employing at least 90 percent "commonality of parts," to serve both the Air Force and the Navy! Five hundred million dollars could be saved, he said, by developing one airplane rather than two.

Now, at that time, the Air Force Chief of Staff happened to be Gen. Curtis LeMay, but LeMay held his fire and waited for the Navy's reaction, which wasn't long in coming.

The Navy pointed out that it needed an *entirely* different kind of aircraft than that required by the Air Force because their missions were different. The Air Force tactical fighter would have to be a large, heavy, offensive machine (90 ft in length and weighing 90,000 lbs), while the Navy needed a much smaller, lighter defensive fighter to ride shotgun for the fleet.

Fig. 9-33. The Lockheed F-104 Starfighter was introduced in 1958 and seemed slightly unbelievable with a razor-thin wing of only 22-ft span and a gross weight of 20,000 lbs. Top speed was 1600 mph, but it was an unforgiving machine and generally unpopular with pilots. (USAF)

Fig. 9-34. The high-altitude U-2 "spy plane" is essentially a jet-powered sailplane packed with sophisticated cameras and other detection devices. It normally operates above 60,000 ft. (USAF)

But McNamara was adamant. The TFX—by then designated the F-111—would proceed as decreed.

Boeing and Convair (the latter with Grumman as a sort of junior partner) responsed to McNamara's specifications, and in November 1962 the services chose the Boeing proposal. Eight Air Force generals and three admirals, plus the Chief of Naval Operations, Adm. Anderson, and Air Force Chief of Staff Gen. LeMay, picked the Boeing designs.

However, McNamara overruled them all because, he said, the Boeing designs contained only 34 percent commonality of parts (by weight), while the Convair designs used 92 percent identical parts.

Backing the McNamara decision were Secretary of the Air Force Eugene Zuckert and Secretary of the Navy Fred Korth, who were also Kennedy appointees.

In the end, the Navy decided to stonewall it, saying that the F-4 Phantom, which it already had, was better suited to the Navy's needs than the Convair F-111B.*

---

*Ironically, the Air Force also began buying F-4s in 1963. McDonnell's versatile Phantom proved to be one of the star performers of the Vietnam war in the air superiority, fighter-bomber, interceptor, grand support, tactical strike, and reconnaissance roles.

The Air Force, however, ended up with 270 F-111 tactical fighters (which fell short of all original performance specifications, and was grounded a number of times until the wing carry-through structure and other weaknesses were modified), and 70 FB-111 "strategic bombers," acquisitions that were considerably eased by the retirement of Gen. LeMay in February 1965, a few days after the F-111 prototype began its flight tests. LeMay had characterized the F-111 as a "jury-rigged . . . inferior stop-gap weapon system." But LeMay could not have remained as Air Force Chief of Staff in any case, because he was bitterly opposed to the policy of flexible response.

The Mitchells, MacArthurs and LeMays must always risk the foreshortening or termination of their military careers—however right they may be—because they cannot be allowed to publicly challenge the decisions of their Commander-in-Chief—however wrong he may be.

Faith, Hope, and Parity

Throughout the '60s and '70s, U.S. defense forces, including the nuclear deterrent forces, steadily eroded in comparison to those of the Soviets; and four different Presidents—Johnson, Nixon, Ford and Carter—sought solace in a series of code words when forced to defend the decline of American arms. *"Equivalency," sufficiency"* and *parity* were imprecise terms used to imply that,

Fig. 9-35. The Strategic Air Command's SR-71 Blackbird can cruise at 2000 mph at 80,000 ft, and is a product of Kelly Johnson's "Skunk Works" at Lockheed. (USAF)

Fig. 9-36. The Convair B-58 Hustler was intended as a replacement for the medium-range Boeing B-47 bomber and entered service in 1960. With a speed in the 1600-mph range it was impressive for its time. But changing requirements, and the fact that SAC was stuck with the FB 111o, caused a phase-out of the 80 Hustlers by the end of the '70s. (General Dynamics)

even if the Soviets had more intercontinental ballistic missiles (ICBMs), there was no need for alarm because, all things considered, the two powers actually were about even in nuclear might. The Congresses of these two decades endorsed this position.

But the assumption that nuclear confrontation is thwarted by this presumed balance of terror is meaningless if the balance exists only in Presidential rhetoric. As valuable as the U.S. spy satellites may be, they cannot probe the contents of roofed structures, and therefore U.S. defense planners cannot know how many ICBMs the Soviets have in standby storage to give them a multiple reload capacity for the ICBMs that are detectable.

At the beginning of the '80s, the U.S. possessed 1,053 ICBMs: 53 Titan IIs in silos at three locations in Arkansas, Arizona and Kansas; 450 Minuteman II Solid-propellant missiles; and 550 Minuteman IIs fitted with multiple independently targetable re-entry vehicle (MIRV) warheads. The ICBMs, with a range in excess of 6000 miles, are pre-programmed to strike strategic targets in the Soviet Union.

The second leg of America's nuclear deterrent triad is the nuclear-powered submarine fleet armed with some 640 nuclear-tipped missiles of medium range.

SAC's manned bombers represent the third leg of the U.S. strategic retaliatory force—290 B-52G and H nuclear missile carriers, 70 FB-111s and 600 supporting KC-135 tankers.

Fig. 9-37. The Military Airlift Command delivers whatever needs to be delivered by air, anywhere in the world, at any time, for the military services. Pictured is one of MAC's emergency hospital aircraft, a Douglas C-9 Nightingale. (USAF)

Fig. 9-38. Lockheed C-130 Hercules is the Air Force combat transport, designed to operate from unimproved airstrips. It does everything from iceberg patrol (for the Coast Guard) to paratrooper drops. (Lockheed Georgia Company)

Fig. 9-39. The Lockheed C-5A Galaxy of MAC is shown with a typical load. It can carry this 256,000 lbs, 2,900 miles nonstop at a speed of 530 mph and land in a distance of 5000 ft. (Lockheed Georgia Company)

The manned bomber has one very important advantage over the ICBM: it can be launched at the first suspicion of attack and then recalled for several hours thereafter if no attack materializes. The ICBM cannot be called back once launched—indeed, it will reach a target in the Soviet Union in slightly over 20 minutes—or it may be destroyed in its silo if for any reason (including a delayed order from the Commander-in-Chief as he agonizes over the decision) it is not launched within the 15-minute warning period provided by satellite and radar surveillance.

The manned bomber is more vulnerable to enemy defenses, which is why the B-52s would penetrate Soviet airspace at 400 mph and only 400 ft above the surface to launch their stand-off nuclear missiles hundreds of miles from their targets.

In 1980, the stand-off nuclear missile carried by the most B-52s was the SRAM (Short Range Attack Missile), as many as 20 per plane (or, more often, depending upon each B-52's pre-selected targets, a mix of SRAMs and nuclear gravity bombs). The SRAM may be launched with the aircraft on any heading, even 180 degrees away from the targets. It flies at 2000 mph and its 18-inch diameter gives it a very poor signature on enemy radar. In tests, the SRAM has repeatedly impacted within 100 ft of its programmed targets. Its only

185

Fig. 9-40. A Navy Tomcat fighter of the "High Hat" squadron, a unit that dates back to the mid-'20's; nowadays part of the air group on the attack carrier *John F. Kennedy*. (Francis H. Dean)

Fig. 9-41. U.S. Navy P-3 Orion anti-submarine warfare (ASW) aircraft makes a mock run on an American sub during exercises held in the Sea of Japan. A perimeter of P-3 bases extending from Sigonella and Souda Bay in the Mediterranean to Norway, Iceland, United States, Japan, Okinawa, the Philippines, Thailand, Australia, New Zealand, Guam and Hawaii make any area in the world accessible to the Orion within 30 minutes' flying time. More than 400 are in service. (USN)

Fig. 9-42. The newest Air Force fighter is the McDonnell F-15 Eagle believed by the Air Force to be superior to anything the Soviets may put in the air during the '80s. (McDonnell-Douglas St. Louis)

Fig. 9-43. The General Dynamics F-16 USAF fighter is a lightweight air combat fighter which performs so well that the gadgeteers and Pentagon Pilots added air-to-surface and all-weather radar and navigation capabilities to broaden its mission. Predictably, the new goodies have forced a quantum leap in cost. (General Dynamics)

Fig. 9-44. Fairchild's A-10 ground support aircraft was literally designed around its tank-killing General Electric GAU-8 seven-barreled cannon. (Fairchild Industries)

weakness is its short range—about 100 miles. It has been operational since 1972.

The new Air Launched Cruise Missile (ALCM) is subsonic, but has a much greater range and therefore significantly increases the B-52 survivability factor. The Cruise Missile program was delayed by the Carter Administration, and as a result full deployment of the ALCM could not be accomplished before 1983. Carter also delayed development of the improved Trident II nuke missile for U.S. submarine strike force, cancelled the B-52's replacement, the B-1, and delayed the MX (mobile ICBM) for three critical years. At last faced with the consequences of these acts—along with those of previous administrations—and a re-election campaign, President Carter endorsed an enormously expensive, environmentally destructive and embarrassingly ridiculous MX railway system in which the missiles were to be shuffled about in a massive shell game that, hopefully, would leave the Soviets guessing as to which shelters contained missiles at any given time. Meanwhile, Mr. Carter

Fig. 9-45. Approximately 100 B-52 nuclear carriers are on alert at all times. New quick-start ability allows simultaneous starting of all engines and a five-minute elapsed time from the scramble order to liftoff. (USAF)

voiced the belief that an eventual nuclear arm limitation agreement with the Soviets was possible. The Soviets, no more concerned with adherence to their future promises than to their past ones, claimed support for such an agreement while going forward with a mobile ICBM program of their own, and concurrently installing new SS-20 medium-range semi-mobile missiles in Western Russia aimed at targets in Free Europe.

Each SS-20 is fitted with three independently-tareted warheads, and a total of 300 SS-20 boosters (900 warheads) were in place by early 1982, giving the communists a clear six-to-one advantage in nuclear weaponry deployed for any kind of a so-called "limited" nuclear confrontation in Europe.

That advantage was, of course, measured against the combined nuclear strength of the NATO partners. This situation so alarmed President Reagan when he took office that it prompted him to seek deployment of ground-launchable cruise missiles in Western Europe to counter this threat. The cruise missile program, along with that of the B-1 bomber, would go forward in the President administration.

Earlier, on the eve of the 1980 elections, in an apparent attempt to gloss over the weaknesses in America's defenses, Carter's secretary of defense,

As the USAF Tactical Air Command entered the '80s, it possessed some excellent new aircraft. The F-15 Eagle had been entering squadron service since the mid-'70s. The first of a planned buy of 733 A-10 ground support planes had come along in the

Fig. 9-46. A Minuteman test firing. The 70,000-lb ICBM is solid-fueled and requires little maintenance. The firing sequence takes just 32 seconds after the order to fire is received. (USAF)

Fig. 9-47. The Titan II ICBM is liquid-fueled and requires extensive maintenance. America's ICBM force consisted of 53 Titans and 1000 Minutemen in 1980, a figure that had remained static throughout the '70s. (USAF)

a man by the name of Brown, decided it was time to reveal the Air Force's "Stealth" bomber program, which had been in the works since late in the Nixon administration. The Stealth bomber, Brown said, would be virtually "invisible" to current Soviet radars.

Brown's revelation impressed the news media and surely sounded reassuring to the taxpayers. But what Brown did not say was that the Soviets already had the key engineering data on the Stealth's radar-eating systems. It had been sold to a Polish intelligence agent for $100,000 by an engineer working for Hughes Aircraft.

Fig. 9-48. The U.S. Navy's nuclear submarine fleet contained 41 vessels in 1980, each armed with 16 nuclear missiles with a 2500 mile range. Test firing shown is of a Polaris A3, launched while the submarine was submerged. The Carter Administration refused to update with the more advanced Tridents. (Lockheed)

late '70s (since President Reagan's large defense budget was almost certain to be cut in the Congress, the A-10 program appeared in jeopardy by mid-1982); and the new F-16 lightweight fighter, 650 of which were promised as replacements for the 675 F-4s acquired during the '60s, was entering service. The F-15 has a top speed in excess of Mach 2, a combat thrust-to-weight ratio of 1.4 to 1, and is expected to be superior to anything the Soviets may put into the air during the '80s. It carries four medium-range missiles and two short-range missiles, along with 900 rounds of ammunition for its 20mm cannon. The F-16 is not as fast or as well armed as the F-15, but is much lighter and more maneuverable.

The F-16 was originally justified as an "economy" fighter, one almost as good as the F-15 for a lot less money. But the initial cost has turned out to be $14 million each, while the F-15 is $17 million. The necessary spares and maintenance equipment add significantly to these figures, not to mention the fact that some highly trained technicians are required to keep them flying.

While such aircraft are capable of some truly amazing performances in the delivery of their ordinance against an enemy, the complexity of these high-technology combat machines is in itself a limiting factor. No matter how miraculous their systems, those out of service for high-tech maintenance have an effectiveness factor of *zero*. And if no more than half of these machines in squadron service can be put into the air at any given time, due to the amount of expert care demanded by their magical black boxes, then our air commanders must plan accordingly.

One lesson learned about airpower in WWII was that the "best" and most effective combat airplanes were simply those that were airborne and ready to fight when needed—a principle clearly established by the pilots flying the unremarkable Douglas Dauntless at Midway, the obsolescent P-40 over North Africa, and the inadequate F4F Wildcat at Guadalcanal and the Coral Sea.

This is a relevant consideration because, currently, the AF and Navy are markedly short of the technical people needed to maintain the sophisticated systems in our first-line combat aircraft, and because the super-gadget advocates in industry and the military are seeking to modify and further complicate both the F-15 and F-16 in efforts to enhance their capabilities.

It is comforting to hear that we have combat airplanes that will do everything but the supper dishes, provided that at least 70 percent of those in service are actually ready to fight at any given moment.

Many Free World observers believe that the greatest likelihood of nuclear attack or nuclear blackmail by the Soviets will come during the '80s, which period will find the United States the most vulnerable because of its badly eroded military strength.

The cost of rebuilding America's nuclear deterrent forces will not really be known until it is done—hopefully before it is too late. We probably will be successful; America has always been a great come-from-behind winner.

Index

A

ABC Ferry Command, 124
Abrams, Creighton, 171
Aeronautics (NACA)
Air Corps Act, 12
Aircraft engines
    Allison V-1710, 34, *54*, 56, 66-69, 103, *147*
    Curtiss Conqueror: *62*; D-12: 32-34, *35*, 44, 56; OX-5: 6, 11, 21
    Daimler-Benz DB 605, *96*
    Hispano-Suiza, 7, 10, 44
    Lawrence Model J, 43-44
    Lo Rhono rotary, 10
    Liberty, 7, 9-12, 17, *22*, 31-32, 34, 39, 44
    Obserursel rotary, *16*
    Pratt & Whitney: R-1340 Wasp: 43, *53*, 55, *61*; R-985 Wasp Junior: *53*, 55; R-1330 Twin Wasp: 55, 67; R-1690 Hornet: 55, *57*; R-2800 Double Wasp: 55, 68-69; J-57: 144
    Rolls Royce Kestrel, 33; Merlin/Packard V-1650, 33-34, 56, *86, 103*
    Wright J-4/J-5/J-6 Whirlwind: *43*, 43-45, 54-55, *61*; R-1: 44; J-3: 44; R-1670: 67; R-1820 Cyclone: 55, *61*, 64; R-3350: *135, 167*
Aircraft Production Board, 9, 11-12, 16
Air Force Reserve, 153
Air Force Systems Command, 176
Air Force Test and Evaluation Center, 180

Air Launched Cruise Missile (ALCM), 188
Air Transport Command, 124
Akagi, 84, 86
Akron, 34, 56, 58-59
Albatross DIII, 6, *13*, 25
Alcock, John, 31
Alexander, Sir Harold, 100
Allen, James, ix
Allison Division (GM), *54*, 56
America, 165
American Air Lines, 53
American Airways, 53
American Volunteer Group, 119-122
Anderson Air Force Base, 166
Andrews, Frank, 60
Anzani, Allesandro, 43
Arizona, 77
Army of the Republic of Vietnam (ARVN), 162-164, 167
Army Reorganization Bill, 12
Arnold, Henry H. "Hap," 12, 60, 64, *71*, 71-72, 74, 108, *112, 128*
Arnold, Leslie, 36
Astoria, 87
Atkinson, Robert, 56

B

Badoeng Strait, 154-155
Baldwin, T.S., ix
Baracca, Francesco, 18
Barner, J.D.,*64*
Battles, campaigns, and operations
    Aisne-Marne offensive, 4
    Aleutians, 82, 85, 117-119
    Arc Light, 166

    Bataan, 79
    Bismark Sea, 89, 91-92
    Coral Sea, 81-82, *81*
    Doolittle raid, 96-97, 122
    Dunkerque, 93
    Eastern Solomons, 90-92
    El Alamein, 96-100
    Guadalcanal, *85*, 96, 89-90
    I-go, 92
    Inchon landing, 150
    Italy, 104-107
    Iwo Jima, 131-132
    Leyte Gulf, 131
    Linebacker II, 172
    Midway, 82-87, 95, 117-118
    Okinawa, 135-137
    Overlord (Normany invasion), 107, 109-111
    Palm Sunday Massacre, 101-102
    Phillipines, 129-131
    Ploesti raid, 108
    Regensburg raid, 108
    Rolling Thunder, 166
    St. Mihiel, 4, 6, 14-15, 23
    Santa Cruz, 90
    Sardinia, 102-103
    Schweinfurt raid, 108
    Skoshi Tiger, 166
    Torch, 95-100
    Vittles (Berlin airlift), 138-140
Baumer, Alber "Ajax", *128*
Bean, Roy, 48
Beech 17/UC-43, *70*
Bell, Alexander Graham, viii
Bell, Lawrence, *141*
Bell: AH-1 Cobra: 169, *173*; P-39 Airacobra: 89, 91; P-63 King

193

Cobra: *127*; UH-1 Huey: 169, *172, 174*; X-1A: *140*, 141
Belleau Wood, 131
Benson, William S., 40-41
Berlin, Donovan, *66, 67*, 69
Billingsby, 38
Bingham, Hiram, 48
Birmingham, 3
Bishop, Billy, 18-19
Bismark Sea, 131
Bissel, Clayton, *128*
Black, Hugo L., 52
Black Committee, 52
Bleriot, Louis, viii
Blue Angels, 63
Bock's Car (B-29), 137
Boeing 247: 62; B-17: 50, *69*, 71, 73, 78, 91, *107, 108, 109, 111*, 113; B-29 Superfortress: 132-135, *135, 136*, 137, *151*; B-50 Superfortress: 142; B-52 Stratofortress: 140-146, *142, 143, 144, 145*, 159, 166-167, 171-173, 176, *177*, 183-185; F4B: *61*; KC-135: 160, 172, 183; P-12C: *61*; P-26: 78, 117
Bowen, T.S., 2
Boxer, 152
Boyington, Gregory "Pappy", 90, 121
Brandt, Floyd, *109*
Brandt, Gerald, 60
Breguet, 15
Brereton, Lewis, 60, 78, 88, 100, 122-123
Brewster Buffalo, 68
Bristol Beaufighter: 91, 100, 102; Fighter: 9
Brooke, Sir Alan, *112*
Brown, Walter Folger, 51-53
Bunker Hill, 132
Burke, Arleigh, 90
Burma Road, 124

C

California, 77
Campbell, David, *132*
Campbell, Douglas, *25*
Cannon, John, 104
Carlsen, Art, 144
Carter, James Earl, 159, 182, 188-190
Casablanca conference, 107
Caudron, 14
Cayley, Sir Geroge, vii
Central Aircraft Manufacturing Company, 119
Cessna L-19, 153
Chadbourne, Thomas, 11
Chaing Kai-shek, 120, *122*, 123-124, 155
Chamberlin, Neville, 71

Chambers, Reed, 24
Chance-Vought F4U Corsair, 68, *131, 132, 136, 149*, 153, 154
Chandler, C.DeF., 2
Chase National Bank, 11
Chenango, 96
Chennault, Clare Lee, 119-121, *122*, 126-127
Chenoweth, Opie, 56, 68
China Air Task Force, 127
China National Aviation Corporation, 124
Chitose, 131
Chiyoda, 131
Churchill, Winston, 74, 94-95, 107, *112*
CIA, 142
Clark, Mark, 104
Clark Field, 76-78
Cleveland, Arthur B., 102
Cockhran, Phillip, 127
Coffin, Howard, 9, 11-12, 48
Coolidge, Calvin, 48
Congressional Medal of Honor, 21, 27
Consolidated B-24 Liberator: 91, 100, *106, 110, 114, 115*; PBY Catalina: 74, 84-85, *130*; B-36 Peacemaker: 142-144, *142*; B-58 Hustler: *183*; F-106: *179*
Constellation, 163
Coral Sea, 166
Craig, Malin, 64, 68
Craven, Thomas T., 41
Curtiss Aeroplane and Motor Company, 11, 44, 55
Curtiss, Glenn, viii, *5*, 30
Curtiss Hawk: 62; BFC-2 Hawk, *61, 64*; C-46 Commando: 124, *124, 125*; CR-2: *34*; F9C-2 Sparrowhawk: *55, 56*, 58-59; F11C-2 Goshawk: *61*; F6C-4 Hawk: *60*; H-12L: *17*; JN-4 Jenny (N-9): 11, *19, 21*, 44; JN-3: 2-3; JN-2: 2, *6*; L: *5*; NC-1/2/3/4: 30-32, *32, 33*; OC-2 Falcon: *59*; P-40: *68*, 69, 74, *74*, 77-79, *77, 80, 86*, 89-91, *94, 95, 97*, 101-102, *118, 119*, 120-122, *120*, 123, *126, 130, 131*; P-1F: *51*; P-36: 50, 66-69, *66, 67*, 71, 74; P-6E Hawk: *62*; R3C-1: *35*; SB2C Helldiver: *137*; SBC-3 Helldiver: *65*; 0-39: *52*; Triad: *4*

D

Daniels, Josephus, 30, 40
da Vinci, Leonardo, vii
Davis-Monthan AFB, 153
Dayton-Wright Company, 11
Deeds, Edward, 9-12

deHavilland DH-4: 7, 9, 11-12, 15, *18*, 29, 32, 60; DH-9: 19
Desert Air Force, 100-102
Dill, Sir John, *128*
Distinguished Service Cross, 27
Doolittle, James, 96, 97, 105, 122
Douglas, Donald, 34-36, 62
Douglas 0-2H: *58*; 0-46: 65; A-4 Skyhawk: *163, 168, 176, 177*; A-20 Havoc: 91; A-26 Invader (B-26): *108, 149*; AD Skyraider: *167, 175*; B-18 Bolo: 78, 117; C-1: *31*; C-9 Nightingale: *184*; C-54: *125*, 126, 140, *141*; DC-2: 52; DC-3/C-47/R4D: 52, 62, 139-140; SBD Dauntless: *83*, 86; TBD Devastator: 85-86; World Cruiser: 34-39, *36, 37*
Duffey, Richard E., 10
Dulles, John Foster, 161
Dunwoody, Halsey, 11
Durgin, C.T., 131, 136

E

Eagleston, Glen, *155*
Eaker, Ira, 105, *178*
Eastern Aircraft Division, 90
Eastern Air Lines, 53
Eastern Air Transport, 53
Eastern FM-1/FM-2 Wildcat: *90*; TBM: *132*
Eckener, Hugo, 32
Eisenhower, Dwight D., 97-98, 100, 105, 116, 151, 159
Elliot, George, 73
Ely, Eugene, 3
Enola Gay (B-29), 137
Enterprise, 63, 65, 82, *83*, 84-87, 89-90
Enterprise (nuclear), 166

F

Fairchild A-10, *188*, 191
Far East Air Force, 129, 152
Farley, James, 53-54
Fernandez, Al, 77
Fisher Body, 11
Fiske, Bradley, 30, 40
Fitch, A.W., 82
Fletcher, Frank J., 82, *82*, 84-87
Flying Tigers, 119-122
Focke-Wulf FW 190, *99*, 106, *109*
Fokker DRI: 6, *16*; DVII: 7; E-1 Eindecker: *8, 16*; Tri-motor: 52
Fonck, Rene, 18
Ford, Gerald, 182
Ford Motor Company, 11, 159, 173
Ford Tri-motor, 52
Forrestal, 161
Fort Sam Houston, 2

Fort Shafter, 73
Fort Sill, OK, 1-2, 18, 29
Foulois, Benjamin, 2
Franklin, 131
Franklin Roosevelt, 163
Fullam, W.F., 30, 40

G

Gabreski, Francis S., *155*
Gambier Bay, 131
Garros, Roland, 6
Geiger, Harold E., 1
General Dynamics F-111: 172, *178*, 179, 181-182; F-16 Falcon: *187*, 191
General Motors, 11, 33, 56
Ghormley, Robert, 88
Gibson, Harvey, 11
Gilkie, Signa, 70
Gilmore, Eddie, 78
Glenn L. Martin Company, 11
Goering, Herman, *100*
Gorrell, Edgar S., 2-3
Great Lakes G-1, *57*
Grumman A-6 Intruder, *164*, 172; F&F Tigercat: *157*; F4F Wildcat: 68-69, *83*, *84*, *85*, 90; F-14 Tomcat: *179*, *186*; F9F Panther: 153, 154; F6F Hellcat: *129*, 132, 133; TBF Avenger, 87

H

Hall, E.J., 9-10
Halsey, William "Bull", 88, 92, 128-129
Hammann, 87
Hancock, 166
Handley Page V/1500, *15*
Hannoveraner, 19, *24*
Harbord, James, 48
Harding, John, 36
Harding, Warren, 41-42, 48
Hart, Thomas C., 76-77
Hartney, Harold, 22-23, 25-26
Harvey, Alva, 36
Hawker Fury: 33; Hurricane: 100
Haynes, Caleb, 122-124, 127
Hazen, Ron, 56
Hedman, Robert "Duke", *120*
Henderson Field, 89
Heron, Samuel, 54-55
Hess, Dean, *152*
Hill, David "Tex", *120*
Hine, Ray, 91
Hiryu, 84, 86
Hitler, Adolf, 5, 29, 50, 64-65, 71, *100*, 113-115
Ho Chi Minh Trail, 166
Hoover, Herbert, 51, 58

Hornet, 82, 84-87, 90, 97
Hotchkiss machine gun, 6, 7
Hoyt, Richard, 11
Hudson, Rock, *152*
Hudson, William, 153
Hudson Motor Company, 9
Hughes Aircraft, 190
Hull, Cordell, 73
Hunsaker, Jerome C., 44

I

Immelmann, Max, *16*
Independence, 164, 166
Ingalls, David S., 16
Intrepid, 131

J

John F. Kennedy, 186
Johnson, Clarence "Kelly", 68
Johnson, Lyndon B., 158-159, 163-170, 173, 182
Jones, Edward T., 54-55
Junkers Ju. 52: 101-102; Ju. 87 Stuka: 97
Jupiter, 41, 44

K

Kaga, 84, 86-87
Kaman HH-43 Huskie, *175*
Kamikaze, 131, *134*, 136-137
Kawisaki Ki-97, 118
Kearny, 94
Keator, Randy, 78
Kelly Bill, 51
Kelly Field, TX, 12
Kelsey, Benjamin, 70-71
Kennedy, John F., 158-160, 162, 176
Kenney, George, 60, 88, 91, 140-144
Kesselring, Albert, 104
Kettering, Charles, 9, 11
Keys, Clement M., 55
Keystone LB-7, *57*
Khan, Gengis, 138
King, Edwin, *104*
King, Ernest J., *112*
Kirkham, Charles, 33
Kirtland, Roy, *2*
Knerr, Hugh, 60
Knox, G.H., 2
Korth, Fred, 181
Kraus, S.M., 43-44

L

Lakehurst Naval Air Station, 46
Lampert-Perkins Committee, 46
Langley, Samuel, viii
Langley Field, VA, 62
Lanphier, Thomas, 91
Lansdowne, Zachary, 46

Lawrance, Charles Lanier, 43-44, 55
Lawrance Aero Engines Company, 43-44
Leighton, Bruce G., 42-44
LeMay, Curtis E., 134-135, *135*, 137, 139, 180-182
Lend-Lese Bill, 71, 93
Leslie, Maxwell F., 86-87
Lexington, 63, *63*, *81*, 82
Lilienthal, Otto, vii
Lindbergh, Charles, A., 31
Little, James, 154
Lockhard, Joe, 73
Lockheed Aircraft, 66-68, 71
Lockheed C-5A Galaxy: *185*; C-130 Hercules: *176*, *184*; F-5 Lightning: *88*, 91, *98*, 105; F-80 Shooting Star: *193*, 148, 152; Starfire: *148*; F-104 Starfighter: 180; P-3 Orion: *186*; P-38: 68-71, *68*, 88, 91-82, 98, *102*, 108-109; SR-71 Blackbird: *182*; T-33: 139, 148; U-2: *181*
Los Angeles (ZR-3), 46, *47*, 58
Lowry, Ed, *52*
Lufberry, Raoul, 22
Luke, Frank Jr., 21-27, *26*, *27*

M

MacArthur, Douglas, 48, 77-79, 88, 92, 128-129, *129*, 148, 155, 157, 159
Macchi C.202, 101-102, 106
Macon, 34, *55*, 56, 58-59
Maddox, 163
Mangels, B., 27
Mannock, E., 18
Mantz, Paul, 153
Manufacturers Trust, 11
Mareth Line, 98, 100
Marmon, 11
Marr, Kenneth, *25*
Marshall, George C., 64,*71*, 71-72, 88
Martin, F.L., 36
Martin, Glenn L., 11, 34
Martin B-26 Marauder: 96, *99*, 111; GMB: *42*
McCain, J.S., 89
McClusky, Clarence W., 86
McCook Field, Ohio, 54-55
McCrary, F.R., 46
McCubbin, George, 16
McDonnell-Douglas F-4 Phantom II: *162*, *163*, *165*, 166, 172, *177*, 181, 191; F-15 Eagle: *187*, 190-191
McDonnell RF-101: 168; XF-85: *143*
McDowall, Charles, 56
McFall, Andrew C., 45
McNamara, Robert, 158-159, *159*, 160, 166-169, 173-181

195

McNarney, Joseph, 60
McNary-Watres Act, 51
McWhorter, E.D., 96
Mead, George J., 44, 55
Mediterranean Air Command, 100, 102-104
Menoher, Charles, 30, 46
Merrils Marauders, 126
Messerschmitt Bf.109: *96*, 100-102, *105*, 106, *109*; Me 110: 106; Me 210: 106
Meyers, Charlie, 20
Midway, 163
MiG-15: *151*, 152, 154, *156*; MiG-21: 166, 172
Mikuma, 87
Military Air Transport Service, 140
Military Units
   1st Aero Squadron, 1-3
   Air Squadron One, 16
   1st Army, 13
   1st Cavalry, 166
   1st Fighter Group, 96
   1st Pursuit Group, 15
   2nd Marine Air Wing, *136*
   3rd Army, 112-113
   3rd Bomb Group, 91
   3rd Pursuit Squadron, 78
   4th Fighter Interceptor Wing, 148, 152, *155*
   4th Fighter Group, 152
   Fleet Air Wing 4, 119
   5th Air Force, 88-89, 91-92, 129, 146, 152
   5th Army (German), 27
   5th Bomb Group, 91
   6th Field Artillery, 1
   6th Phillipine Pursuit Squadron, 78
   7th Air Force, 92, 128
   7th Army, 103
   7th Bomb Group, 91, 126
   7th Division, 119
   7th Fleet, 163, 166
   8th Air Force, 98, *103*, 104-109
   8th Army (British), 95-96, 98, 100, 103
   8th Fighter Group, 91, 94
   Torpedo Squadron 8, 86
   9th Air Force, *97*, 100, 104-113
   Marine Day Squadron 9, 17
   Marine Fighting Squadron 9, 17
   10th Air Force, 89, 107, 123, 126
   Navy Patrol Wing 10, 78
   11th Air Force, 117-119
   Task Force 11, 82
   12th Aero Squadron, 19
   12th Air Force, 96, 98, 100, 104
   Attack Squadron 12, *163*
   12th Bomb Group, 100, 126
   13th Air Force, 89, 92, 129, 152
   13th Cavalry, 2
   14th Air Force, 107, 120-122, 128
   14th Fighter Group, 96, 106
   15th Air Force, 98, 104
   Task Force 16, 84-87
   17th Photo Squadron, 91
   17th Pursuit Squadron, 78
   Task Force 17, 82, 84-87, 90
   18th Fighter Group, 90, 91
   19th Bomb Group, 78, 91
   19th Tactical Air Command, *109*, 112
   20th Air Force, 128, 132-135, 137
   20th Bomber Command, 132-135
   20th Fighter Group, *103*
   21st Bomber Command, 132
   21st Pursuit Group, 78
   22nd Bomb Group, 91
   23rd Fighter Group, 120-122
   24th Fighter Group, 91
   24th Pursuit Group, 78
   27th Aero Squadron, 22-23, 26
   29th Pursuit Squadron, 78
   31st Fighter Group, 96, 105
   33rd Fighter Group, 96, 126-127
   33rd Fighter Squadron, 94
   Task Group 34.2, 96
   35th Fighter Group, 91
   42nd Bomb Group, 91
   44th Fighter Squadron, *127*
   47th Bomb Group, 96
   49th Fighter Group, 91
   51st Fighter Group, 126, *131*
   VF-51, 154
   Task Group 52, 131, 136
   55th Fighter Group
   56th Fighter Group
   57th Fighter Group, *97*, 100-102
   Task Group 58, 131, 136
   58th Fighter Group, 91
   58th Bomb Wing, 132
   64th Fighter Squadron, *97*, 101
   69th Bomb Squadron
   78th Fighter Group, *108*
   79th Fighter Group, 100
   80th Fighter Group, 126
   82nd Airborne Division, 109-110
   82nd Fighter Group, 102, 106
   85 Squadron (RFC), 18-19
   91st Bomb Group, 107
   94th Aero Squadron, 19, 21
   98th Bomb Group, 96, 100
   99th Fighter Squadron, 102
   101st Airborne Division, 109-110
   148th Aero Squadron, 19, 21
   Marine Helicopter Rescue, 161, 154
   213 Squadron (RAF), 16
   Marine Fighting Squadron 214, 90, *149*, 154
   Marine Scout Bombing Squadron 232, 84
   Marine Fighting Squadron 233, 89
   301st Bomb Group, 96
   307th Bomb Group, 91
   310th Bomb Group, 96
   311th Fighter Group, 126
   311 Squadron (RFC), 19
   319th Bomb Group, 96
   320th Bomb Group, 96
   322nd Bomb Group, 100
   Marine Fighting Squadron *323*, 154, 155
   324th Fighter Group, 100-101
   325th Fighter Group, 100, 102-103, 105-106
   341st Bomb Group, 126
   343rd Fighter Group, 118-119
   347th Fighter Group, 90, 92
   358th Fighter Group, *114*
   376 Bomb Group, 100
   407th Bomb Group, 118
   439th Troop Carrier Group, *115*
   459th Fighter Squadron, 127
   475th Fighter Group, 91
   509th Composite Group, 137
Minh, Duong Van, 162
Minh, Ho Chi, 160, 162, 169-171
Minuteman II, 183, *190*
Minuteman III, 183
Missouri, 137
Mitchell, William "Billy", 6, 12-15, 19, 22, *27*, 30, 32, *38*, 39-42, *41*, 45-48, 50, 60, 80
Mitschner, Marc, 131, 136
Moffett, William Adger, 40-46, 55-59
Mogami, 87
Monroe Doctrine, 28
Montgomery, Bernard, 96, 98, 100, 104
Moore, Joseph, 77-78
Moran, Charles, 153
Morane-Saulnier Bullet, 6, *7*
Morgan, J.P., 48
Morrow, Dwight, 48
Morrow Board, 48
Mussolini, Benito, 104
MX missile, 188

N

NAF TS-1, 44
Nagumo, Chuichi, 84-86
NASA, 62
Nassau, 119
National Advisory Committee for Aeronautics (NACA), 62
National Guard, 152-153
National Liberation Front, 162
National Security Act of 1947, 12, 142
National Socialist (Nazi) party, 28-29
Naval Aircraft Factory, 44
Navy Air Transport Service, 126
Nelson, Erik, 36-37, *38*
Neutrality Acts, 50, 93
Newcomb, Simon, viii
Nieuport 17, *14*, 20

Nike-Zeus ABM, 176
Nimitz, Chester W., 82, 84, 88, 90
Nixon, Richard M., 171-173, 182
Norstad, Lauris, 142, 144
North American A-36: *54*, B-25 Mitchell: 89, 91, *97*, *101*; F-86 Sabre: *148*, 152, 153, 156; F-100 Super Sabre: *165*, 166, *169*; P-51 (F-51) Mustang: 68, *69*, 109, *146, 150, 152*; P-82 (F-82) Twin Mustang: 56, *147*, 152; T-6 Texan: *147*
North Atlantic Treaty Organization (NATO), 157, 160, 166, 176, 189
Northrop, John K. "Jack", 62
Northrop F-5: *166*; P-61 Black Widow: *133*
Northwest African Air Forces, 100-101, 103

O

Ogden, Henry, 36, 38
O'Hare, Edward "Butch", *84*
Oklahoma, 75
Older, Charles, *119*
Orenco D, 7, 30
Ostfriesland, 42, 46

P

Packard Motor Car Company, 8-9, 11, 44
Pan Americna Airways, 123
Patrick, Mason, 13, 15, 19, 30, 32, 34, 36, *38*, 39, *41*, 46
Patton, George S., 109, 112-113
Pawley, William D., 119-120
Pearl Harbor, 39, 48, 50, 68, 71, 73-77, *75, 76*, 77, 87, *93*
Pershing, John J., 2, 4, 13-15, 29-30, 47
Pfalz DIII, 6
Phillipine Sea, 154
Polaris A3, *191*
Portal, Sir Charles, *112*
Porter, Finlay, *112*
Potter, Stephen, 16
Pound, Sir Dudley, *112*
Powers, McArthur, 102
Pratt and Whitney Tool Company, 55
President's Aircraft Board, 48

R

Randolph, 134
Ranger, 63, 82, 95, 96, 176
Read, Albert C., 31, *33*
Reagan, Ronald W., 189, 191
Reed, Joe R., *58*
Rentschler, Frederick Brant, 44, 54-55
Republic F-105 Thunderchief: *160*, 166, *169*, 170, *171*; P-47 Thunderbolt: 69-70, *104, 108, 114*
Rhee, Syngman, 146
Rickenbacker, Edward, 18, 24, *25*
Ridgeway, Matthew, 155
Roberts, Ivan, 25
Rockwell B-1, 188, 190
Roma, 58
Rommel, Erwin, 95-96, 98, 100-101
Romulo, Carlos, *129*
Roosevelt, Franklin Delano, 49, 54, 63-64, 71-72, 74-75, 81, 87, 93-95, 104, 107, *112*
Rosendahl, C.E., 58
Royal Aeronautical Society, viii
Royal Air Force, 17-19, 31, 96
Royal Australian Air Force, 91-92, 105
Royal Flying Corps, 13, 17, 19
Royal Navy, 19
Royal New Zealand Air Force, 91
Ryujo, 90

S

St. Lo, 131
Salmson, 3, 15, *23*
SAM missiles, 172
Sangamon, 96
Santee, 96
Saratoga, 63, 82, 89-90, 131
Scott, G.H., 31
SE-5a, 6, 18-19
Seversky P-35, 64, 78
Shenandoah (ZR-1), *45*, 46-47, 58
Shoho, 82
Shokaku, 82
Siciliy, *151*, 154
Siedman, Robert, 107
Signal Corps, U.S. Army, ix, 1, 11-12
Simplex Automobile Company, 10-11
Sims, William S., 30, 40-41, 43
Slocum, H.J., 2
Smith, Lowell, 36-37, *38*
Smithsonian Institution, viii
Sopwith Camel, 6, 19-20
Soryu, 84, 86
South African Air Force, 100, 105
Southeast Asia Treaty Organization (SEATO), 162
Spaatz, Carl "Tooey", 60, 97-100, 103, 105, *111*, 142, 144
Spad VII, 6-7, 22-26, *26*, 27
Springs, Elliot White, 18-21
Spruance, Raymond A., 84-85, *84*-87
SS-20 missile, 189
Standard Aeroplane Company, 11
Staten, Chester E., 27
"Stealth" bomber, 190
Stilwell, Joseph, *128*
Stimson, Henry L., 71
Strategic Air Command, 140, 144, 159, 183
Stratemeyer, George, 155
Street, Clair, 32
Sullivan, Mark, 47
Supermarine Spitfire, 70, 96, 100-102, 105
Suwannee, 96
Symington, Stuart, 144

T

Tactical Air Command, 176
Tanabe, Yahachi, 87
Taylor, Douglas, 30
TFX (F-111), 176-181
Thatch, John, *84*
Thomas Morse MB-3, 7, 44
Tibbits, Paul, 137
Ticonderoga, 163
Titan II, 183
Tojo, 87, 94
Tonkin Gulf Resolution, 164
Tower, John, 30-31
Treaty of Versailles, 5, 28-29, 41
Trenchard, Sir Hugh, 13-14, 18-19
Trident
Trident II, 188, *190*
Triumph, 154
Truman, Harry S., 41, 137, 139, 142, 146, 148, 155-157, 160, 173
Tunner, William, 126, 140
TWA, 53, 62
Twining, Nathan, 105

U

United Air Lines, 53, 62
United Nations, 148, 155
United Nations Security Council, 146
U. S. Air Service, ix, 12, 14-15, 18, 29-30, 32, 46
U.S. Army, viii-ix, 1
U.S. Post Office Department, 51
USS Langley, 44, 63, 82
USS Maryland, 45

V

V-1 (Fiesler Fi. 103), 113
V-2, 113
Valley Forge, 154
Vance, Cyrus, *159*
Vandenberg, Hoyt, 144
Vickers Vimy, 31
Vickers Wellington, 100
Villa, Francisco "Pancho", 2-3
Vincent, Jesse, 8-10
Virdin, Ralph, 71
Vireo, 87
von Arnim, Juergen, 98
von Richtofen, Manfred, 18
von Zeppelin, Count, viii

Vought A-7 Corsair II: 174; VE-7: 44-45
Vultee L-5, *153*

W

Wade, Leigh, 36, 38, *38*
Wagner, Boyd D., *79*
Wainwright, Jonathan, 79
Walker, Walton, 155
Wasp, 63-64, 82, 89-90, 94
Wayne, John, 22
Webb, Jerry, *151*
Weeks, John, *38*
Wehner, Joseph Fritz, 23-25, *26*
Welch, George, 74
Wells, Edward, 144

Westover, Oscar, 68
West Point, 14
West Virginia, 76
Weyland, O.P., 112
Whitten-Brown, Arthur, 31
Wienecke, Otto, *52*
Wiggen, Albert, 11
Willgoos, Andrew V.D., 44, 55
Willis, Robert H., 2
Willys, John North, 11
Wilson, Woodrow, 3, 9, 12
Wright B, *2*
Wright brothers, vii-ix, 5
Wright Aeronautical Corporation, 10, 44, 54-56
Wright Field, 55-56, 66, 68
Wright Flyer, viii-ix

Wright-Martin Company, 11, 44
Wright Military Flyer (Model A), viii-ix, 1
Wright-Patterson AFB, 55
Wurtsmlth, Paul "Squeeze," 91

Y

Yamamoto, Isoruku, 82, 85, 91-92
Yeager, Charles, *141*, 152
Yorktown, 63, 65, 82, *83*, 84-87

Z

Zuckert, Eugene, 181
Zuiho, 131
Zuikaku, 131